THEORY OF GARDENS

ex horto
DUMBARTON OAKS TEXTS
IN GARDEN AND LANDSCAPE STUDIES

THEORY OF GARDENS

JEAN-MARIE MOREL

JOSEPH DISPONZIO,
introduction and notes to the translation

EMILY T. COOPERMAN,
translation

DUMBARTON OAKS RESEARCH LIBRARY AND COLLECTION
WASHINGTON, D.C.

Library of Congress Cataloging-in-Publication Data

    Names: Morel, J.-M. (Jean-Marie), 1728–1810, author.

    Title: Theory of gardens / Jean-Marie Morel, author; Joseph Disponzio; Emily T. Cooperman, translator.

    Other titles: Theorie des jardins. English

    Description: Washington, D.C.: Dumbarton Oaks Research Library and Collection, [2018] | Series: Ex horto: Dumbarton Oaks texts in garden and landscape studies | Translation of Jean-Marie Morel's Theorie des jardins (1776). | Includes bibliographical references.

    Identifiers: LCCN 2018015866 | ISBN 9780884024538

    Subjects: LCSH: Landscape gardening—Early works to 1800.

    Classification: LCC SB471.M8513 2018 | DDC 712.09/033—dc23

    LC record available at https://lccn.loc.gov/2018015866

Cover illustration: The Philosopher's Pyramid at Ermenonville, from Alexandre de Laborde, *Description des nouveaux jardins de la France et de ses anciens châteaux* (Paris, 1808–1815). Dumbarton Oaks Research Library and Collection, Washington, D.C.

www.doaks.org/publications

CONTENTS

FOREWORD

Jean-Marie Morel (1728–1810), a leading French landscape designer and theorist, is now mainly remembered as the author of *Théorie des jardins* (1776; second edition, 1802), one of the fundamental eighteenth-century texts in the history of landscape architecture. In his own day, Morel earned professional distinction as a foremost champion of the "English" landscape gardening style in France and was involved in over fifty garden projects executed for major patrons, including such notable sites as Malmaison and Ermenonville. A proponent of the approach to landscape design that tended to downplay the degree of human intervention in a country that was then still a stronghold of the formal garden tradition, Morel had a career that spanned a long and turbulent period of French history, from the *ancien régime* through the French Revolution, the Terror, and the rise of Napoleon. With his background as an engineer, he also played an instrumental role in shaping the profession of landscape architecture, opening up a new professional domain by coining the term *architecte-paysagiste,* the precursor to the modern designation "landscape architect."

Although very little remains of Morel's legacy as a landscape designer, his contribution as a theorist should be of compelling interest to landscape historians and designers alike. What makes his treatise stand out among other eighteenth-century French publications on picturesque garden theory is his interest in the natural processes that underlie the formation of landscape, with special attention to landform, hydrology, and seasonal variation. An awareness of the character of each landscape, according to Morel, was particularly important because of the emotional response that it was likely to elicit. While incorporating lessons from the comte de Buffon's writings on natural history and the new "scientific" outlook on nature propagated by the authors of the *Encyclopédie,* Morel's approach also showed the impact of his design practice, with an express concern to relate the garden to its natural surroundings. Morel's unique theoretical contribution was, therefore, an attempt to develop an approach to garden design grounded in the new understanding of natural processes, which brought together picturesque theory and landscape practice, taking into account a wide range of environmental factors that had an impact on the work of an *architecte-paysagiste*.

Although widely influential in professional circles, Morel's *Théorie des jardins*, even at the time of its publication, was not very well known to general audiences. This translation of the 1776 edition makes it available in English for the first time. It is published as part of the Dumbarton Oaks series ex horto, which is intended to provide access to the foundational literature of garden and landscape studies through translations of classic and rare texts on garden history and on the philosophy, art, and techniques of landscape architecture. Architectural historian Emily T. Cooperman, the translator of *Théorie des jardins*, has done an admirable job making Morel's elegant eighteenth-century French prose accessible to modern English-language readers, while Joseph Disponzio, a leading international authority on Morel, has provided the introduction and critical apparatus. We have elected to translate the first edition rather than the second; it is more concise and it omits a lengthy list of botanical materials, but it also has the virtue of situating Morel in his original intellectual contexts.

Our hope at Dumbarton Oaks is that this joint effort will help bring attention, beyond the circle of French garden specialists, to one of the key eighteenth-century texts in picturesque garden theory, making it available to students of landscape architecture as well as to historians of science and the environment. Morel not only anticipated the professional identity and practice of landscape architecture but also foreshadowed one of the discipline's most significant principles in his attention to the distinctive processes of landscape formation and their impact on the character of a place.

JOHN BEARDSLEY
Director, Garden and Landscape Studies
Dumbarton Oaks

INTRODUCTION

JOSEPH DISPONZIO

When it was published in 1776, Jean-Marie Morel's *Théorie des jardins* (*Theory of Gardens*) received near unanimous praise. It was recognized as an important addition to the corpus of theoretical texts appearing in France during the 1770s that dealt with the still relatively new natural or picturesque style of gardening—commonly known as English—that was quickly eclipsing the regular or symmetrical style associated with André Le Nôtre.[1] The acclaim was warranted, for Morel deftly crafted a theory of gardening that synthesized the aesthetics of empirical sensibility with an understanding of natural systems; in the process, he laid the foundations for an environmentally based approach to landscape design. In tacit recognition of Morel's achievement, one contemporary reviewer wrote that previously there had been the "art of gardening," but now there was its "science."[2]

Among the laudatory reviews, however, one demurred: Jacques-Henri Meister, writing in the important *Correspondance littéraire,* wryly commented that the book had been more talked about than read.[3] One might say that Meister's pithy comment still holds true today, for while *Théorie des jardins* is still "talked about," it is fair to say that it is among the most influential works on landscape theory that few people have ever read.

It is not that *Théorie des jardins* is unknown. It has appeared in every major English and French garden bibliography since its publication, and it is routinely quoted and paraphrased in garden literature. But a citation of the work often appears more as a perfunctory obligation than a well-considered synthesis based on a full read of the text. Those who have "read" Morel—especially French garden theorists of the nineteenth century, such as Lalos, Boitard, Viart, Richou, and Vergnaud—quote him throughout their works with little or no attribution; indeed, he often appears as an éminence grise whose theories have been absorbed but not credited. In the twentieth and twenty-first centuries, he has been given more attention by writers on French literature than on garden theory, with the exception of minor citations of his book or discussions of specific aspects of his theory related to his division of gardens.[4]

Morel's name has faded, but his influence has not. By dint of his five-decade career, which spanned the birth, growth, development, and maturation of picturesque gardening, his garden theory and landscape practice helped solidify and establish it as a distinct profession, independent of architecture. Indeed, he coined the term *architecte-paysagiste* (landscape architect) to designate a professional practicing in the new design idiom. His major published work, *Théorie des jardins*,[5] not only laid the practical foundations for the new profession by outlining the scope of its practice but also helped to establish its theoretical foundations. In his book, Morel systematically constructed the professional territory of the new garden designer by usurping activities and responsibilities previously given to the architect. Although Morel cannot be considered an environmental scientist as understood today, his *Théorie des jardins* established and underscored the importance of natural processes as they impacted the creation of landscapes; this understanding is the basis of the environmental approach to landscape architecture that has become a central tenet of the profession today. Perhaps most importantly, Morel's theory helped to reconceptualize the approach to modeling land, thus changing how landscapes were conceived and designed. While there may be little recognition of his contribution, his theories infiltrated the discourse on landscape architecture, thereby influencing and redirecting its future course.[6]

⤚⤙

Jean-Marie Morel (Figure 1) was born in Lyon, France, on August 21, 1728, and died on October 7, 1810, in Écully, a suburb of his native city. He lived most of his life, however, elsewhere. Through the last decades of the Old Regime, French Revolution, Reign of Terror, Consulate, and First Empire, with the exception of his imprisonment in Lyon during its siege, Morel rarely stopped working. His design legacy of more than fifty landscapes includes gardens for a "who's who" of French nobility, wealth, and power, beginning with the prince of the blood, Louis-François de Bourbon, prince de Conti, and ending with Napoleon. The château d'Arcelot, outside of Dijon, is the best preserved of his extant landscapes, which also include Ermenonville, designed for (and with) the Marquis René Louis de Girardin, and Malmaison, designed for the Empress Joséphine.

He worked until a week before his death, at which time he was the undisputed "patriarch" of French landscape design, enjoying a stature in France on par with that of Lancelot "Capability" Brown and Humphry Repton in England. His death made national news, with obituaries running in every major French journal, including Napoleon's *Le moniteur universel*. None other than J. C. Loudon posthumously lauded him as the "Kent of France" in *An Encyclopædia of Gardening*— high praise from the British encyclopedist of garden history, theory, and practice.[7] In the mid-nineteenth century, Morel's reputation was sufficiently intact that his name was included among the selling points on a sales poster for the château de

Figure 1

Jean-Marie Morel (1728–1810).

Saint-Mury, outside of Grenoble. But shortly thereafter, his name and reputation faded, so much so that the honorific "Kent of France" is removed in the posthumous, 1865 edition of Loudon's *Encyclopædia*.

Why Morel entered an ill-deserved obscurity can only be conjectured. No doubt, the ephemeral nature of gardens is contributory, in that gardens are among the most delicate of art forms, subject to demise even as they are being constructed. That the overwhelming majority of his gardens have been destroyed, and that those that survive (though compromised) are in private hands, has surely contributed to the lack of recognition of his work.[8] But print is more lasting than vegetation, making *Théorie des jardins*—read or not—his most enduring work.

Morel's Practical and Intellectual Formation and the Age of Enlightenment

To fully appreciate Morel's magnum opus, we need to understand its context. Because his life and career neatly paralleled the birth and maturation of the theory and practice of picturesque gardening, Morel was both witness to and participant in the transformation of these events. Moreover, his life (and, likewise, the birth of the picturesque) coincided with one of the most tumultuous and intellectually stimulating eras in modern history, the Age of Enlightenment, when virtually every aspect of human knowledge was reevaluated or otherwise called into question. Morel was a keen and receptive student of his era, and *Théorie des jardins* owes its strength to his ability to understand and apply the lessons of a changing world order to a rigorous and sound theory of landscape design.

We know little of Morel's education prior to 1754, when he began an apprenticeship as an *ingénieur géographe* (geographical engineer) near his hometown. His duties included surveying and mapping landscapes as well as drawing plans for roads and bridges. After this initial field experience, he was sent to Paris for advanced study at the prestigious École royale des ponts et chaussées, where he remained from 1758 to 1760. During this period, he also studied under France's preeminent teacher and theorist of architecture Jacques-François Blondel. This training was crucial to his future calling. In an era when engineering was still a practice of manipulating the constituent parts of landscape (earth, wood, water, and rock), the requisite technical knowledge of the practice of landscape gardening was entirely subsumed under the title of geographical engineer. Moreover, the education of a geographical engineer in the eighteenth century was a field apprenticeship that emphasized practice over theory. Instruction centered on identifying, interpreting, and recording both the natural and man-made components of landscape in situ. This included natural landforms, hydrologic features (lakes, streams, springs, and groundwater tables), vegetative cover (forests, meadows, and fields), and individual species of trees and plants; the agricultural landscape of productive forests, cultivated fields, and arable land; and the constructed and inhabited landscape of cities, towns, and villages. In brief, a geographical engineer learned how to *read* a landscape and its constituent parts. The data collected in the field was then analyzed and synthesized into a coherent whole and drawn up in a topographical survey plan.

The making of a survey plan is a methodical process that records the landscape, tree by tree, rock by rock, stream by stream, spot elevation by spot elevation. When all the survey points are connected, the composite picture is not a unitary composition but a diverse field of fragments whose logic is revealed by the natural processes that determined them. Thus understood, landscapes are not something derived from abstract aesthetics regulated by divine proportions, as can be claimed for architectural space, but as its antithesis, something seemingly chaotic, yet naturally ordered. Beneath the topographic variety of landscape lie the internal mechanisms that create them.

In learning how to survey and graphically represent a landscape from its constituent parts, Morel developed an understanding of how landscapes were formed, composed, and structured, all of which conformed to and were determined by natural law. Thus, his training led directly to an appreciation of both the natural processes that formed the landscape and the forces that altered it. He developed a critical understanding of the nature of landscapes and an attendant sense of landform process, which—when coupled with the aesthetic imperatives of design that he learned from Blondel—would inform his garden theory and practice. No doubt, his education at the École royale des ponts et chaussées helped focus his field experience, allowing for the application of the techniques, practices, and methods used in recording and evaluating landscapes to the art of designing them.

As noted, the years of Morel's practical and professional development coincided with the transformation in the discourse of knowledge that characterized the Enlightenment. Jean Le Rond d'Alembert, one of the intellectual spokesmen for the age, wrote in 1759 that "a very remarkable change in our ideas is taking place, a change whose rapidity seems to promise an even greater transformation to come."[9] Denis Diderot, the other intellectual expediter of the age, put it more dramatically: "A new order of things" was born.[10] One of the most significant aspects of this "new order" was the methodology of empirical science: observation was to be the starting point of all inquiry. This Newtonian-Lockean heritage cannot be underestimated, as it pervades all intellectual occupation in the eighteenth century, from pure science to philosophy to garden theory.

The "new order" is evident in one of the greatest publishing ventures of the age, the *Encyclopédie, ou, Dictionnaire raisonné des sciences, des arts et des métiers*, edited by Diderot and d'Alembert, whose first volume appeared in 1751, a few years before Morel began his apprenticeship in Lyon. The dozens of entries devoted to the natural and physical sciences are solidly grounded in the presuppositions of empirical science, stressing that the observation of nature will reveal the universal laws of the material world. Of importance, and very likely required reading for a geographical engineer, was Nicolas Desmarest's entry on physical geography. It emphasized that only through the direct observation of nature could a theory of the earth be formulated. Implicit here is a methodology that mandates observation prior to action in the design of landscapes.[11]

Earlier in the century, the Abbé Noël-Antoine Pluche did much to increase an awareness of the natural world with the publication of his multivolume work, *Le spectacle de la nature, ou, Entretiens sur les particularités de l'Histoire naturelle qui ont paru les plus propres à rendre les jeunes gens curieux et à leur former l'esprit,* between 1732 and 1750. Pluche was not a scientist, but he was an effective writer and a skilled assimilator of natural history, making it accessible to a general audience. His works readied a receptive readership for the *Histoire naturelle, générale et particulière, avec la description du Cabinet du Roi,* the forty-four-volume work by Georges-Louis Leclerc, comte de Buffon. With its first volume appearing in 1749 and the others following over the next forty years, this monumental work was the only publishing venture of the era to rival the *Encyclopédie* in importance and size. It was a phenomenal success, with ten editions of the entire work published in the eighteenth century alone, and it was translated into English, German, Dutch, Italian, Spanish, Portuguese, and Latin. It is noteworthy that *Histoire naturelle* and *Le spectacle de la nature* were among the most popular books of the day, and their influence features prominently in *Théorie des jardins.*[12]

The natural sciences were not the only areas of knowledge undergoing fundamental re-evaluations. In philosophy, the publication of John Locke's *An Essay Concerning Humane Understanding* (1690) upended Cartesian rationalism, catapulting empiricism as the preferred methodology for interpreting and understanding the world and human behavior. Locke's philosophy maintained that all mental activity—whether the accumulation of knowledge or the production of feeling—was dependent on the sensory stimuli of the external world, not driven by innate ideas, as René Descartes had argued. Locke's important and influential work precipitated the fundamental reevaluation of how the world was perceived, understood, and investigated; it laid the foundations for the subsequent dismantling of Cartesian systems, especially as they applied to the understanding of the natural world.[13]

An Essay Concerning Humane Understanding was translated into French in 1714, and Locke quickly found a disciple in the Abbé Étienne Bonnot de Condillac, who refined his philosophy in *Traité des sensations* (1754), perhaps the most cogent treatise on the nature of the senses. Like Locke, Condillac argued that human reason and emotions result from external stimuli. Together, the metaphysics of Locke and Condillac primed the ground for explorations of human emotions and the senses, something furthered by Edmund Burke's *A Philosophical Enquiry into the*

Origin of Our Ideas of the Sublime and Beautiful (1757), which was translated into French in 1765. The work was of central importance to the aesthetics of sensibility, and, while it was not directly concerned with gardening, it nonetheless had a major impact on eighteenth-century garden theory. Burke's exploration of the senses and how they are produced, affected, and controlled freed beauty from the hegemony of classical proportions, thus providing a theoretical approach for a new way of gardening independent of rigid aesthetics. His philosophy allowed greater sway of emotion over reason—something that Roger de Piles had already voiced in his prescient *Cours de peinture par principes avec un balance de peintres* (1708). It is from Burke and de Piles that Morel drew his most evocative language.

Enlightenment history focuses primarily on the philosophical battle between Cartesian rationalism and Newtonian-Lockean empiricism, but an equally significant battle was being waged between the followers of a mechanical understanding of nature and the proponents of the life sciences. Diderot was one of the foremost *philosophes* to promote an organic nature of the universe. In his *Pensées sur l'interprétation de la nature* (1754), he ridiculed the *géometres* of the era and correctly recognized that a decisive turning point in the sciences was at hand. But his metaphysics was grounded in the science of Buffon.

Buffon called nature a vital force—"une puissance vive"—that encompassed and animated everything; it was a creative energy of perpetual change that came from within, not some static mechanical force measurable from without.[14] His work in the natural sciences revealed a complex world in continual transformation, a world understood as a system of organic interaction and mutability of natural phenomena. In directing his efforts to the newly emerging life and earth sciences, his achievement was nothing less than outlining their structure independent of the authority of mathematics, which could not meet the descriptive requirements of natural history.

Implicated here, and something that can only be outlined in the present essay, is the utter transformation of the meaning and understanding of nature in the eighteenth century.[15] It is no exaggeration to state that "Nature" was the datum of all philosophical inquiry. It was at the heart of the speculation on the relationship between human beings and God. Through the course of the century, the Gordian knot that held God, Nature, and Man as one became unraveled. By the end of the century, Nature had achieved an autonomous status, and, as such, began to be investigated in its own right, thus paving the way for the rise of scientific disciplines such as biology, chemistry, and geology.

It cannot be a coincidence that the development of a new gardening tradition coincided with these paradigmatic events, in particular, the rise of a sensationalist metaphysics and a new organic outlook on the natural world. Gardening, an art form so intrinsically tied to both culture and nature, cannot escape the fundamental shifts in the intellectual environment that nurtures and sustains it. The

Enlightenment legacy of changes in aesthetics and metaphysics as well as its idea of nature and its understanding of the natural world (not to mention the social, political, and economic developments in the world) almost by default insured that the art of landscape design would undergo dramatic change.

And indeed it did. As is well known, throughout the course of the eighteenth century, the regular style derivative of André Le Nôtre was replaced by what was considered a more "natural" style, now commonly subsumed under the rubric English, natural, or picturesque garden. The earliest writings on the changing currents in the garden date to the early eighteenth century, when Joseph Addison, writing in the *Spectator*, began to challenge the existing order of garden design. It wasn't until some decades later that William Kent executed the first designs in the new English manner. Shortly thereafter, Lancelot "Capability" Brown gave traction to the new style, perfecting it into the form universally recognized today.[16] While the practice of the new style was advancing, the theory of it lagged. But all of that changed in the seminal decade of the 1770s, when a multitude of important texts were published on the new style.

Thomas Whately's *Observations on Modern Gardening* (1770) was the first theoretical work on picturesque gardening. It was so popular that it received a second edition within its first year of publication; French and German translations were published in 1771, the year of its third edition. François-de-Paule Latapie, a protégé of Montesquieu, was the French translator, and he included a lengthy and influential introduction that presented an historical perspective on the new gardening.[17] The German translation was by Johann Ernst Zeiher.

In 1774, Claude-Henri Watelet issued his *Essai sur les jardins*, the first French book on the picturesque. Following in rapid succession were Antoine-Nicolas Duchesne's *Sur la formation des jardins* (1775; second edition, 1779); Morel's *Théorie des jardins* (1776); and René Louis de Girardin's *De la composition des paysages* (1777; English translation, 1783). Less theoretical in nature, but no less important were William Chambers's *Dissertation on Oriental Gardening* (1772), published simultaneously in English and French, and Louis Carrogis de Carmontelle's *Jardin de Monceau* (1779). To these can be added C. C. L. Hirschfeld's five-volume *Theorie der Gartenkunst*, which was published simultaneously in French and German between 1779 and 1785, and Georges-Louis Le Rouge's compendious, multivolume series, *Jardins anglo-chinois à la mode*, which was issued between 1776 and 1788.[18] Until the English translation of Watelet's *Essai sur les jardins* in 2003, Girardin's book had been the only French work translated into English.[19]

The publication of these texts within a single decade is suggestive of a turning point in the writing of landscape history. There is no mistaking the new, original, and wholly self-contained quality of the works. To varying degrees, they incorporate ideas drawn from the new aesthetics, philosophy, and natural science of the day. They are mostly devoid of plans and technical information, and they contain no plant lists; instead, they are heavily weighted by pure landscape description in a direct appeal to the imagination.

The common thread in these works is the rejection of anything resembling André Le Nôtre's style and its derivatives. All of the authors professed a "more natural" manner of modeling land, one that eschewed major and minor axes, symmetry, regular geometries, and clipped vegetation. Such regular and contrived means of constructing gardens were deemed incapable of creating the variety of landscape characters that was at the basis of the new theory. On a metaphysical level (though few claimed it as such), all of the authors were operating in the realm of empirical sensationalist philosophy—that is, their goal was to design gardens in emulation of natural scenery that moved the soul only through the manipulation of natural features such as earth, rock, water, and vegetation. But they did not necessarily agree on what the new landscape should look like.

Each author accepted that artifice should be subordinated to nature in the creation of a garden, but the degree to which "Art"—evidence of human intervention—was to be apparent in the landscape was by no means an accepted norm. Whately in England and Morel in France favored the least evidence of human agency in the landscape composition; they considered the elements of nature, artfully manipulated, sufficient. For Chambers and Carmontelle, garden design required an apparent artistry, as nature alone was not enough. At the heart of such debate was the artistic theory of mimesis, which (at a minimum) required that art, by definition, be distinguishable from nature. In practical terms, one only need compare Capability Brown's Blenheim to William Chambers's Kew, or Morel's Guiscard to Carmontelle's Monceau, to appreciate the lack of uniformity in an ostensibly common gardening style. With an emphasis on pure landscape features, Brown and Morel go to elaborate lengths to mask the hand of man, while Chambers and Carmontelle fill their compositions with demonstratively artful and exotic contrivances.

Despite their disagreements over the look of the garden, the authors of the new theory books agreed that designing in the new style required a new design professional. Garden design in the regular style had traditionally been within the province of architecture, yet each author avoided using the professional designation "architect" in describing the designers of the new gardens. The French authors agreed that Whately's use of "gardner" was not acceptable because the term in French —jardinier—was restrictive in suggesting a laborer, not a designer. But they could not agree on a term; indeed, each used a different substantive for the new designer. Girardin used "artist," while Duchesne employed "form giver" (formateur). Morel emphatically wrote that jardinier was not the correct term, but he offered no alternative: "By Gardener, I understand the tasteful Artist who composes Gardens, not he who tends them." As a measure of how important professional designation was to him, and as evidence of his career-long preoccupation with professional identity, Morel revisited the question some twenty-six years later in the second edition of his *Théorie des jardins* (1802), where he lamented that there were still no proper terms for the person who designed in the new genre or for the type of garden designed.[20] However, by 1804, he had settled on a name for the practitioner, *architecte-paysagiste* (landscape architect), a term apparently of his own invention.[21]

Implicit in the discussion over nomenclature is the understanding that the architect was incapable of meeting the design requirements of the new genre. Garden design until then was predicated on the selected arrangement of regular geometries drawn on flat surfaces in accordance with the rules of proportion, perspective, and taste. Instruction in these matters could be found in books such as Antoine-Joseph Dézallier d'Argenville's *La théorie et la pratique du jardinage* (1709) and Stephen Switzer's *Ichnographia Rustica; or, The Nobleman, Gentleman, and Gardener's Recreation* (1718), or in the numerous treatises of Jacques-François Blondel, including *De la distribution des maisons de plaisance* (1737) (Figure 2).

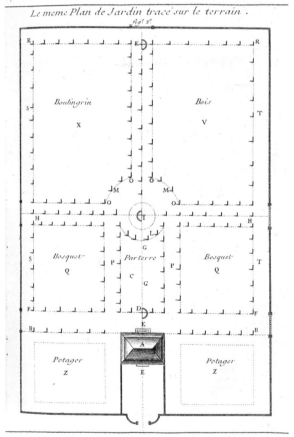

a

b

Translating these designs into the field posed no problem as long as the ground was itself flat, be it a horizontal or an inclined plane. But once the topography was to respect or emulate a "natural" condition, as was required by the dictates of the new style, the designs of regular shapes became ill-suited to the desired site configuration. And once symmetry and formal arrangements were banned, as was also dictated by the new style, the traditional garden designers faced a serious challenge. Architecture theory of the era was simply incapable of satisfying the requirements of the new aesthetic. Faced with the rapid transformation of garden design, the architect's training could not bend theory to practice, thus resulting in its replacement. The vacuum created by the expulsion of the architect from the garden was filled by a new occupational entity as yet unnamed.[22]

To judge by their critical reception, the new garden theory texts were recognized for their innovation. Those of Whately, Watelet, and Morel received overwhelmingly favorable reviews in the most important literary and scientific journals of the day, including the *Journal des savants, Mercure de France,* and *Gazette*

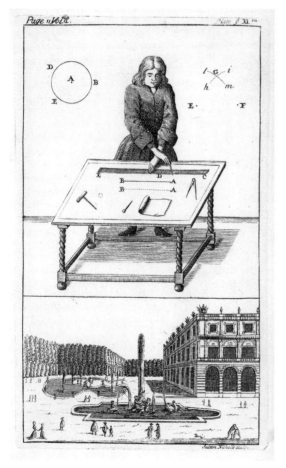

Figure 2

Examples of eighteenth-century designs of gardens, from Antoine-Joseph Dézallier d'Argenville's *La théorie et la pratique du jardinage* (Paris, 1709) (a–b) and Stephen Switzer's *Ichnographia Rustica; or, The Nobleman, Gentleman, and Gardener's Recreation* (London, 1718) (c).

c

universelle de littérature. In particular, the stress on natural history was given implicit recognition. Whately's *Observations on Modern Gardening* received a lengthy, two-issue review in Abbé Rozier's *Journal de physique*, the most prestigious scientific periodical of its day. Whately's book, groundbreaking though it was, was not as rigorously scientific as Morel's *Théorie des jardins*, which, as noted, was recognized for its "scientific" approach in one review.[23]

Morel's *Théorie des jardins*

Against this backdrop, we can now consider *Théorie des jardins*. By Morel's own admission, the work was "the fruit of twenty years of study and ten years of practice," a statement suggestive of his awareness of the events unfolding around him, as well as a declaration of his qualifications for writing such a work. He prepared well for his book by reading those which preceded his. He admired *Observations on Modern Gardening*, but he found the book's structure weak, and he was dismissive of *Essai sur les jardins*, which he found discursive and unmethodical.[24] He would correct these shortcomings in his book by crafting a theory as tightly structured as it was logical in exposition, as scientifically grounded as it was aware of subjective factors that affect human emotions, and as comprehensive in scope as it was focused on its single objective: the creation of landscapes that emulate nature.

Théorie des jardins is an ambitious and complex work that addresses both the theory and practice of the new style, which Morel described as picturesque or natural. As practice, Morel set out to write the rules and scope of the new gardening style as well as the responsibilities of the new garden design professional. As theory, he constructed a sophisticated notion of landscape continuum—the field as it were of the practice—based on an understanding and study of natural laws.

His book has several main foci. Like his contemporaries, Morel accepted that garden design was a liberal art, and must thus favorably stir human emotions. Secondly, he recognized that picturesque gardens must be both conceived in accordance with the natural processes that dictated landscape formation and designed (primarily with natural elements) in a manner that respected the character of a site. The design must always be subordinate to nature. Third, he emphasized that gardens must provide for and display the hierarchical structure of society, one made legible through a system of garden archetypes, each pegged to a particular segment of society and the natural character of the site.[25] Lastly, more so than any of his contemporaries, he identified the professional territory of the new garden designer, giving clear limits of where the architect's purview ended and the garden designer's began. In sum, Morel's theory provided for a garden design that activated the senses, designed in accordance with natural laws, and attempted to provide landscapes of social representation in accordance with accepted cultural norms, all the while establishing the responsibilities of the new professional entity.

Morel began his book by condemning regular or symmetric gardens. In addition to his dislike of rigorous symmetry, which he found boring at best, he objected to the spatial discontinuity that occurred when symmetric gardens ended and the natural surroundings began. He preferred continuity between the designed property and the natural surroundings—that is, the garden closer to the house should appear more "designed" (i.e., exhibit human agency) and progressively become less designed as one receded from the dwelling. At the extremity of the property, the character of the garden should merge with that of the surroundings. This notion of transitions in landscape from house to surroundings was central to his conception of landscape continuum, something evident in nature landscapes.

Morel's dismissal of the symmetric garden, and its designer—the architect—was the first salvo in his quest to wrest garden design from the province of architecture and to redirect it to a new design professional. At every turn, he underscored the limits and inadequacies of the application of architectural theory to picturesque gardening, and he claimed areas of current architectural practice for the new garden professional. In so doing, he consistently and incrementally expanded the domain of the emergent landscape designer, thereby carving a space for a new professional entity. Banishing the architect from the garden was an essential first step in its establishment. By virtue of a decade of practice and even more years of thinking about picturesque gardening, Morel placed himself in the center of the new professional territory that he was himself in the process of creating.[26]

Once his authority and his project was established, Morel let it be known that his theory would not be narrowly conceived. Addressing *Le spectacle de la nature*, the title of his second chapter, Morel situated his garden theory in the broader realm of natural history, the understanding of which was essential to successful landscape design. His was not to be a theory confined to discrete, self-contained gardens, but one that built landscapes that were components of, and identical in conception to, a much larger natural sphere. Utilizing the title of Pluche's enormously influential work was a blatant—and shrewd—move of subject recognition, but Morel relied less on the amateur abbé for his inspiration than on the naturalist Buffon.

The nature Morel invoked was the protean Nature of Buffon: infinite and unknowable, magnificent and mysterious, rich in her forms and variety, subject to endless modifications, always changing yet subject to internal laws (organizing principles, as it were) that dictated landscape forms. The Nature of Buffon was the dynamic agent that animated Morel's theory. Indeed, dynamics became a hallmark of his design sensibility. Although his discussion of the spectacle of nature was brief, it set the tone for his entire work, particularly its reliance on a vocabulary and thought derivative of Buffon and others, especially Diderot, who was himself influenced by Buffon. Echoing the naturalist, Morel noted that while nature may hide behind a veil of disorder, she is upon inspection quite regular in her methods: "Under her guise of disorder, she veils the most useful views, the most regular workings, and the most wisely composed plans." Having identified the problematic (garden design), identified the player (an as yet unspecified garden design professional), and indicated the source of the solution (nature), Morel set about constructing his theory.

First, he crafted its structural core, naming four garden archetypes or *classes* that constituted the basic divisions of designed landscapes: the *countryside* (*le pays*), an all-inclusive landscape of natural effects; the *park* (*le parc*), a less rustic (*champêtre*) landscape more closely associated with a country seat; the *Garden proper* (*le Jardin proprement dit*), a landscape more amenable to visible human interventions; and the *farm* (*la ferme*), a landscape that combined utility and pleasure: "One may thus include, under four general classes, all the Gardens that take Nature as model." Morel ascribed to each *class* a relative size and character, and each was subject to an infinite variety of compositional modifications, which he characterized as *types*. That is, each archetype or *class* of garden could be subdivided into a subclass or *type*. He stressed that the natural character of a site would necessarily determine the overall character of the garden, or conversely, that the garden's character must never contravene the character of the site. As he would repeat throughout his book, a respect for a site's natural character was central to his theory.[27]

Having primed the reader on his concept of landscape continuum, Morel conceived the garden as a transitional space between the house and its surroundings, in which the design becomes progressively more natural the farther from the house one gets: "the sweetest scenes and those most carefully tended must be followed by those that are the most rural and simple." The *classes* were called to service as the means of effecting this transition. Nearest to the house would be the *Garden proper*, whose character would exhibit a certain degree of apparent design, especially in proximity to the dwelling. At its extremity, the *Garden proper* would take on a character closer to that of the *park*. Likewise, the *park* would be closer in character to the *Garden proper* when in proximity to it, and it would progressively take on the character of the *countryside* as it approached this, the most natural of the *classes*. Similarly, at its extremities, the *countryside* would be virtually indistinguishable from the *park* and the surrounding landscape:

> From these definitions, it may be seen that these classes are not so far apart that a large *park*, depending on how it is treated, may not approach a small *countryside*, especially at its edges. A *Garden proper* of a certain extent and nobility in its composition may tend toward a small *park*.
>
> The *park* must join with the *countryside* at the edges and to the *Garden proper* at the center. It is by this association that the pleasures of one will be united with the beautiful effects of the other, and the nobility of the style will be allied with Nature's graces.

The *farm*, functionally and aesthetically different from the other *classes*, can be comfortably located at the extremity of the *park* or within the *countryside.*

Thus conceived, the *classes* were tools of design instrumentation for mediating between the house and horizon. They were the means of linking the house to the garden and the garden to the surrounding landscape. As theory, it was a powerful concept of landscape continuum. Morel was clearly addressing an ideal, but his approach was well within garden design traditions. In the primordial garden, a wall separated the garden from the surroundings, a spatially discontinuous condition. During the Renaissance, the wall fell, so to speak, giving rise to the concept of the three natures—garden, cultivated landscape, and natural landscape—with the implied progression from one nature to the next.

The concept of the three natures, though executed differently, is evident throughout postmedieval garden history. In her book *Italian Villas and Their Gardens* (1904), Edith Wharton succinctly expressed the concept, noting the "subtle transition from the fixed and formal lines of art [the villa] to the shifting and irregular lines of nature [the garden]."[28] Though less obvious, such design transitions are also evident in French gardens of the seventeenth and early eighteenth centuries, in which parterres became progressively less elaborate as their distance from the château increased. Thus, working within the history of gardening, Morel's *classes* likewise presented a successive transition from the obviously designed landscape surrounding the house to a more *champêtre* landscape farther beyond. By allowing for an infinite degree of stylistic modifications and expression, concurrent with the decreasing evidence of human intervention, the *classes* taken successively formed a seamless transition from the province of art to the domain of nature.

In addition to their design function, Morel added a layer of social representation to his *classes*. Following accepted design norms of the era, and drawing on the architectural theory of Blondel,[29] Morel recognized the hierarchy of French society and the "distinctions of social order that depend irrevocably on the present state of things." The putative social classes—"the powerful, the rich, the simple citizen, and the man of taste"—each had their individual tastes, needs, means, and habits; Morel ascribed a garden *class* to each social class. The *park* valorized the château of the man of wealth who needed to demonstrate his "greatness and power." The *Garden proper* was for the man who wanted his "elegance and taste" to be evident. The *countryside* was reserved for the "man of taste," who was curiously unencumbered by excessive wealth and who was desirous of a country retreat as near to a natural condition as possible. The *farm* was reserved for those who wished to exploit their land for revenue. Once the appropriate *class* was determined, the designer had great latitude to develop the garden within the parameters establishes by Morel.[30]

Associating a layer of social representation to each *class* added needless confusion to Morel's theory. And, indeed, his *class* classification system was called into question, prompting Morel to give it a spirited defense in the preface to the second edition of *Théorie des jardins*. In truth, he completely avoided the question of how his theory would function in practice: How could one insure the sequence of the *Garden proper, park,* and *countryside,* with the *farm* located appropriately in the landscape? The only way to understand his conflated layers of responsibility for the *classes* is to separate them. First, the *classes,* individually or as a whole, must suggest a design transition between the house and the property limit. Second, a garden's character must suit the social position of the owner, all the while respecting—to the extent possible—the natural character of the site.

Morel then devoted several chapters to the parameters, processes, and elements that the designer had at his disposal to create picturesque gardens. His brief chapter "Of the Materials of Nature" introduced themes, including the professional purview of the garden designer and the physical laws of nature that the designer must understand and obey in order to create gardens, that he would return to again. The chapter established an important part of his theory: in as much as the garden designer's task was to emulate nature, he must recognize and understand how the natural landscape was composed, organized, and arranged. Nature was a system of physical laws that the designer must "consult" in order to create landscapes that emulated nature.

Morel included a brief chapter on climate—only one paragraph long—that might have seemed superfluous, were it not for the central importance of climate in garden design. It was a given that one must work with, not around.[31] The chapter was a logical precursor to his subsequent chapters on the seasons, in which he offered descriptions of natural landscapes throughout the year. These chapters presented landscape scenes that evoked the different characters that garden designers should strive to emulate for year-round enjoyment. They also contained some pertinent gardening advice: don't plant evergreen trees that block the morning sun; plant deciduous trees to block summer's sun; recognize the different blooming times of plants, shrubs, and trees; and site houses midslope, etc. Implicit in the sequential organization of the chapters—spring, summer, fall, and winter—was the notion of the perpetual cycle of nature, with her unending processes and constant modification. Morel reinforced this idea with a vocabulary redolent of the infinitesimal change and continuity of nature and her perpetual alteration: leaves dry "little by little"; their colors "se nuancent" and pass successively from one shade to another; and evening's light fades "insensiblement."

Continuing on the same theme, he described how the designer must create liaisons among groupings of plants, shrubs, and trees, and he must manage their transitions from the shortest shrub to the tallest tree. Everything in nature progresses orderly from one state to another, in nuanced steps. Just as he had discussed the transition of the garden's overall design from house to horizon, he likewise described the transitions among nature's elements.

In his chapters on the seasons, Morel broached concepts of human understanding. In a paraphrase of Condillac, he posed the rhetorical question: "But perhaps she [Nature] has only established the succession of the seasons with the view to enhance one by the others." The experience of the seasons was enhanced because that which precedes influences the appreciation or reception of that which follows. Although he denied it, Morel was operating in the realm of sensationist metaphysics, and he claimed ignorance of how such operations of the mind function. Nonetheless, throughout his book he returned to the theme.

Terrestrial concerns were addressed in chapters on land formation, water, vegetation, rocks, and structures—all of which were the fundamental components of gardens. In these chapters, Morel's study of Buffon and the empirical philosophers became most evident. His chapter on landform, "Of Terrain," combined evocative descriptions of the natural landscape with well-considered and informed lessons on geological formations. Nowhere is Morel's training as a geographical engineer more evident than in this chapter, which is heavily laden with descriptions of natural processes. The length of the chapter (one of the longest in the book) is indicative of the importance that Morel gave to the subject and is a tacit acknowledgment that all landscape design begins from the ground up.

Moreover, understanding how land is formed is of utmost importance because it dictates landscape character, which was a central concern to Morel. Yet, as he discussed, landform was a natural creation largely beyond the capability of man to alter or change. The garden designer could not create landform, but could only enhance it and work with it—a crucial lesson that Morel reinforced at the end of this chapter, when he related landform to his four *classes* and their respective characters. The lesson is clear: to create gardens that are in keeping with the natural site character, the designer must understand the natural mechanisms that created it. Accordingly, Morel devoted a great deal of the chapter to the means by which natural landscapes are created.

More than any other contemporary author of picturesque theory, Morel incorporated recent geological discoveries, including lessons in the hydrodynamics of water and its role in the formation of mountains and mountain valleys. We learn of the inverse proportional relationship between the speed of a river's flow and a mountain valley's width; of the role that substrates played in the speed of a river's flow; of the equal and reciprocal angles of mountain valley's slopes; and of the corresponding salient and retreating angles of a mountain valley's disposition. In an apposite metaphor, Morel compared the division and subdivision of water into rivers, streams, and rivulets in a landscape to the vascular structure of the human body: "These are as many channels that, like the vessels of the human body, divide and subdivide, and branch and bifurcate, to carry freshness and life, and to perfect forms everywhere."[32]

As a measure of the difference—and scientific distance—between Morel and his closest rival, the Englishman Whately, we need only compare their respective discussions of landform. Whately maintained that land is either flat, concave, or convex, a vocabulary derivative of painting theory. Morel dispensed with descriptions and went directly to natural process. Other than catastrophic events, rain is the most important determinant in the formation of land. As rain accumulates, it forms rivers, which, in turn, erode the earth: "Water is indisputably one of the principal agents by which the terrain receives almost all its modifications." But Morel went further, by connecting rain to vapors, clouds, and the wind to the endless natural cycle of evapotranspiration. In doing so, Morel took a singular element—rain—and connected it to a global process, the water cycle: "The perpetual circulation of water (which is endlessly reduced to vapor and pumped off by the sun's action), a universal principle of activity and movement, is a physical effect well known and remarked by even the least attentive men. Light mists, which are transformed into clouds by the force of the winds that raise them above our heads, condense, fall as rain, and are distributed to all the points of the globe's surface."

Throughout this rather exceptional chapter on landform, which was notable in a volume ostensibly on "garden theory," Morel reinforced his mantra that the visible landscape is the result of natural processes, and to each form there is an associated process that created it: "all of the forms . . . must bear the imprint of its action," and "causes have much contributed to their form." The more general principle is that while the natural landscape may look chaotic, it is the opposite, as for each "irregularity" in the natural world, there is a rule that governs it. Nothing in nature is arbitrary; the garden designer must keep this in mind. It is upon the understanding of natural processes dictated by natural laws that Morel founded his theory of landscape design.

In his subsequent chapters on water, vegetation, and rocks, Morel addressed the constituents of picturesque gardens that are under the direct influence of the designer. By turns didactic and evocative, each chapter examined the material and metaphysical qualities of these natural elements and considered how each contributed to the creation of landscape character and, consequently, how each effected human emotions. He began his chapter on water by writing that "water is to the landscape what the soul is to the body," thus setting the tone for the chapter and establishing the importance of the liquid for setting the mood and character of a landscape. He investigated water in its myriad forms—moving, stagnant, falling, and even vaporous—and noted the range of emotions associated with each state. But such purely descriptive (and, at times, poetical) language quickly yielded to more lessons in natural processes. He discussed islands—the only garden theorist to do so—and noted that their forms are not arbitrary, but governed by the natural processes that create them. River islands are created by the hydrodynamics of the river's flow and are, thus, constrained in their shape, while lake islands are the result of drowned depressions and, thus, can take on any configuration. Returning to water's flow, he noted that large rivers have fewer, but broader, meanders than smaller ones, and he warned against the scouring effect of water at the base of torrents and falls. He reiterated the obvious, but important, law that nature never allows water to run uphill, his point being that water must be comfortably sited according to the natural disposition of the site.[33]

Morel devoted considerable attention to vegetation, from rock lichen to the noble oak. He catalogued plant qualities from the subtlety of a trembling leaf to the solidity of a massive tree trunk, from the harmonious blend of fall foliage to the contrast of exotic flowers, all the while relating each to their effect on landscape character and, consequently, on human emotion. Water may animate a landscape, but vegetation provides for its adornment and embellishment. Trees, for which he had a special affection, hold the greatest potential of all living material to stir emotions. With trees, one can create an atmosphere of silence and solitude or a visually disorienting experience of a sharp chiaroscuro. In one remarkable passage, he depicted a dark, dank, old-growth forest in language bordering on the Burkean sublime, then followed his evocative description of this primordial vegetal realm with an observation, derivative of the empirical philosophy of Locke and Condillac: "The objects that compose them, however insensate and inanimate, in working on the intellectual faculty, succeed in elevating our mind to the most sublime contemplations."

As he often did throughout *Théorie des jardins*, Morel followed such metaphysical statements with straightforward landscape design advice. He wrote at length on the problem of designing the transition between an open field or lawn and an existing, mature forest. All too often this shift is an inelegant straight line—an abrupt transition, as it were—that he objects to. His solution was to create strong undulations at the transition, by planting it with a variety of trees and shrubs as well as isolating "specimen trees"[34] pulled from the canopy.

A brief chapter on rocks dispatched with this most vexing of nature's elements. Rocks are difficult to work with, as their character is too strong to bend to the needs of the designer. By their nature, they cannot be created, and they are moved only with great difficulty. But Morel acknowledged that they have their place in certain landscape *classes*, and maintained that they are best worked with by excavating or filling around them and by associating them with water or plantings.

Structures in the landscape ("des bâtimens") are the last of the garden elements that Morel treated in *Théorie des jardins*. He was preoccupied with them, and the lengthy chapter, the longest in the book, is evidence of his concern. As garden elements that are most under the influence of human agency, they are the most susceptible to having a negative impact on a garden's character if their purpose, placement, and use are not properly understood. The breadth with which Morel covered them might speak of a misplaced erudition if it were not for the subversive reasons he had for demonstrating his knowledge. He showcased his understanding of current architectural theory not to support the architect's place in the design of gardens, but to hijack it, so to speak, by repositioning the responsibilities previously given to the architect to the new garden designer. When he discussed the variety, uses, and placement of structures in a landscape, he was, more importantly, outlining the professional territory of the newly emerging garden design professional.

The scope of practice that he presented touches on objective and subjective criteria. Objective criteria include site selection based on physical parameters of healthfulness (*salubrité*), solar orientation, vegetative cover, topography, and proximity to roads and water—more or less the standard set of site selection criteria that any landscape designer would be concerned with today. By assigning these responsibilities to the new garden designer, he was not necessarily usurping the architect's responsibilities; instead, in a time when professional territory was fluid, he was making a claim for them within the garden designer's field of practice.

But when Morel discussed the subjective criteria of structures, he entered the domain of architecture. In one brief paragraph, he noted that the garden designer—not the architect—should be responsible for the structure's form, mass, style, details, and tint, all of which contribute to the structure's character. These parameters must be in accord with the character of the site. Once established, they cannot be changed without consequence. For instance, if the building is to be expanded to accommodate new functions, its size and mass will change. Rather than add new floors, which would affect the height, size, mass, and character of the building, Morel suggested constructing an entirely new structure nearby. Driving his reasoning was his interest—obsession, one might say—with character: the character of the structure and the character of the site must be in harmonious accord. Morel calls this accord *convenance,* which in the art of gardening is naturally, and thus universally given, as opposed to architectural *convenance*, which is based on custom and practice.[35]

In discussing the architectural structures called follies or *fabriques*, Morel addressed the topical aesthetic debate of the day: association theory. Thomas Whately had first broached the subject in *Observations on Modern Gardening*. He favored a landscape devoid of architectural follies, especially when such structures, through their design, strongly suggested or were associated with a subject, place, time, or person. He wrote:

> All these devices are rather *emblematical* than expressive; they may be ingenious contrivances, and recall absent ideas to the recollection; but they make no immediate impression, for they must be examined, compared, perhaps explained, before the whole design of them is well understood; and though an allusion to a favorite or well-known subject of history, of poetry, or of tradition, may now and then animate or dignify a scene, yet as the subject does not naturally belong to the garden, the

allusion should not be principle; it should seem to have been suggested by the scene: a transitory image, which irresistibly occurred; not sought for, not labored; and have the force of a metaphor, free from the detail of an allegory.[36]

Morel concurred with Whately's aesthetic theory on garden follies. But one might say that he went further: Structures in a landscape must be strictly limited; they must be present only for evident, functional purposes, and must not be exotic (e.g., no Chinese pavilions, Tartar tents, or Greek temples); and they must be placed in accordance with, and in enhancement of, the site character. In a not too veiled attack on contemporary garden designer and writer Louis Carrogis de Carmontelle, whose Jardin de Monceau (known for its abundance of *fabriques*) was being constructed as Morel was writing his theory, he wrote: "What is more nonsensical than the association of all the types—ancient and modern, Greek and Gothic, Turkish and Chinese—in a single Garden? How does one claim to bring together, without offending common sense, the four corners of the earth in one small space, and all the centuries in one moment?" Following his critique of Carmontelle, Morel asked the rhetorical question: Where should such follies be placed? His answer—in "le jardin anglais"—is a sly nationalistic plug in keeping with what was among the French a pejorative reference to natural-style gardens populated with architectural follies, such as Stowe.[37]

Morel reproved of emblematical devices and warned of their detrimental effects on taste. His believed that nature, enhanced by the designer, must be the driving force of the emotional effect a garden has on the senses. In emulation of the artistic theorist Roger de Piles, who championed that a painting must first appeal to the gut, rather than to the mind, Morel favored the pure, unmitigated experience between the observer and enhanced nature.

Before concluding his chapter on structures, Morel offered some practical advice, especially regarding the main house and its relationship to the site and its surroundings. He reiterated standard site selection criteria known in architectural treatises dating to Vitruvius, such as siting the house midslope rather than in a depression or on a ridge. And he warned against placing the house in a position that affords a splendid vista, for such views quickly lose interest once the prospect is taken in. Morel was particularly interested in how the house meets the ground, and how one accesses the garden from within the house. His preference was the least encumbered means possible: no terraces, steps, or other architectural structures should mediate the transition from house to garden. Grand reception rooms should be on grade with the garden to allow for an effortless flow between inside and out. If there is a moat surrounding the house, it should be filled in to provide for direct and comfortable access. These examples once again demonstrate Morel's interest in smooth transitions across a landscape continuum, whether it be exhibited on a large scale, as with the *classes*, or on a smaller scale, as with the transition from garden to house.[38]

Having emphasized the overriding natural factors, which are generative of landscapes, and having presented detailed discourses on the physical elements of garden design, in keeping with the rigorous logical structure of his book, Morel concluded with five successive chapters focusing on garden *classes*, which serve as examples, as it were, of his theory. Two chapters concern gardens (Ermenonville and Guiscard)[39] that he designed or was involved with; these gardens are representative of the *countryside* and *park*, respectively (Figures 3 and 4). Chapters on the *farm* and the *Garden proper* follow. The concluding chapter, which is confusingly entitled "Des Genres" ("Of the Types"), does not relate to his four archetype (*class*) divisions; rather, it deals with a set of gardens that are dependent on emblematic effects (i.e., architectural follies, not natural scenery) to establish their character. His chapters on the four *classes* are used to demonstrate, if not substantiate, his theory, while his concluding chapter is intended as a cautionary note on the abuses that natural garden design can be subjected to.

Le CHÂTEAU D'ERMENONVILLE du côté du Nord.

ERMENONVILLE'S HOUSE on the Nord side. ‖ Das SCHLOSS von ERMENONVILLE gegen Norden.

Figure 3

Le château d'Ermenonville, from Alexandre de Laborde, *Description des nouveaux jardins de la France et de ses anciens châteaux* (Paris, 1808).

Pl. 87

Le CHÂTEAU DE GUISCARD, pris du côté de l'Étang.

The CASTLE OF GUISCARD, taken from the Pond side. ‖ GUISCARD'S SCHLOSS von der Seite des Teiches.

Figure 4 ——————————————————————————————

Le château de Guiscard, from Alexandre de Laborde, *Description des nouveaux jardins de la France et de ses anciens châteaux* (Paris, 1808).

The chapters on the *countryside* and *park* include extensive descriptions of the natural landscape character, which the garden designer must recognize in order to create a garden appropriate to the site. Ermenonville is a *countryside* because of the site's natural variety and expansiveness, while Guiscard, which is less rich in its natural landscape variations, is blessed with natural grace and beauty befitting the *park*. It is more restricted in its design variations than the *countryside*, but it can support an array of common design interventions guided by good taste. The chapters on the *farm* and *Garden proper* are straightforward discussions of the landscape character appropriate to each *class*. Because the *Garden proper* is the most dependent on obvious design interventions, its site character is of less importance. For the *farm,* the presence of arable soil and productive fields takes precedence. Because they are most given to caprice and human inventions, the *jardins de genre* have great latitude in being independent of the site constraints.

For the most part, the chapters on *classes* do not add anything new to the theory that Morel presented in the preceding pages, but they do embellish, elaborate, and reinforce what he wrote through descriptions and metaphors. For example, he likened the *countryside* to an epic poem: the *countryside* is "the equivalent of the epic Poem in the Art of Poetry." Moreover, the length of each chapter demonstrates the importance of the archetypes (*classes*) in his theory. As noted previously, they are its structural core, and, as such, he was insistent that his reader understand not only their centrality but also their essence. Perhaps, in more practical terms, as a creator of landscapes Morel wanted to demonstrate his ability to practice what he preached, much as Watelet had done in *Essai sur les jardins*, the concluding chapter of which was on his own garden at Moulin Joli.

Morel addressed the challenges that any landscape designer might face with preexisting conditions. At Ermenonville, he was confronted with a poorly sited, graceless château, which was set within a landscape of disparate and contrasting parts. It was his job to make it into a unified whole while preserving its original character, and he praised himself on his work: "Thus, a disagreeable location became a charming landscape, a marshy and unhealthy site was changed into a cheerful and airy valley, and an unfortunate place was transformed into one of the most interesting situations." At Guiscard, the property included a château and land of roughly 330 acres.[40] It had a well-preserved, formal garden that Morel systematically dismantled, turning it into a natural garden; his chapter recounted how. The professional point he was making is that bold strokes must be made, at great expense, over long periods of time in order to refashion an existing site into a proper natural garden.

Important in these concluding chapters is Morel's return to the metaphysics of feeling and artistic mimesis. Throughout his book, he broached these subjects, but as he neared its conclusion, he returned to them with an urgency and focus not seen before. In the penultimate chapter on the *farm*, he entered into a five-page riff, indebted to Condillac, on the mechanisms of human understanding. We learn through the senses by constantly comparing and contrasting physical phenomena; Morel adapted this idea to a comparative sequencing of landscape scenes. He said as much in his chapters on the seasons, but now he elaborated with a specific example of a designed landscape:

> nothing is perfectly isolated in Nature's scenes. Each effect, each feature depends on what is around it, and affects us differently by what accompanies it. Everything that presents itself to our eye has a kind of connection to what we have just seen, and even with what we assume we must see. Let us note in passing that when it is tricked this foresight is the source of contrasts and exciting transitions. Finally, objects trace a sequence of simultaneous and successive images in the head according to their association,

bringing worth to one another, and strengthening the present impressions and preparing for the effects of those that must follow.

This remarkable passage is unprecedented in any garden theory work of the era, and Morel, recognizing his tangent, quickly apologized: "These ideas may appear slightly metaphysical, and for many people my frame will be merely a dream . . . Let me return to vegetable gardens."[41]

But he returned to the theme in the last chapter. Feigning ignorance of "that part of Philosophy" dealing with human understanding and sensations, he asked rhetorical questions concerning "how insensate and often immobile beings put his senses in motion, and how, then, pure sensations produce feelings." Through some roundabout reasoning, he steered his argument to the theory of imitation in the arts and its application to garden making, all for the purposes of supporting and validating his "natural" approach to the garden.

Only at the end of his book did Morel engage the differences between painting[42] and gardening; contemporary garden theorists had done so upfront. Postponing the discussion focused attention on natural gardening, independent of any presumed influence or connection to painting. Indeed, more than his fellow garden writers, Morel distanced natural gardening from painting; despite any similarities between painting and natural garden design, they are different art forms, each with their own respective internal artistic logic. On very practical level, one cannot enter or move through a painting as one does a landscape, and one cannot change perspectives by simply moving. A painting is a moment in time—"un seul moment du jour"—incapable of eliciting the sensations of seasonal succession and changes that a landscape can.

The more theoretical point, however, is that painting is a true imitative art; natural gardening is not. Here, Morel entered questionable—and contradictory—artistic grounds. Although he elevated garden design to the liberal arts, he denied it the very criteria that constitute art. Art, by definition, must show the human agency that produces it; the natural garden—or the kind that Morel favors—must hide ("cacher avec soin") any such intervention: "In the entire course of this work I have proved that when the means are apparent, they destroy pleasure and interest, whatever merit they might announce in the Artist who has put them to use. In great Art, these means are never suspected, and in no case should the strings and machines be seen, but should instead be veiled with the most scrupulous attention and the greatest skill."

Morel never confronted the contradiction in artistic theory, as he clearly did not see one. Yet, in distancing natural garden design from painting, and removing it from the imitative arts, he established its independent status.[43] Moreover, he used this mimetic argument as a foil to argue against *jardins de genre*. Returning to themes already introduced in his chapter on building, he vehemently reproved these thematic gardens predicated on a variety of man-made effects. As a set-up, he named four garden *types*—*le poétique* (poetic), *le romanesque* (romantic), *le pastoral* (pastoral), and *l'imitatif* (imitative)—only to condemn them. Each is subject to, and driven by, a set of design elements that have little to do with natural elements and site conditions. Rather, architectural follies and evident man-made interventions are at play. For example, *le poétique* draws from mythology and fables; this garden *type* is brought to life, so to speak, through buildings, statuary, and other devices. Implicit in his condemnation of such gardens is the need for advanced learning or knowledge, as it were, of the themes at play. Seconding Whately, Morel proffered the superiority of his *jardins de la nature* because such preordained knowledge is not necessary. No reflection is needed, just an ability to see and feel. In a sense, just as he had argued for the unmediated physical spatial transition from house to garden, and from garden to surroundings, Morel dispensed with any intellectual mediation between the designed garden and the human response.

After almost four hundred pages of a tightly crafted and rigorous theory of natural gardening, one might think that Morel's concluding chapter warrants a spirited valediction. Curiously, it is nothing of the sort. Rather, it is a blend of defense and caution. Reacting to the (apparent) predominant trend of the day, which favored *jardins de genre* over natural gardens, Morel clearly feared for his approach. He noted that in any "revolution"—and he considered the changing style in garden design as such—the first "steps" are misguided and false, and that "the simplicity of Nature is only reached after having exhausted all these combinations, just as the truth is only met after having traveled a long circuit of errors. Such are the workings of the human mind." But he implicitly placed his gardening style at the end of this progression, where art has returned to the truth. Acknowledging that the world of gardening was in flux, Morel was not at all confident that truth would triumph. As if exhausted by his own efforts, he ended *Théorie des jardins* on a less than sanguine note: "Should it not be feared that these examples of a type so frivolous, so opposed to good taste, in multiplying with impunity before the eyes of a Nation enlightened by the truth but in love with novelty, should prolong the infancy of an Art that is still in the cradle?"

The Second Edition

In 1802, twenty-six years after the initial publication of *Théorie des jardins*, Morel reissued the work in a revised and augmented second edition (Figure 5). Although he maintained that his theory was intact, the second edition contains many alterations, and is, in fact, largely rewritten. Among the most obvious differences are the two volumes of the second edition; it has an expanded title, *Théorie des jardins, ou, L'Art des jardins de la nature*, which speaks more directly

THÉORIE DES JARDINS,

OU

L'ART DES JARDINS

DE LA NATURE.

Seconde édition, revue par l'Auteur, enrichie
de Notes, et suivie d'un Tableau Dendrologique,
contenant la Liste des Plantes ligneuses indigènes
et exotiques acclimatées, etc. etc.

PAR J.-M. MOREL,

Ancien Architecte, Membre ordinaire de la Société
d'Agriculture, de Botanique et des Arts utiles du
département du Rhône, et de l'Athénée de Lyon.

Il entretint les Dieux, non point sur la fortune ;
Sur ses jeux, sur la pompe et la grandeur des Rois ;
Mais sur ce que les champs, les vergers et les bois
Ont de plus innocent, de plus doux, de plus rare.
La Fontaine. Fable de Philemon et Baucis.

TOME PREMIER.

A PARIS,

Chez la Vᵉ PANCKOUCKE, Imprimeur-
Libraire, rue de Grenelle, Nᵒ 321, faubourg Saint-
Germain, en face de la rue des Sts.-Pères.

AN XI. — 1802.

C'est l'art de la Nature.
Préface, Page I. et suiv.

Figure 5

Frontispiece and title page of *Théorie des jardins, ou, L'art des jardins de la nature,* 2nd ed.,
(Paris, 1802).

to the art form under consideration and sharply focuses his intent; the quotation from Milton's *Paradise Lost* on the title page of the first edition is replaced
by a quotation from La Fontaine's *Fable of Philemon and Baucis,* a sign of independence from English precedents; a new frontispiece (the first edition did
not contain one); a dedication to Empress Joséphine, his then patron; a new,
128-page preface; a new appendix (*Tableau dendrologique*) containing a list of
trees, shrubs, and plants suitable for natural gardens; and a letter from an uniden-
tified Italian artist who had questioned Morel's attack on symmetric gardens,
along with Morel's lengthy rebuttal.

Most important in the second edition is its new preface, in which Morel provided a literature review of current French and English texts on picturesque gardening, including works by William Mason, Horace Walpole, Thomas Whately,

William Chambers, Claude-Henri Watelet, Abbé Jacques Delille, Adrien de Lezay-Marnésia, and Jean-Antoine Roucher, and gave an account of several English gardens that he had visited since writing the first edition, including Blenheim, Hagley, Kew, The Leasowes, Oatlands, Stourhead, Stowe, and Woburn Farm. Implicit in his statement that he did not change the substance of his theory between editions is the idea that his theory could stand on its own, even after his travels to England. Also of interest is that, in the new preface, Morel defended his garden archetypes, which had been subject to harsh criticism by some of the writers just mentioned.

In the new edition, Morel expanded the footnotes and restructured them as endnotes; removed sections that he deemed to be inessential; rethought some vocabulary; rephrased discussions for clarity; and, on occasion, changed a word or two for stylistic purposes. Some changes respond to criticisms he received to his first edition, such as it being too "metaphysical," containing too many technical words, and having a vocabulary drawn from science. Indeed, the word "metaphysics" is removed from the second edition, while "laws of physics" is replaced by "physical causes." Many descriptions of natural processes are removed altogether. Nonetheless, the second edition is still a well-considered synthesis of empirical sensationist philosophy and an understanding of natural law.

It might be said that the biggest difference between the two editions is accessibility—that is, the second edition is more "user-friendly." In a gesture that betrays the changed social climate of France, the language of the second edition is "Republicanized." Words that spoke of a pre-Revolutionary social order are struck in favor of a vocabulary aimed at a rising bourgeois class. Likewise, many of the changes were intended to appeal to a greater audience. By 1802, Morel had a solid reputation and did not have to prove himself among his contemporaries; nonetheless, he had to find clients. The *Tableau dendrologique*, a first of its kind in a garden theory book,[44] is perhaps the clearest indication of his desire to appeal to a potentially new client base. It is suggestive that the *theory* of *Théorie des jardins* has now been supplemented with more easily grasped and specific practical matters.

Morel ends his second edition with only the slightest concession to advancements in the art form that he was so instrumental in establishing. Citing the continued spread of gardens of stylistic types which were not "based in Nature" (i.e., his theory of garden design), he feared that the art form that had only "just left the cradle" was at risk for a prolonged infancy: "Should it not be feared that these examples of a type so frivolous and opposed to truth, multiplying with impunity under the eyes of an enlightened Nation, but covetous of novelty, will prolong the infancy of an art that has only just left the cradle?"[45]

Notes

1 Throughout this introduction, the reference to "André Le Nôtre style" shall mean any variation on the style of gardening based on the symmetrical arrangement of regular geometries around major and minor axes. It is the general style that predominated prior to the advent of the natural, picturesque, or English style of gardening. It is understood that there was a great deal of variation in the "André Le Nôtre style," but the reliance on axes, symmetries, and regular geometries was still the primary means of organizing space.

2 "We have had gardens, and even the art of gardening, but we haven't had the science of gardening; we can consider M. Morel as the creator of this science." (Nous avions des Jardins, & un Art même des Jardins; mais nous n'en avions pas la science; c'est cette science dont on peut regarder M. [Morel] comme le créateur.) *Affiches, announces, et avis divers,* July 17, 1776.

3 "The *Theory of Gardens* by M. Morel has made much noise; but it is a book that has been more praised than it has been read." (La *Théorie des jardins,* par M. Morel . . . a fait assez de bruit; mais ce livre a été beaucoup plus prôné qu'il n'a été lu.) *Correspondance littéraire,* November 1776.

4 See the bibliographic essay for an overview of Morel and garden literature.

5 See the bibliographic essay for an overview of Morel's published works.

6 "We must not equate the fading of a name with the extinction of a person's influence. In so doing, we propagate one of the many errors inspired by our generation's fundamental confusion of celebrity with stature . . . under certain definite circumstances . . . a loss of personal recognition through time actually measures the spread of a person's impact as innovations become so 'obvious' and 'automatic' that we lose memory of sources and assign their status to elementary logic from time immemorial." Stephen J. Gould, review of *Buffon: A Life in Natural History,* by Jacques Roger, *New York Review of Books,* October 22, 1998.

7 J. C. Loudon, *An Encyclopaedia of Gardening* (London: Printed for Longman, Rees, Orme, Brown, Green, and Longman, 1835), §337. Loudon's comparison of Morel and William Kent is curious, as Morel's style is more akin to Capability Brown than Kent. Indeed, Morel is most easily characterized as the "French Brown." It suggests that he viewed the Frenchman as having a primacy of sorts among French practitioners and theorists, similar to Kent's nominal reputation of establishing the English school of garden design.

8 For a discussion and list of Morel's gardens, see Joseph Disponzio, "Jean-Marie Morel: A Catalogue of His Landscape Design," *Studies in the History of Gardens and Designed Landscapes* 21, nos. 3–4 (July–December 2001).

9 Jean Le Rond d'Alembert, *Essai sur les éléments de philosophie,* quoted in Ernst Cassirer, *The Philosophy of the Enlightenment* (Princeton: Princeton University Press, 1968), 3–4.

10 "Rerum novus mascitur ordo." Denis Diderot, *Le Rêve d'Alembert,* in *Oeuvres philosophique,* ed. Paul Vernière (Paris: Garnier frères, 1964).

11 Demarest's eleven-page article in the *Encyclopédie* was divided into two parts: methodology and observation, and description of the mechanisms that form the physical features of the earth.

12 On the popularity of Pluche and Buffon in eighteenth-century France, see Daniel Mornet, "Les enseignements des bibliothèques privée (1750–1780)," *Revue d'histoire littéraire de la France* 17, no. 3 (1910):449–96. For a brief discussion on the publication and reception of books on science in the eighteenth century, see Daniel Roche, *France in the Enlightenment*, trans. Arthur Goldhammer (Cambridge, Mass.: Harvard University Press, 1998).

13 I condense a complex history here; Cartesianism never fully died out in France. See Aram Vartanian, *Diderot and Descartes: A Study of Scientific Naturalism in the Enlightenment* (Princeton: Princeton University Press, 1953); Colm Kiernan, "Additional Reflections on Diderot and Science," *Diderot Studies* 14 (1971):113–42; and Colm Kiernan, *The Enlightenment and Science in Eighteenth-Century France*, 2nd ed., Studies on Voltaire and the Eighteenth Century (Banbury: Voltaire Foundation, 1973).

14 "une puissance vive, immense, qui embrasse tout, qui anime tout." Georges-Louis Leclerc, comte de Buffon, *Histoire naturelle* (Paris: Impr. Royale, 1764).

15 The literature on "Nature" is enormous; see Arthur O. Lovejoy, "'Nature' as Aesthetic Norm," *Modern Language Notes* 42, no. 7 (1927):444–50, reprinted in *Essays in the History of Ideas* (Baltimore: Johns Hopkins University Press, 1948). For a comprehensive review of the meaning and idea of nature in France during the eighteenth century, see Jean Ehrard, *L'idée de nature en France dans la première moitié du XVIIIe siècle* (Paris: SEVPEN, 1963); and Daniel Mornet, *Le sentiment de la nature en France, de J. -J. Rousseau à Bernardin de Saint-Pierre* (Paris: Librairie Hachette, 1907).

16 The change in garden style on both sides of the English Channel in the eighteenth century was the result of multiple factors—social, political, and literary—in addition to the foci presented in this introduction. These other influences have been extensively covered in the vast literature on the rise of the picturesque garden.

17 In a chauvinistic plug, as well as a true characterization of rationalist France, in his introduction to his translation of *Observations on Modern Gardening*, Latapie suggested that while the English may have been the first to write on the new style, the French were the first to *think* about doing it: "To Kent goes the glory for having introduced the natural style of composing gardens to his country, but he wasn't its inventor; the style had already been conceived by the famous Dufresny." (Kent a eu la gloire d'introduire dans sa patrie la méthode la plus naturelle de composer des jardins, mais il n'en est pas l'inventeur . . . il avait été prévu en France par le célèbre Dufresny.) Latapie's remark remained current in French historiography of the "English" tradition through the nineteenth century.

18 These were only the more prominent books published. Others included François-Henri, duc de Harcourt, *Traité de la decorations des dehors, des jardins et des parcs* (*Treatise on the Decoration of the Outdoors, Gardens, and Parks*) dating to 1775, but not published until 1919 by Ernest de Ganay; Guy de Chabanan, *Épitre sur la manie des jardins anglais* (*Letter on the Mania of English Gardens*), published in the *Correspondance littéraire secrète* in January 1775, with numerous re-editions; and *Lettre sur les jardins anglais* (*Letter on English Gardens*), published by the anonymous "M[onsieur]. L.I.G.D.M." in the *Journal encyclopédique* in October 1775. To these can be added countless poems, prose works, and essays devoted to the new genre. For a comprehensive list, see Ernest de Ganay, *Bibliographie de l'art des jardins*, ed. Geneviève Bonté (Paris: Bibliothèque des Arts Décoratifs, 1989).

19 René Louis de Girardin's book was translated by Daniel Malthus as *An Essay on Landscape* (1783; reprint, New York: Garland Publishers, 1982). See Claude-Henri Watelet, *Essay on Gardens: A Chapter in the French Picturesque*, trans. Samuel Danon (Philadelphia: University of Pennsylvania Press, 2003). Hirschfeld received an abridged translation in 2001: C. C. L. Hirschfeld, *Theory of Garden Art*, trans. and ed. Linda B. Parshall (Philadelphia: University of Pennsylvania Press, 2001).

20 "ni ses productions, ni l'artiste qui le professe, n'ont pas encore obtenu dans notre langue un nom qui les distinguât du légumier et de celui qui cultive." Jean-Marie Morel, *Théorie des jardins, ou, L'art des jardins de la nature* (Paris: Chez la Ve Panckoucke, 1802), xxv.

21 The term first appeared next to Morel's name in the *Almanach de la ville de Lyon* for the years 1803–4. In the previous year's *Almanach*, his name was appended with *architecte et paysagiste*. (*Paysagiste* at the time meant a *painter* of landscapes, not—as it implies today—a landscape designer.) There is every reason to believe that Morel self-defined as such. For more on Morel's coining of the term *architecte-paysagsite*, see Joseph Disponzio, "From Garden to Landscape: Jean-Marie Morel and the Transformation of Garden Design," *AA Files* 44 (Autumn 2001):6–20; and Joseph Disponzio, "Landscape Architect/-ure: A Brief Account of Origins," *Studies in the History of Gardens and Designed Landscapes* 34, no. 3 (Fall 2014):192–200.

22 Many self-professed and trained architects, such as William Chambers, François-Joseph Bélanger, Richard Mique, and Pierre-Adrien Pâris, designed in the new idiom. But with the exception of Chambers, none wrote on garden theory. The point is not that architects were creating picturesque gardens, but that the new garden style posed technical and mechanical challenges to the architect's training. It should come as no surprise that the early practitioners and theorists of picturesque gardening—such as Kent, Whately, and Watelet—were not trained architects; in a sense, they were not burdened by a training that was of little help in designing in the new style.

23 The word "science" in the eighteenth century suggested a general, systematized knowledge of a subject, not the rigorous hypothesis-experiment-proof field of study as it is known today.

24 In the preface to the second edition of *Théorie des jardins,* Morel gave a critique of virtually all of the writers on picturesque theory, including Chambers, Whately, and Watelet. Of Whately, he wrote, "[he] has given the best book on the subject" (le meilleur ouvrage sur cette matière). But he was severely dismissive of Watelet: "The essay will be more pleasing to the informed reader because of its agreeable style and its moral precepts, than it will be of use to the gardener-artist for the lessons it contains. Not because, in and of themselves, the precepts are not correct, but because they are too lightly treated and unconnected; they do not have the liaison, rapport, and order that facilitates understanding. Either because of inexperience or lack of facility, the author, who is otherwise interesting, does not walk with a solid step into the career he has undertaken to explore." (Cette essai sur les jardins . . . plaira plus au lecteur lettré, par l'agrément du style et par la morale qui y est répandu, qu'il ne sera utile à l'artiste-jardinier par les leçons qu'il renferme. Non qu'en eux-mêmes la plupart des préceptes ne soient bons; mais parce qu'ils y sont trop légèrement esquissés; qu'ils n'ont pas entre eux cette liaison, ces rapports, cet ordre qui en facilitent l'intelligence; et que, soit inexpérience, soit légèreté, l'écrivain, d'ailleurs intéressant, ne marche point d'un pas ferme dans la carrière qu'il a entrepris de parcourir.) (cii)

25 Such a hierarchy may seem odd to the modern reader, but a legible social structure, quite visible through the build environment (especially architecture), was an accepted norm in the eighteenth century.

26 Morel argued against architectural practice on the strictest of rational grounds: the theory and practice of architecture, which is predicated on geometry for its forms and mechanics for its practice, are not just antithetical to the new garden art, they are incapable of the new design imperatives. La Harpe found Morel's argument compelling enough to quote large excerpts from it in his review of *Théorie des jardins*; see La Harpe, "Sur la théorie des jardins, de M. Morel," *Mercure de France*, September 1776. Neither Whately nor Watelet specifically addressed the architectural profession. Only Chambers mentioned the need for a professional identity in the new gardening. Morel considers the theme at greater length and depth in chapter eight.

27 A garden's character was a preoccupation with most garden theorists of the 1770s, but they differed on how to achieve it. Unlike architectural character, which was dictated by custom, landscape character was dictated by nature, and could only be nuanced, but not created. One could, however, work against a site's character. Morel was the most conservative; for him, a garden's character must conform to the surrounding landscape setting. The talented designer must recognize the site character and work with it. For others, such as Watelet, the designer could create character through artistic means, especially using architectural follies (*fabriques*). Morel reproved of such artificial devices; see discussion below.

28 Edith Wharton, *Italian Villas and Their Gardens* (New York: Da Capo Press, 1904), 7.

29 In French architectural theory, the concepts of *convenance* and *bienseance* dictated the rules by which a building would self-evidently be representative of function, purpose, or social status. In particular, *convenance* is a broadly conceived concept that governs the "look" of a building with regard to its function and purpose. Thus, the palace of a king must be designed to specific requirements that suggest the seat of the monarch. Likewise, the château for a prince, or a home for a wealthy entrepreneur, must be expressed in its architecture. Morel, a student of Blondel, adapted these concepts to his garden theory.

30 Morel was alone among the garden theory writers of the late eighteenth century to address social distinctions in his landscape theory. Although he would rephrase or sometimes omit passages pertaining to this aspect of his theory, he would not substantially change it in the second edition.

31 Whately and Watelet seldom used the word "climate," if at all.

32 All these examples are drawn from Buffon, Desmarest, or some other eighteenth-century source. See notes to the text for specific references.

33 The length of Morel's discussion on water, and the degree to which he covers it, suggests his training as an engineer-surveyor and his expertise on the subject. He wrote a memorandum (published posthumously) on the hydrodynamics of the flow of the Rhône River (see "Mémoire sur la théorie des eaux fluentes, appliquée au cours du Rhône," *Archives historique et statistique du Rhône* [Lyon, 1825]). His discussion throughout *Théorie des jardins* is evidence that he incorporated discoveries of the natural world into his garden theory.

34 In landscape design terms, a specimen tree is one planted in isolation, not within a forest canopy, thus allowing for the tree to grow to its full potential. Morel did not use this terminology, but he makes use of such trees, pulling them from the canopy as a design device in the transition from field to forest.

35 In general, architectural *convenance* is governed by custom and, therefore, is arbitrary. Morel, in a twist, removed the arbitrariness from his "convenance dans l'art des Jardins" by suggesting that the relationship between the building and the site will be governed by the site's character, which is not arbitrary but rather set by natural conditions.

36 Thomas Whately, *Observations on Modern Gardening* (London: T. Payne, 1770), 119–20.

37 Stowe was one of the most well-known and published English gardens in France. But it was criticized as having too many *fabriques* or architectural follies; in time, a garden with a superabundance of structures was pejoratively called, among the French, a "Jardin Anglais" or "Jardin Anglois-Chinois."

38 In practice, Morel followed his own theory at the gardens of Arcelot (Côte-d'Or), where the main hall of the château is on grade with the garden, and at Guiscard (destroyed) and Heudicourt (Eure), where the château's medieval moat was filled in.

39 Morel took a considerable amount of credit for the garden of Ermenonville, perhaps more so than is warranted. He undoubtedly worked on it with René Louis de Girardin, its owner, but we simply do not know to what extent the park, as created, was his work alone. There is little question, however, that Morel's presence at Ermenonville informed Girardin's own approach to his garden.

Introduction

40　This is the only specific land measure cited in *Théorie des jardins*, thus it is an important datum for understanding the relative size of the *park*.

41　In the otherwise praiseworthy reviews of *Théorie des jardins*, Morel was often criticized for his metaphysical digressions, which might explain why he removed the passage cited above (as well as others) from the second edition.

42　Morel was specifically speaking of landscape painting.

43　Morel's removal of natural gardening from the imitative arts was seconded by Antoine-Chrysostome Quatremère de Quincy: "If, among the number of the fine arts it be allowable to cite one which has not as yet been agreed upon to call an art of imitation, I allude to *landscape gardening*, more especially in the irregular style, it is with a view to show that, in accordance with the spirit of this theory, it is of itself excluded from the imitative scale. In fact every element necessary to constitute imitation is absent from it ... What pretends to be an image of nature is nothing more nor less than nature herself." *An Essay on the Nature, the End, and the Means of Imitation in the Fine Arts*, trans. J. C. Kent (London: Smith, Elder and Co., 1837), 170. (Si l'on se permet de citer à la suite des beaux-arts, ce qu'on n'est pas encore convenu d'appeler un art d'imitation, je veux dire le *jardinage*, surtout du genre irrégulier, c'est pour faire voir que dans l'esprit de cette théorie, il se place de lui-même en dehors de l'échelle imitative. Là effectivement, tous les éléments de ce qui constitue l'imitation disparaissent ... La prétendu image de la nature, n'y est autre chose que la nature elle-même.) *Essai sur la nature, le but et les moyens de l'Imitation dans les beaux-arts* (Paris: Treuttel et Würtz, 1823), 148. Compare his words with those of Morel: "Nature's beauties have no need, in pleasing us, to recall the talents of the Artist, because it is not in imitation, but in themselves that reside the interest and pleasure to which they give rise."

44　Hirschfeld included extensive plant lists through the several volumes of *Theory of Garden Art*—he was the first to do so—but his plant lists are more randomly placed and do not comprise a synthetic *tableau* of plants, trees, and shrubs.

45　"N'est-il pas à craindre que ces exemples d'un genre si frivole, si oppose au vrai but, en se multipliant impunément sous les yeux d'une Nation éclairée sans doute, mais avide de tout ce qui est nouveau, ne prolongent l'enfance d'un art qui sort à peine du berceau?" Morel, *Théorie des jardins* (1802), 2:176.

BIBLIOGRAPHIC ESSAY

JOSEPH DISPONZIO

Théorie des jardins has appeared in all the major English and French bibliographies of gardening and garden theory books, including Narcisse Vergnaud, *L'art de créer les jardins* (Paris: Roret, 1835; 2nd ed., Paris: La Librairie Encyclopédique de Roret, 1839); Louis Bouchard-Huzard, *Traité des constructions rurales et de leur disposition*, 2 vols. (Paris: Ve Bouchard-Huzard, 1860; 2nd ed., Paris: Ve Bouchard-Huzard, 1869); Henry Sargent Codman, "A List of Works on the Art of Landscape Gardening," *Garden and Forest*, March 12, 1890, reprinted in *The Codman Collection of Books on Landscape Gardening* (Boston: Boston Public Library, 1899); Mrs. Schuyler van Rensselaer, *Art Out-of-Doors: Hints on Good Taste in Gardening* (New York: Charles Scribner's Sons, 1893); and Ernest de Ganay, *Bibliographie de l'art des jardins* (Paris: Bibliothèque des Arts Décoratifs, 1989; 2nd ed., Paris: Ed. de l'Imprimeur, 2005).

The volume is not entirely absent from landscape literature, but until the recent past it appeared as a fleeting apparition in French garden history, rather than as a central presence. Morel's theory features prominently in many early nineteenth-century works of French garden literature, where his ideas, and often his words, are widely plagiarized, including J. Lalos, *De la composition des parcs et jardins pittoresques* (Paris: Chez l'auteur, 1817) (with five editions published through 1832); Pierre Boitard, *Traité de la composition et de l'ornement des jardins* (Paris: Audot, 1825) (with multiple re-editions); Amédée de Viart, *Le jardiniste moderne: Guide des propriétaires qui s'occupent de la composition de leurs jardins, ou de l'embellissement de leur campagne* (Paris: Chez Petit, 1819; 2nd ed., Paris: N. Pichard, 1827); and Richou, *Art de composer, de distribuer et décorer, à peu de frais, toute espèce de jardins* (Paris: Audin, 1828).

Late nineteenth-century French garden design texts likewise do not give credit to Morel or simply glide over his contribution. He is mentioned in Alfred-Auguste Ernouf, *L'art des jardins: Histoire, théorie, pratique de la composition des jardins, parcs, squares…* (Paris: J. Rothschild, 1868), and Édouard André, *L'art des jardins: Traité général de la composition des parcs et jardins* (Paris: G. Masson, 1879), but he is given no serious consideration. He is not mentioned in Adolphe Alphand, *Les promenades de Paris* (Paris: J. Rothschild, 1867–73), although the book includes illustrations of his landscapes. Armand Péan, *L'architecte paysagiste: Théorie et pratique de la création et décoration des parcs et jardins* (Paris: A. Goin, 1886), comes closest to a serious consideration of Morel's contribution, noting that he was instrumental in signaling the change in garden style in the eighteenth century; the book includes some specific features espoused by Morel.

In the early twentieth century, Morel was cited in a series of articles—still worth reading—on French picturesque gardening by Albert Maumené in the review *La vie à la campagne*. Ernest de Ganay devoted a lengthy article to Morel's contribution at Ermenonville in the *Gazette illustrée des amateurs de jardins*, also dating from the early 1900s; he also mentioned him in passing throughout his unedited, unpublished collection of notes on deposit at the Bibliothèque des Arts Décoratifs in Paris. Ganay gave Morel credit for being the first to formulate a theory of English gardening in *Les jardins de France et leur décor* (Paris: Larousse, 1949), 195. Daniel Mornet frequently mentions Morel in *Le sentiment de la nature en France* (Paris: Librairie Hachette, 1907), but always in the company of other French eighteenth-century picturesque garden designers. Pierre de Nolhac is a rare exception who took note of the difference between Morel's two editions of *Théorie des jardins* in a chapter devoted to "Les jardins du dix-huitième siècle," in *Versailles au XVIIIe siècle* (Paris: L. Conard, 1926), although his discussion of Morel is entirely in footnotes.

Perhaps not surprisingly, books devoted to his hometown, Lyon, give Morel more notice. In particular, he is often cited for his participation as a member of the artistic, cultural, and intellectual establishment of the city: Julien-Bernard-Dorothée de Mazade-Percin, *Lettres à ma fille sur mes promenades à Lyon,* 4 vols. (Lyon, 1810); François-Marie de Fortis, *Voyage pittoresque et historique à Lyon, aux environs et sur les rives de la Saône et du Rhône,* 2 vols. (Paris: Chez Bossange frères, 1821–22); and Louis Trénard, *Lyon, de l'encyclopédie au préromantisme,* 2 vols. (Paris: Presses universitaires de France, 1958).

Morel has featured prominently in French literature studies, especially of the romantic era. Robert Mauzi, *L'idée du bonheur dans la littérature et la pensée françaises au XVIIIe siècle* (Paris: A. Colin, 1967); André Monglond, *Le préromantisme français,* 2 vols. (Grenoble: B. Arthaud, 1930); and Roland Mortier, *La poétique des ruines en France: Ses origines, ses variations de la Renaissance à Victor Hugo* (Geneva: Droz, 1974), have all mined Morel for his sensationist writing to support arguments for romantic aspirations of picturesque writers of the eighteenth century. In English, Paul Ilie used Morel for his evocations of the sublime in *The Age of Minerva,* 2 vols. (Philadelphia: University of Pennsylvania Press, 1995).

Morel has received more serious attention in the recent past, in part spurred by the increased interest in French picturesque gardening as a result of the important exhibition catalogue *Jardins en France, 1760–1820* (Paris: Caisse nationale des monuments historiques et des sites, 1977). The following works have addressed Morel in more than just a perfunctory manner: Monique Mosser and Georges Teyssot, eds., *The Architecture of Western Gardens* (Cambridge, Mass.: MIT Press, 1991); Janine Barrier, "Jardins et littérature à l'époque des Lumières," in *Les temps des jardins*, ed. Florence Collette and Denise Péricard-Méa (Seine-et-Marne: Conseil général de Saine-et-Marne, 1992); Antoine Picon, "Le naturel et l'efficace: Art des jardins et culture technologique," in *Le jardin, art et lieu de mémoire*, ed. Monique Mosser and Phil Nys (Besançon: Editiones de l'Imprimeur, 1995); Antoine Picon, *L'invention de l'ingénieur moderne: L'école des ponts et chaussées, 1747–1851* (Paris: Presses de l'École Nationale des ponts et chaussées, 1992); Jean-Pierre Le Dantec, *Jardins et paysages* (Paris: Larousse, 1996); and Michel Baridon, *Les jardins: Paysagistes, jardiniers, poètes* (Paris: R. Laffont, 1998). Yves Luginbühl stressed Morel's importance to the conception and representation of landscapes in *Paysages: Textes et représentations du siècle des Lumières à nos jours* (Lyon: La Manufacture, 1989). Elisabetta Cereghini wrote a dissertation ("Jean-Marie Morel: Un architetto paesaggista nella Francia del XVIIIe secolo") on Morel for the Istituto universitario di Architettura (Venice) in 1991, but the work remains unpublished, and—as evidenced by unsuccessful attempts to access it—unavailable. Cereghini, however, has published one article and one biographic entry on Morel. Several master's theses have been devoted to gardens by Morel, including those by Catherine Berthoux (Savigny-lès-Beaune), Christophe Bourgouin (Arcelot), and Valérie Collardeau (Saint Trys).

The English literature on Morel is less extensive. When he is mentioned, it is almost always with reference to his role at Ermenonville, or as the author of *Théorie des jardins*, without further discussion. Loudon's discussion is, by far, the longest nineteenth-century English text devoted to Morel. Of note, in an article on landscape gardening dating from 1888, Mrs. Schuyler van Rensselaer placed *Théorie des jardins* at the head of a list of recommended and noteworthy books on the subject, but as the list is neither chronological nor alphabetical, it is unclear why Morel is placed at the top; see "Landscape Gardening," *American Architect and Building News* 22 (January 7, 1888):3–5. He is sometimes given fleeting mention in general texts, such as Albert Forbes Sieveking, *Gardens Ancient and Modern* (London: J. M. Dent, 1899). Marie Luise Schroeter Gothein does not mention Morel in the compendious *Geschichte der Gartenkunst*, 2 vols. (Jena: E. Diederichs, 1914). Oswald Sirén, *China and Gardens of Europe of the Eighteenth Century* (New York: Ronald Press, 1950), gives him serious consideration. Morel is not mentioned in Christopher Hussey, *The Picturesque: Studies in a Point of View* (London: Cass, 1927), although his contemporary Girardin is. Christopher Thacker, *The History of Gardens* (Berkeley: University of California Press, 1979), notes Morel's role in assisting Girardin at Ermenonville. Morel is not mentioned in Norman Newton,

Design on the Land: The Development of Landscape Architecture (Cambridge, Mass.: Belknap Press of Harvard University Press, 1971), which for a generation or two was the standard textbook used by students of landscape architecture in the United States. Morel is, likewise, absent in the more recent text of Philip Pregill and Nancy Volkman (*Landscapes in History: Design and Planning in the Western Tradition* [New York: Van Nostrand Reinhold, 1993]), but he does make an entry in Elizabeth Barlow Rogers, *Landscape Design: A Cultural and Architectural History* (New York: Henry N. Abrams, 2001). More serious discussion of Morel is given by Dora Wiebenson, who placed him in the context of the field, but, curiously, dismissed his contribution. Her book, *The Picturesque Garden in France* (Princeton: Princeton University Press, 1978), is still the only one in English devoted to the subject. Kenneth Woodbridge, *Princely Gardens: The Origins and Development of the French Formal Style* (New York: Rizzoli, 1986), cites Morel's belief that symmetric gardens derived naturally from the architect's training, and that these regular gardens had their place in the public realm. Robin Middleton emphasized Morel's influence on late eighteenth-century French architecture theory in the introduction to Nicolas Le Camus de Mézières, *The Genius of Architecture; or, The Analogy of That Art with Our Sensations*, trans. David Britt (Santa Monica, Calif.: Getty Center for the History of Art and the Humanities, 1992), and in the review of Werner Szambien, *Symétrie, goût, caractère: Théorie et terminologie de l'architecture à l'âge classique, 1500–1800*, in *Burlington Magazine* 131 (January 1989):44–45. John Dixon Hunt has given Morel serious consideration in several recent books, especially *The Picturesque Garden in Europe* (London: Thames and Hudson, 2002) and *A World of Gardens* (London: Reaktion Books, 2012). Brigitte Weltmar-Aron is the rare scholar who has clearly read Morel and given his work more than casual study; see *On Other Grounds: Landscape Gardening and Nationalism in Eighteenth-Century England and France* (Albany: State University of New York Press, 2001). Morel has been discussed in at least one American PhD dissertation; see Richard Stephen Hopkins Jr., "Engineering Nature: Public Greenspaces in Nineteenth-Century Paris" (PhD diss., Arizona State University, 2008). The present author completed his dissertation ("The Garden Theory and Landscape Practice of Jean-Marie Morel" [PhD diss., Columbia University, 2000]) on Morel, and has published widely on the French master garden designer. He is currently preparing a full study on Morel.

Published works by Jean-Marie Morel

Théorie des jardins. Paris: Chez Pissot, 1776.

> Reprint, Geneva: Minkoff, 1973, with the erroneous inclusion of eleven plates which are not in the original. The plates are from René Le Berryais, *Traité des jardins, ou, Le nouveau de La Quintinye* (Paris: Chez P. Fr. Didot jeune, 1775).

Théorie des jardins, ou, L'art des jardins de la nature, 2nd ed. Paris: Chez la Ve Panckoucke, 1802.

> "Seconde édition, revue par l'Auteur, enrichie de Notes, et suivie d'un Tableau Dendrologique, contenant la Liste des Plantes ligneuses indigènes et exotiques acclimatées, etc., etc. 2 volumes."

> Includes a new preface, frontispiece, and dedication to the Empress Joséphine.

Théorie des jardins, ou, L'art des jardins de la nature, 2nd ed. Paris: Chez D. Colas, 1806.

> "Seconde édition, revue par l'Auteur, enrichie de Notes, et suivie d'un Tableau Dendrologique, contenant la Liste des Plantes ligneuses indigènes et exotiques acclimatées, etc., etc. 2 volumes."

> Frontispiece, dedication, and text identical to the 1802 edition, with the following changes: The title page has been reset, and the font size changed; the publisher is Chez D. Colas, Imprimeur-Libraire, and the year of publication is 1806.

Théorie des jardins, ou, L'art des jardins de la nature, 2nd ed. Paris: Chez L. Colas, 1818.

> "Seconde édition, revue par l'Auteur, enrichie de Notes, et suivie d'un Tableau Dendrologique, contenant la Liste des Plantes ligneuses indigènes et exotiques acclimatées, etc., etc. 2 volumes."

> Same as the 1806 edition, with the following changes. The dedication to Joséphine is removed; the publisher is changed to Chez L. Colas, Imprimeur-Libraire and the date of publication is 1818.

> The publisher and publication date are printed on a strip of paper affixed to the title page of the 1806 edition, covering the underlying publisher's name and date of Chez D. Colas, Imprimeur-Libraire, 1806.

> The 1818 edition is housed in the Franklin L. Moon Library of the State University of New York, College of Environmental Science and Forestry, Syracuse, New York. It is from the collection of Fletcher Steele. By all accounts, it appears to be a unique copy, as it is not listed in major library catalogues, including that of the Bibliothèque Nationale, New York Public Library, British Library, or Harvard University Library. It is not returned in a Google book search.

Tableau Dendrologique, contenant la Liste des Plantes ligneuses indigènes et exotiques acclimatées. Lyon: De l'Imprimerie de Bruyset, 1800.

> The *tableau* was appended, unchanged except in format, to the second edition of *Théorie des jardins*.

"Mémoire sur la théorie des eaux fluentes, appliquée au cours du Rhône," *Archives historiques et statistiques du Département du Rhône* (1825).

Work attributed to Jean-Marie Morel (but not likely by him)

L'art de distribuer les jardins suivant l'usage des Chinois. London, 1757.

Work attributed to Morel, but more likely by the botanist Dr. Jacques-François-Nicolas Morel, founder of the Botanical Garden of Besançon.

Tableau de l'école de botanique du Jardin des plantes de Paris, ou, Catalogue général des plantes qui y sont cultivées et rangées par classes, ordres, genres et espèces. Paris: Didot le jeune, 1800.

Tableau de l'école de botanique du Jardin des plantes de Paris, ou, Catalogue général des plantes qui y sont cultivées et rangées par classes, ordres, genres et espèces. Paris: Chez Méquignon l'aîné, 1801.

In addition to these published works, Morel authored numerous unpublished memoirs, essays, and papers for the learned societies of Lyon to which he belonged, including the Académie des sciences, belles-lettres et arts de Lyon and the Société d'agriculture de Lyon.

For a full list, see Joseph Disponzio, "The Garden Theory and Landscape Practice of Jean-Marie Morel" (PhD diss., Columbia University, 2000).

TRANSLATION

EMILY T. COOPERMAN

THEORY OF GARDENS

In a narrow room nature's Whole Wealth, yea more
A heav'n on earth . . .
—*Paradise Lost*, book IV

FOREWORD†

I t is indeed difficult to bring about the reception of a new opinion, however reasonable it may be, when it is counter to received ideas. The regularity of forms and their symmetry have been laws so generally adopted in the composition of gardens that I would not have dared, a few years ago, to bring a work that fights these into the light of day. But today let the blindfold of prejudice be removed, and let the trials and experiments be multiplied sufficiently so that we may see Garden Art finally break the shackles of the routinism that has enchained it from its birth, and so that this Art can raise itself to the rank of the most appreciated liberal arts[1] by the knowledge that it assumes, the talents that it requires, and the good taste to which it is susceptible. I no longer hesitate to make public these reflections, which are the fruit of twenty years of study and ten years of practice. If these thoughts can contribute to easing the progress of this Art, one of the most agreeable and interesting, I will have attained the goal that I set for myself.

TO THE READER: Notes added by the original author, Jean-Marie Morel, are marked by an asterisk (*) and appear as footnotes. Translator notes (added by Emily T. Cooperman) are indicated by a dagger (†). Commentary by Joseph Disponzio is found in the endnotes, and is marked in the text by Arabic numerals.

† TRANSLATOR'S NOTE: Inconsistencies in Morel's original capitalization have been made consistent throughout the translation.

OF SYMMETRICAL GARDENS

I

Our tastes, even our most widely accepted opinions, are often mere prejudices fortified by blind habit and perpetuated by slavish imitation. These opinions give our prejudices an imposing authority that silences reason and restrains our own contradictory sense. Among the large number of examples that support this truth, I would only cite our symmetrical gardens in order not to stray from the subject that I propose to address. Despite their monotony and uniformity, despite the tedium that these gardens have caused us to suffer during their existence over more than a century, the overwhelming force of convention and fashion have subjugated us so firmly that even those with taste barely dare acknowledge how vexing these pressures are. Beyond the anticipated Reader of this work, no one will imagine that things can be improved, and all new innovations in this type will be at the very least charged with being odd. Perhaps after a long time we may come back to the truth of a delightful Art that is not inimical to our happiness, since its goal is the association of the pleasing and the useful, its aim is healthy exercise as well as peaceful entertainment, and it offers the most necessary and innocent distractions to the busy City Dweller. It will be seen in the following how, as a tasteful Art, it can also become the most interesting.

When it is remembered that the Garden Art was born at the moment when the Arts were reaching perfection, it is undoubtedly surprising that such a favorable period did not save it from the pitfalls of false taste. The eyes of all of Europe were opened to Nature, which should have served as a guiding rule, but her true principles were exchanged for geometric forms. Geometry, however, while a useful and profound science and the foundation of all others, is absolutely foreign to refined and delicate feeling—the true guide in a career in the Fine Arts. The general confusion was such that everywhere the cold symmetry of geometric figures was preferred to the sublime and varied, yet also simple and touching beauties that Nature's spectacle[2] offers us in such enticing patterns; and the coldness of the ruler and the methodical compass was substituted for simple and free pencil drawing. I believe I have discovered the source of the peculiar and universal misapprehension.

As soon as the Architect took over the creation of gardens, it should have been anticipated that he would confuse the principles of the two Arts,* since he was overly accustomed to the regular forms whose use accords with and is so well adapted to the Architect's works. He sought, by mutual correspondence, to link the building, which he made his primary subject, to the Garden, which to him seemed to be merely an accessory. Led by the habit of making forms symmetrical and by calculating spaces, he wanted to subjugate Nature to his methodical schemes, believing he was embellishing her; but he disfigured her. He composed a Garden like a house: he compartmentalized it into rooms, cabinets, and corridors, and formed divisions in it with arbor walls pierced by doors, windows, and arcades. The piers of these walls were laden with all the ornaments intended for buildings.

As a consequence of this false analogy, Architects gave round, square, and octagonal forms to these Garden rooms, as they did for those in buildings, decorated them as if they were private apartments, with vases, niches, and hangings, and in them they placed statues, the very appropriately unfeeling inhabitants of such a melancholy abode. They furnished them like rooms, with tapestries of greenery, trellises, painted perspectives, beds, and earth seats covered with grass. They went so far as well to build theaters and dormitories, and finally conceived the detailed labyrinth.

Architects, when Gardeners were required,** always cut a tree as if it were a stone—into vaults, cubes, and pyramids, and they subjugated water, which is so mobile, to these outlines, when its irregular and free course gives it all its charm. They did not fear exposing a dwelling to unhealthiness by enclosing water within four walls. They were rebuffed neither by the unpleasantness this caused once the water was stagnant and constrained, nor by the difficulty in retaining it in pools where stone, lead, clay, cement, and all sorts of coatings were put to the task of bending

---

* Architecture was a science before it was an Art. At its birth, Architecture, as the child of need, addressed only what was of the first necessity. Experiment first yielded knowledge of the most appropriate building materials. Architecture then sought the stability that it could acquire only as the sciences of exact measure, such as Arithmetic, Geometry, and Mechanics, moved toward perfection. It is more than likely that the symmetrical distribution of the forms of buildings was a result of the application of these sciences by the Architect. As these are founded only on ratios and proportions, it appeared to him that, when one part created stress, it had to be opposed on the other side by an equivalent resistance in order to create equilibrium. To this equivalence of reciprocal forces, which established the resemblance between corresponding parts, was joined the homogeneity of materials used in construction. Thus, symmetry necessarily became the first rule in decoration, while it also resulted from the laws of stability. The agreement between all of the components of decoration (which is nothing other than, as may be seen, a symmetrical distribution of parts combined according to need, rationality, and stability) became known as order. But stability has limits determined by Physics, which calculates the strength of materials as well as their resistance, and taste, which must consult architectural materials as we have admitted, determined the number of orders to be used to be four. Beyond this number, those with superfluous strength and too-heavy proportions err, on the one hand, through excess, and those that are too light or insubstantial sin, on the other, by their lack. It is therefore in the correspondence of symmetrical forms combined with the rules of stability, and in the relationship between its goals and needs that Architecture finds its principles, its techniques, and its beauties. How could the Architect have confused these with the principles proper to Gardens, which are based on the ingenious arrangement that Nature presents to us in forms free and unbounded by the shackles of method, with no rule but sentiment and no principle but taste? This confusion nevertheless exists, and even has its defenders.[3]

** By Gardener, I understand the tasteful Artist who composes Gardens, not he who tends them.[4]

a too-fluid element to their will. These means were almost always insufficient and should have deterred Architects by their lack of success and disabused property owners from the fashionable effects gained by them because of their expense.

Finally, they pushed the application of their principles to the point of cutting the terrain in terraces whenever it was not perfectly level. They held up the earth with walls, and sometimes by embankments as stiff and inflexible as the iron from which they were fashioned. They created circulation with ramps and stairs. Too preoccupied by their method, they paid no attention to the fact that level ground lacked undulations, its uniformity depriving it of the cheerful effect of the play of slopes and heights and the mixture of valleys and hills that is so pleasant. While need justifies stairs between the floors of a building, nothing is more inconvenient than climbing and descending steps in a Garden. Of all the ways of reaching one point from another, this is the hardest and least natural.

Almost all of our country houses, however, are placed on terraces and detached from Gardens. They are connected only with the help of a stair to a methodical parterre, which must be traversed while exposed to the heat of the sun, on soil with moving sand and raked earth that offers only a tiring walk and tedious sterility, in order to finally arrive at dark and symmetrical groves where shadow renders midday oppressive and the evening damp, since, at all moments of the day, invincible obstacles prevent air from circulating and the sun's healthy and beneficial rays from penetrating.

If conveniences have been neglected, pleasant things have been no better treated: views in particular, which are so necessary in rendering a dwelling and Gardens congenial and cheerful. To expect interesting scenes, to hope for prospects and varied points of view from a plan, which, drawn on a desk in a study, combines regular forms in a symmetrical arrangement that could be applied to any location and placed on any kind of ground with neither knowledge of local conditions nor regard to site, soil, and environment, is an error too palpable to bother refuting.

After denaturing the terrain, they disfigured the trees. They subjected them to the same form, laid them out at equal distances, restricted them to a single height, and required them to be the same age. The trees are so exactly alike in our Gardens that one wonders, when seeing them, if they were not cast from a common mold. Nature unrestrained would have varied them, and modeled them with the informal graces stamped on her productions. From their infancy, however, unpitying maneuvers by scythe and hand scissors have subjugated some to form a square; others have been pruned into balls. They have subjugated others to extend their branches into a fan or flattened them into a fence. They slice, cut, and show no mercy even to the most minor branch or tiniest extra leaf that tries to escape. The most magnificent and varied feature of our Gardens becomes, under their barbaric iron, the poorest and the most shapeless. In vain does its lack of vigor and stubborn tendency to retake its native form announce its repugnance: it will be cut, maimed, and martyred until it perishes under the murderous instrument that torments it ceaselessly. To thus mutilate the most beautiful productions of Nature—is this embellishment, correction? It is, rather, disfigurement and insult.

Regular and symmetrical forms being limited, and having served as a rule in Gardens, the latter must, and in fact have, resembled one another. We have not only been deprived of an abundant source of richness and variety in altering trees' natural form and avoiding mixing species. As soon as their cold and methodical creators have placed an allée on one side, they trace on the other its twin either parallel to it or on a like angle. When they place a grove on the right, they must have a corresponding one on the left. In their prospects and compositions, they repeat themselves perpetually: they plant a long and narrow allée at the midpoint of the house, at a right angle to its facade, and on a line they call the principal axis. This permits one to see beyond it, as if through the tube of a telescope, only that object which chance has placed there, whatever that may be. Too bad for the viewer if this sacred line does not present anything of interest in that direction; we must look there and not elsewhere. On one side or the other perhaps a pleasant view might have been encountered, or a far distance that would have pleasantly completed the scene. In sacrificing symmetry on the right or the left, a pleasant perspective might have been procured that would have enlivened the prospect and embellished the site. Alas! So many beauties and precious pleasures will have been lost for not having been found directly in front of the château. In truth, it is tempting to believe that these Designers do not know that the organ of sight moves in the orbit that encloses it; that the head may pivot freely; that the vertebrae permit a variety of inflections of the body; and that, through the combination of all these movements, the viewer, without changing position and even independent of the assistance of his feet, may scan the circle of the horizon in almost all of its circumference.

From the sameness of all our Gardens, and from this uniformity in all its parts, arises the boredom felt in those parks made at great expense. Here, pleasure has been sought through the surfeit of luxury and grace through regularity, ornaments, statues, vases, and bronzes have been lavished, and water, spouting in thin trickles and following with effort a route opposed to the one Nature would have traced for it, thrusts itself toward the area from which it should have fallen. To this gaudy monotony must be attributed the natural instinct that forces even the property owner to take leave of his unnatural Gardens, causes him to traverse them by the shortest route, to go walking along the hedgerows of his village and on the rough paths that share the fields of his district, and to climb the hillsides of the neighborhood by oblique and torturous paths. Attracted to the natural beauties that surround him as much as he is repelled by the tedious uniformity of his park, he prefers the river's edge, where clear water, free in its course, has fashioned uneven and varying banks. He seeks to penetrate a neglected woodland, unspoiled by the hand of man, where groups of trees and thickets intersected by clearings let light and shadow play by their happy arrangement. Swept along by charms that are always new, he passes through a vast lawn maintained and enlivened by the livestock of the parish, or he descends into a dale enriched by a meadow continually refreshed by a stream that freely follows the slope and its meanders.

To the many reasons to reject symmetrical Gardens founded on feeling and taken from the rules of taste, I would add only one more: the too-narrow limits that the type necessitates. However extensive the property possessed by a particular owner, even a Prince or Monarch, its boundaries will be perceived quickly, since where Art finishes, Nature begins. The line that separates them marks the boundary by a break that is all the more noticeable since it is always indicated by a wall, whose straight course and angular returns spoil and disfigure the landscape in which the Garden is inscribed by their coldness and hardness. In vain one imagines that part of this unpleasantness might be saved by openings or by what are called "ha-has." This crude finishing never deceives, but its invention proves that all obvious enclosures are displeasing, because it always produces a secret uneasiness that leads to a desire to broach these limits, whether this discomfort should arise from that near universal feeling for liberty, or whether one suspects that the objects these enclosures hide might be more pleasant than those they confine. This supposition is always true in the Gardens that taste disapproves and Nature rejects.

Must it be concluded from what has just been said that symmetry and Art's ornaments need be excluded from all the places given the name of Garden? No: there are some that will tolerate symmetry, and even some that require it. Symmetry goes well in those gardens that are annexed to palaces[*] and mansions: nothing outside impedes this type of decoration.[5] The nearly always regular form of the terrain and its limited area, and the importance of the building whose influence must make itself felt in the confined space that surrounds it, collaborate in subjecting such sites to symmetrical schemes. He who allows himself not to be deceived by the term will see in these sorts of Gardens only decorated courtyards, of which the first aim is to provide light and air to the city residence, a precaution without which time spent there is not very healthy.

Symmetry is also applied with success in the composition of public Gardens. These are only squares planted with trees within the bounds of the city, where citizens gather, not to enjoy the spectacle of Nature, but to take some momentary exercise, and where they assemble to display their wealth and satisfy their

---

[*] This is the case at Versailles. The trees of its superb gardens have recently been taken down. I believe it would lack appropriateness to change their style. First, because this residence of our kings is not a castle, even if it carries this name; it is, rather, a magnificent palace. Second, because, as a royal residence, its gardens are public, and it will be understood that they should fall within the category of symmetrical gardens. Third, because the luxury of the arts, the richness of materials, in a word the beauties of artifice, announce human power, unlike the beauties of Nature which will never be submitted to it.

In replanting the gardens of Versailles on their ancient traces, it would be necessary to ... but it is not of this style that I have proposed to speak.

curiosity. The greatest ornament of these sites exists in this general gathering. The boredom that they provoke, when they are poorly frequented, is the proof of this. Here are required a level ground, trees well aligned, and a walking surface that is good in all weather. Here all the Arts of imitation and decoration must be called in to help. Here, finally, the layout must be such that strollers of one or the other sex, whose goal is to put themselves on display, will both see all at a glance and appear at their best, since they are simultaneously both spectators and spectacle.

These are the Gardens that should be given over to Architects. They are part of their designs and are subject to the authority of their principles. It is certainly by dint of an insidious extension that they have transported a garden type into the countryside that is misplaced there and should never have left the cities where it was born. This liberty is the source of the error and false taste that has reigned too long in the composition of our country Gardens, where only the image of free Nature should be perceived. When we seek asylum in the fields, it is not in order to find there the constraints of regularity, cold symmetry, and the dressings of Art. On the contrary, it is there that we take refuge by fleeing these so as to rid ourselves of the importunate weight of court display, anxiety, and the discomfort of the city.

I finish with this reflection: a château is not a palace, and a farm is not an urban mansion. In the end, a city house is an entirely different thing from a rustic one. This difference is clear in the character of buildings, in their surroundings, in their placement, and in their embellishments. Let us therefore leave symmetry to the city Garden, and let us pose as axiomatic that in the country the simple graces and varieties of Nature are preferable. Let us seek the precepts of an Art still new among us, an Art worthy, by the exquisite taste that it requires and the pleasures it will procure for us, to train the Artists of our nation. Let us endeavor to find its principles and let us see by what techniques the scattered beauties of Nature may be distributed about our country residences without altering or disfiguring them; and how taste will bring these beauties together and Art will unite them without heaping them up.

OF NATURE'S SPECTACLE[6] AND THE ADVANTAGES OF THE COUNTRY

II

Of all the objects that strike our eye, there are none with as lively an impression, none that hold so universal a sway in the heart of man as the spectacle of Nature. Vast and majestic, this spectacle astonishes and impresses. It is both pleasant and interesting, it charms and attracts us. Thus Nature, always simple and magnificent, draws on the relationship and proportions of her parts and sublime effects that she presents to us and the unassuming graces that adorn her. Diverse in her forms, rich and well-proportioned in her unequal dimensions, she varies herself infinitely. At times solemn and serious, at times gay and cheerful, here noisy and agitated, elsewhere silent and tranquil, she embraces all characters, and presents pictures of every kind to us. Sometimes strong and vigorous in her style, clearly decisive in her colors, she strikes us with the boldness of her transitions, and surprises us with the strangeness of her contrasts. Often regular, soft and dissolving, she pleases us by the elegance of the whole and the softness of her contours, and enchants us by the sweetness and agreement of her tones. Like a theatrical scene, she masters all our sentiments; she moves us by secret means and hidden connections that delight the sensitive man, that good taste perceives and grasps, and that the attentive and intelligent Artist recognizes and puts into his work. Under her guise of disorder, she veils the most useful views, the most regular workings, and the most wisely composed plans. If she seems frightful in her tumults, afflicted in her disasters, she soon consoles and reassures us by the immensity of her productions. In opening her breast to our needs, she procures ease and richness for us, and with her gifts leads us unceasingly from hope to bliss.

Independently of all of Nature's beauties and charms, the countryside—theater of her magnificence and liberty—offers its lucky inhabitants innumerable resources: life flows by there in fruitful and pleasant occupations without worry and remorse. The soul is sound and the heart at peace there; a sojourn there calms the violence of destructive and maleficent passions, and maintains honest feelings by sweet infusion.[7] The frail and sickly man recovers his strength and his health, and the vigorous and hale man conserves them there. The countryside provides relaxation to the working citizen, and a retreat for the soldier who has completed his perilous career; it is the refuge of a happy man and the most certain resource for the poor man. The philosopher loves, contemplates, and occupies himself with it. The wise man knows its cost and enjoys it. The enlightened rich man finds the true happiness there that had been promised in vain by the false favors of fortune. There are found the delights of old age and the hopes of youth. Poets sing of it, painters imitate it. Its attraction is felt in every heart and it is independent of the whims of fashion and variation in opinions. In a word, the countryside has had and will have admirers in all countries and all eras, and the more that customs are simple and pure, the less taste will be corrupted and the more its pleasures will be sought.[8]

Were a Reader to be found who, preferring the tumult of cities, is so insensitive to its many charms and advantages, let him close this book and go no further. He would be unable to understand its language. For him, Nature is dead.

DIVISIONS OF GARDENS

III

Let us leave to Philosophy the care of researching and fixing the fundamental principles that enlighten the human mind and guide it with a firm step in its slow and uncertain progress. Philosophy alone, with the help of analysis and Logic,[9] can set the edifice of the sciences and the Arts on a solid and durable base. Let us content ourselves in presenting a few reflections on the Art of Gardens, and let us show that, as all the other Arts, it has its own laws and rules. On the new pathways this Art has just opened, still uncertain of its true principles, it floats at the will of capriciousness and fantasy. Principles, however, place boundaries beyond which all production becomes license. Rules, taken as a point of departure, facilitate study, speed up progress, and prevent errors.[10] In vain the objection will be raised that rules, in the tasteful Arts, hobble the Artist who follows them. The man of genius will know well how to bend and even break them when needed. He will apply them without difficulty to his sublime productions. With so few paths opened in Garden Art, rules will be—at least for others—the guiding principle, until time and experience, which refine taste and perfect human understanding, either confirm or reject those rules.

Fertile ground, clear and limpid water, a meadow dotted with flowers, woodland shade, and pure air doubtless were objects that charmed humankind and were first to fix its attention. But Nature almost never brings together all her beauties and pleasures in a single place. She does not always arrange the effects she presents to us in the best and most interesting manner. To bring them together, put them under their most favorable aspect, and in the end, to make them their own, has been the task of those who have been sensitive to her charms. Such were the principles, we have been told, on which the Gardens of Alcinous[11] were formed, and they could perhaps be ours again, if inequality of fortune and differences of rank had not extended their influence to things to which they are least susceptible. Doubtless, the beauties of Nature, whose enjoyment belongs to all, by this very fact have ceased to please those men too preoccupied with their own superiority or wealth. Doubtless, the habit of seeing these beauties or the need to share them with the common man has rendered them dull for these men. Thus, they have needed contrived Gardens, with artificial and conventional beauties. They have wanted, by means of expense and refinement, to procure by these techniques what belonged only to them, and the common people could not attain. I will, then, accept these distinctions of social order that depend irrevocably on the present state of things and will confine myself to the division of Gardens, trying nonetheless to distance myself as little as possible from Nature, the invariable model of good taste, to whose irresistible charms men always return, whatever the strength of their own prejudices may be.

The powerful, the rich, the simple citizen, and the man of taste have different customs, manners, ways of seeing, and, I even dare say, different feelings. These differences necessarily bear upon their enjoyments. Each class has its particular turn; its tastes and habits are subject to its means and other causes, which are hardly necessary to discuss here. Men of rank have great possessions, rights, estates, vassals; to make manifest their grandeur and their power, they must have châteaus and *parks*. He for whom an estate with fields is useful and remunerative contents himself with *farms* and cultivation. Those with wealth to spare wish to distinguish themselves through elegance and splendor; they claim for themselves the Arts appropriate for embellishing their possessions. The luxury of these Arts, which requires care and refinement, announces and consumes their excess. It is for these men that the *Garden proper* was invented, as well as the pleasure-house. The man of taste, heedless of these distinctions and wanting to bring Gardens back to their first origin, seeks to bring together the beautiful effects of Nature about him, and to combine them with all the wealth of the country. He only sets out to arrange and perfect the favorable site and make what is called the *countryside*.†

One may thus include, under four general classes,[12] all the Gardens that take Nature as model, and her beauties as their aim: the *park*, the *Garden proper*, the *countryside*, and the *farm*. These four classes encompass all the types of Garden through the infinite number of modifications of which they are capable. The specific and distinctive character of each is: the variety of the *countryside*, the nobility of the *park*, the elegance of the *Garden proper*, and the simplicity of the *farm*.

The *countryside* assumes no specific type, or, more precisely, it takes in all of them. It is so allied with what surrounds it that it knows no limits. It takes in from afar all that comes into view. It has no principal point that serves as the center of a composition to which it refers. The manor house of the property owner is only a feature in the general ensemble. Its cheerful prospects and somber views; the cultivated and the wild; its vast scenes, bold effects, and its most picturesque perspectives arise from its resources. It adopts what Nature offers that is most

---

† TRANSLATOR'S NOTE: Morel's term is *pays*, which he uses to discuss the countryside as a type of landscape and as a garden category. There is no equivalent contemporary category for this kind of garden, in contrast to the other categories defined by Morel.

surprising and singular, as well as what is most ordinary and simple. It is for the *countryside* that the greatest contrasts and all the riches of variety must be reserved: as in Nature, it takes its beauty from the freedom of its progress and its apparent disorder. Like Nature, it rigorously excludes the small details, affected refinements, and all that allows intention in its arrangement and design in its execution to be perceived. I would happily call this class, destined to present Nature in her majesty and beauty, the preeminent Garden.

The *park*, less vast in its purpose, supposes neither as much grandeur in its effects nor as much carelessness in its execution: its site demands fewer undulations in its general view; its transitions must be less bold and less frequent. The principal scenes will be made for the château. The importance of the owner must be announced by the nobility of this building, by the style of the composition, and the extent of the estate. Woods must present themselves in large and deep masses. The lawns will be vast and the lines that bound them broadly drawn. The water features will be imposing in the volume of that water, in their form, and in their arrangement. But, within this class of Garden, all its features, their form, and their location—in the end, all that make it up—must present effects that are avowed and recognized by Nature. Whatever the type that might be adopted for it, the *park* requires grandeur in its entirety and nobility in its arrangement.

The *Garden proper*, smaller still in its extent, is particularly distinguished by its elegance, its richness, and its neatness. It lends itself to details. It is content with a small number of scenes, but these must be luxurious and cheerful. It avoids strong contrasts, rough or wild perspectives, and terrain that is too rough. It fears hard and severe forms; it prefers delicate touches, soft contours, and careful transitions. It can separate itself, up to a certain point, from the exact truth: for this class of Gardens is the least severe in the imitation of Nature. But, whatever liberty this type of composition may allow, it is necessary, even in these deviations, that her workings be found, that her effects are recognized, and that finally, she is displayed there, but in all her sweetness and provided with all her graces—in a tableau in miniature.

The *farm*, whose main purpose is economy and utility, is identified by its rustic atmosphere, its informality, and its lack of pretension. Like a simple, artless Shepherdess, its simplicity will be its only ornament. Its scenes can be rustic, but never wild: it takes its character from its situation. Its principal prospect will be formed from the different components of its cultivations. The main house and the various, well-situated buildings that surround it may form an agreeable ensemble when they are arranged in a picturesque manner, and when the enclosures that surround them and the neighboring trees are happily grouped. The tracks and paths that divide useful fields or wide pastures, when planted and arranged with taste and laid out with intelligence, become walks; meadows and orchards become Gardens. This class will have the inestimable advantage of bringing together the pleasant and the useful by the variety and products of its cultivations.

From these definitions, it may be seen that these classes are not so far apart that a large *park*, depending on how it is treated, may not approach a small *countryside*, especially at its edges. A *Garden proper* of a certain extent and nobility in its composition may tend toward a small *park*. The *farm*, a particular class far removed from the three others due to its aim and purpose, would never be confused with them, but it may make a good effect in the *countryside* and will figure very well at the edge of a *park*. With regard to the *Garden proper*, its elegance and delicacy may seem opposed to all connection with the carefree and rustic tone of the *farm*, but there are cases when opposing these will provide a lively contrast. Thus one may, if not link them directly, then at least connect them through ingenious transitions.

Once the class has been determined from the general distinctions that have just been established, the character of the site will always decide the type. The Artist, who, in his first arrangements, having misunderstood this essential precept, will make an irreparable error, and from this point his project will be lost beyond remedy. He will only escape this misstep by examining his terrain from all points, in all seasons, and perhaps at different times of day. He will inspect it from all angles to know all its advantages, to grasp it in its totality, and to sound out its details. Above all, he will develop a considered account of the feelings it has given rise to in him, in order not to mistake its true character. This beginning is important; success depends on it. Without these preliminaries, the Artist will proceed without a goal; he will act without reason and will have worked ingloriously.

If, on the other hand, he has perfected his talent for reflection and experiment, and formed his taste by the study of design and the contemplation of the grand effects of Nature, his only model; if he has learned how to observe her in her constant and varied workings; if he has perceived the Art she uses to give herself foregrounds and far distances, and how she arranges her transitions and operates her contrasts; if he has been attentive to the ingenious way she sets out her distances, to the effects that her scenes take from light and shadows, to the brilliance of her perspective, in the air as much as on the ground, then he will have acquired much. He must still, however, know the materials that compose and embellish her perfectly. When I have placed them before his eyes so that he will study them attentively, then he may take up the pencil and design.

OF THE MATERIALS OF NATURE IV

The materials of which Nature is composed consist on the one hand of those in a state of constant variation[13] that man will never be able to control, and on the other of those that are stable and permanent. Among those counted in the latter are some over which he has no sway, but which he may seize when they are at hand, and others that are under his dominion, and which he may use at will.

Climate, the effects produced by the sun relative to the seasons and at different moments of the day, the moving clouds and varying colors that decorate the sky with ceaselessly renewed tones—all these are among the materials of Nature that lie beyond the grasp of the Artist. He can neither command them nor change them at his pleasure, but he must consult them and keep them in mind in his arrangements, since they are part of the whole and the complement to his tableaux. There are other materials over which he has more power, such as the respective terrain in his various developments, and the productions that clothe it, from the superb oak down to the creeping grass, the water, and finally, the rocks. Here is all that Nature brings into play to compose the innumerable scenes that she presents to us. These are the colors with which she charges her palette, and the canvas on which she mixes them.

Although buildings, the work of human industry, are of a different order, they must nevertheless be counted among the materials that work toward forming a landscape. Need led to their birth, and the conveniences of life have caused them to multiply so much that there are few sites in which they do not occur as notable features in the composition, and they are often the principal subjects. It is from this point of view that the Artist Gardener must envisage and place them. It is up to him to prescribe their form and fix their massing, to determine their placement, their color, and their style. In this, the Architect is subordinate to him, since, as objects in the view, buildings are part of what composes his Gardens.[14]

It is the small number of these materials that Nature brings together with such Art and taste and the judicious order with which she arranges them that provide the prodigious variety of effects that surprises us and produces the superb pictures that enchant us. But the Artist who handles them must know how to use them and to study their forms, must understand the places that she assigns to them, must scrupulously conserve the proper character and conventions for each, must observe the appropriate proportions, and finally, must consult the laws of Physics that establishes their reciprocal relationship.[15]

OF CLIMATE

V

Each climate has its own particular beauties and means. Nature is not the same in the countries situated under the burning sun of the torrid zone and in those in the middle of the frosts of the north. Far from the extremes of the one or the other, let us abandon the observations that are specific to them. Let us only occupy ourselves with remarks on the climate's temperature where we live, and that which the country where we are located will furnish us. We will see its effects in the seasons, which are the subject of the following chapter.

OF THE SEASONS

VI

There are very lovely scenes in Spring; there are some that are preferable in Summer. The Autumn has its own effects. Even Winter, the season when Nature is lifeless, can still have certain charms and attractions, to which those who spend their lives in the country are not insensitive.

Of Spring

§. I.

The Spring is the awakening of Nature; she then has all the freshness and grace of youth. The green of lawns is tender, as is that with which the trees adorn themselves. The colors of the flowers are vivid and varied, and they exhale sweet odors everywhere. Seeds and all vegetation grow. The first rays of the sun are sweetly warm and active. The air is pure. Beautiful days are reborn. Birds sing melodiously, and mix with the bleating of the flocks attracted to the fields by the tender, new grass. All of these things render Nature active and animated, and present the most interesting spectacle and enchanting picture. Then, not one of our senses is not agreeably affected, bringing delightful emotion to our soul.

But in our climate, this amiable season is often stormy and uneven; in its inconstancy it sometimes returns us to the rigors of Winter, which it has just followed. However inviting the charm of new things may be, man does not dare to leave his abode. It is thus appropriate, in order to facilitate his enjoyment, to surround him with flowers, that charming production that might be called Nature's coquetry. The Gardener will therefore place flowering trees, shrubs, and bushes around the manor house and within the owner's sight, and he will arrange them so that their appearance, form, and colors mix tastefully to yield a beautiful assortment that is the result of a pleasing disorder. He will distribute these plantings in groups sized to their distance and according to the effects he seeks to obtain. He will separate the groups so that they will contrast pleasingly according to the variety of their masses, or he will bring them close together so that their crowning branches form a bower shaded by their interlacing. At the center of the clumps he will place trees and bushes whose trunks and stems grow upward, and whose flowers appear at their tops, so that they are seen clearly and to their best advantage. He will vary the outline of the masses and their distances, and carefully avoid the tendency to symmetry and regularity. However much they might displease is balanced by the pleasure our sight takes in wandering over a gathering of pleasant and selected trees laid out in groups. Those gatherings that we discern cause us to seek out, by their attractiveness, others that they hide, and invite us to go and see them in the hope of a new pleasure. Here the Gardener entertains pyramidal forms, and there ones that are rounded as much in plan as elevation. Elsewhere the massing is lighter, farther on it is tighter and thicker. Sometimes the principal groups will be composed of smaller individual groups, or they will be detached without being entirely separated. By such techniques a fortunate effect can always be obtained from hollows and outcroppings, and by the piquant mixture of light and shadow.

It is useful to know the flowering period of each species, so that flowers distributed accordingly succeed each other and extend the pleasure they provide.

All the clumps will not only have the proportions they must have as individual objects, but also, in their arrangement, the Gardener will consider their connection with the scenes and views of which they are part: since flowers fade and the groups of trees that bear them remain. However denuded they may be of their ornament, they must still figure and play a graceful role in the entirety of the general picture.

In addition, if the Composer has learned how to connect these masses to other clumps by carefully managed transitions, and to place them in gradations from the smallest bush to the highest forest tree; if the clearings that divide them are happily contrasted either in their form or size; if the lawns, which serve as the foundation for all these plantings, are refined and well maintained; if walking in them is soft and easy and the slopes gentle, then a most delightful grove will be obtained. Its prospect will present the sweetest picture: in almost all the seasons of the year, it will create the most engaging walk and the most frequented refuge. In the Spring, one will go there to seek out the desired warmth of the sun. In Summer, shelter from the intensity of its rays will be found there. The violent Autumn winds will encounter obstacles, and their efforts will be broken by the groups scattered about in abundance. The air will circulate freely there, however, and maintain its coolness without humidity: the sun's action, whose influence will make itself felt alternatively on one side, while on the other shade will temper its rays, will lead to pleasurable enjoyment in all the moments of the day. A simple resting place, a comfortable bench, a proper retreat, discerned between the trees and placed in a solitary and shaded location, will invite the stroller to relax there. He will dream there with delight.

In a grove of this type, the Gardener who wishes to bring together all the beauties that Spring produces will obtain magnificent effects from young fruit trees mixed artistically into the clumps. The immensity of the flowers with which these plants are covered in the beginning of the season creates a wondrous effect. The flowers are followed by fruit whose lively colors render the green of the leaves brighter, and which receive in exchange a greater splendor. Shrubs must also not be neglected: the berries, the fruit clusters, the leaves, and the barks are colored with a thousand different tints that in Autumn recall the flowers of Spring.

If, to animate the picture, a happy accident would have brought a stream snaking its way through the lawn, sometimes shaded, slow, and silent, and sometimes in the open, agitated, and murmuring; if the Gardener has arranged pleasant viewpoints close by in order to have it slip away and reappear in turn, so as not to disturb the tranquil atmosphere and the slightly mysterious tone of this type of composition; were he to know how artfully to bring in and trace solid and practicable paths so that in walking them objects will present themselves from the most favorable aspect; then, he will have made a true springtime Garden. He will have brought together all that is most delightful of this sensuous season, and this ensemble will leave nothing to be desired.[*]

Of Summer

§. II.

The sun, in moving forward on its path, brings Summer and its heat with it. Vegetation is then in its greatest vigor, and greenery attains its highest degree of perfection. It is summer that Nature seems to have chosen to display before us all of her luxury and magnificence. Attentive to our well-being, she prepares shelters for us against the intemperance of this burning season. As the heat rises, trees, the most beautiful production of all vegetation, achieve their full development. Their shade, while it is less extensive, is darker and thicker. They receive and stop the nearly vertical rays of the sun at their top; the abundance of their leaves absorbs these and blocks them from being transmitted to us. From the trees' assembly and adjacency are formed the woods that protect us by their ever-cooling shade in sanctuaries impenetrable by the obtrusive heat.

This season brings together other advantages missing from the others. In Spring and Autumn, out of the twenty-four hours of the day, we can barely enjoy the three or four that precede and follow midday. In Summer, each part of the day has its own character and particular beauties: the coolness of the morning; the brightness of noon that seems to pull a sort of majesty from the silence that reigns in all Nature with the cessation of work, when all animals surrender themselves to rest, and silence is even respected by the birds who then suspend their games and

---

[*] This grove as it has just been described does in fact exist and is part of the Guiscard Gardens.

song; and finally the temperature and calm of the evening. These three periods are no less distinct in time than different in their effect.

The long days of Summer are followed by beautiful nights. A Summer's night brings together part of the pleasures of a beautiful day: it has the coolness of the morning, the silence of midday, and the calm of the evening.

The Artist who has noted these very perceptible nuances and the moments to which they belong will take the greatest advantage from them. He will seek to bring them out by the distribution of his scenes and disposition of his massing. He knows that air that is pure and moving lightly at the moment when twilight spreads sweet serenity to the soul, and that the still languid song of the birds, whose concerts celebrate the morning dawn, bestows the hope of a beautiful day. He foresees that if he obstructs the east side with heavy and high plantings, that the shadows of vertical objects, which reach into the far distance, will alter the gaiety of the morning from which it derives its charm. These plantings would deprive the morning of the beautiful effects of the rising dawn, when it ushers in the first rays of the sun that gild the summit of the mountains and that are soon reflected in every direction by the cool and bright dew that they must have to quench their thirst.

He will not forget that the excess of sun at midday requires, in contrast, plantings that are thick and close together. By presenting to our view the side of these plantings opposite to the sun, the shadows that cover them will temper the sun's overly strong brightness, and those they cast on the ground will seem, by coming and going in front of us, to offer a more immediate pleasure. Thus for those moments of fatigue and repose he will purpose his woods, grottoes, and shaded waters: in sum, all that produces, maintains, and promises hope of refreshment, and provides relaxation. He will have convinced himself that the most expansive and broad views are preferable on the northern aspect, since heat reflected from there will be more bearable. The views will be all the better if the objects that are too faintly drawn by the great distance and seemingly lost in the vacant air are brought out by lively touches, if, without losing any of their harmony, these objects are emphasized and rendered more discernible by the reflection of the light, and, if, finally, the best position to take pleasure from a certain vista is that from which the viewer has his back to the sun when it is at its highest point.

Ever attentive to serendipity, the artist will also have noted that the shadows of the waning of the day, as in its beginning, lengthen and burnish large areas. Far from displeasing, however, this feature confers an effect upon the scene that adds to the calm of a beautiful evening. Consequently, the masses of trees, placed and combined skillfully according to the view, will guarantee to those most habitual walks all the oblique and ever-tiring rays of the setting sun.

He will, however, set aside some points of discovery, from which a broad sky will sometimes provide the scene of a magnificent sunset, when, through colored clouds, thousands of rays will escape, and, by their copious refrangibilty,[16] spread out their greatest majesty and dazzle. In these superb moments, the atmosphere is on fire, the earth burns, and all of Nature, as if in flames, takes part in the hot and vigorous tints of the light. The rays, squeezed by the dark cloud that covers and pushes them back, make an effort to break free, on one side falling on the horizon, which shines from their luster, and on the other launching themselves swiftly into the skies in sparkling traces: a truly sublime spectacle worthy of the radiant star that produces it. Such is this star's magic that the places it thus illuminates never again appear the same. These are other landscapes, the objects in them transformed, and the scenes changed. The illusion endures until the light, modifying itself in all its tones, weakens to imperceptibility,[17] and until that which has propagated it also escapes and both are lost in the shadows of the night.

Finally, for his night effects, the intelligent Gardener will fashion a valley discovered with soft tone and tranquil character. There, in the vast mirror of the waters of a lake, or on the surface of a wide and peaceful river, the dark blue of a beautiful sky and the brilliance of the stars will be repeated, and sometimes the flickering image of moon and the pale clouds that accompany it will depict themselves painted there.

Would he like to vary his scenes? He will obtain agreeable and very lively effects from this weak light when its rays glide and play among the foliage, contrasting with the darkness of the verdure and penetrating the groves strewn with light clumps where shadows draw contours and dark and solid protrusions on the shaved grass that serves as a carpet.

In the midst of a calm and tranquil night, the image of repose and peace, who has not felt in such places the luxurious feeling of a delightful reverie? And who does not care to recall once more its pleasant memory?

Of Autumn

§. III.

The beginnings of Autumn touch so closely on Summer, which it follows, that they share almost all of Summer's beauties and preserve a great part of its attractiveness. If the days are shorter, their heat is more bearable. Walks are more frequent and longer. The vigor of the month of August revitalizes Nature, which has languished and been suppressed under the burning rays of the Summer sun. She spreads a new liveliness on all that grows. Dried out trees recover their first beauty, and lawns, refreshed by more abundant dew, regain all their green. This season also gives us flowers, which, although less delicate and later, are lacking neither brilliance nor pleasure; they even have a particular kind of nobility. Nature has endowed them with a vigor that prolongs their life beyond that which she gives to her too-fleeting

Spring flowers. It is about this time that the shrubs' berries and fruit clusters color with brilliant hues. Fruits then begin to ripen. Their form and colors embellish the trees that bear them: they bring pleasure through the memory of their flavor, and then by the hope of seeing them ornament our tables. The orchards that are so blooming and beautiful in Spring please us anew in this rich season by the abundance they promise us.

And when, finally, Autumn nears Winter, Nature, as inexhaustible in her resources as she is varied in her effects, presents us with a spectacle that is entirely new. The leaves dry out little by little, it is true, but before they abandon the trees where they were born, they tint themselves in a variety of colors. Each species has its special hue and passes successively through different tones, from pale green and light yellow to the darkest brown and the most lively and deepest rosiness. The mixture of these tints, enhanced by those few trees that remain green, present the view of a rich perspective. The play of tree trunks, the pattern of the branches, and the varied colors of the barks are then better seen, and lend elegance to the whole, revealing clusters of unequal scale. A general mass is too heavy and uniform without these distinctions. The choice in the mixture of trees and moments of accidental beauty will be the goal of this particular study. The Artist who surrenders himself to this will find his reward in all the surprising effects he will obtain from it.

The most advantageous position for such vistas will be in a wooded amphitheater, in which each tree is partly hidden by the one before it, and only covers half of that behind it. The contrasting forms of the parts that show themselves and the varied hues with which they are colored will create a great pleasure when the assortment is managed with taste. Taste requires that the masses be large, unequal, and varied, and that they blend by a well-considered gradation of tone. Sometimes these masses must run together, and sometimes they must disconnect through oppositions. With these precautions, the effects will be pleasing, but uniform lines that trace parallel bands, and distributions that are too equal in the tone and form of the masses must above all be avoided. The diversity of trees, and particularly their height differences, will give the means to obtain variety. Those that stand out the most will provide the best-lit points, while those that are shorter will be shaded and deprived of light by the shadows with which the most dominant cover them. This last effect, which is derived solely from the way in which they are lit by the sun, will follow its daily progress, and move as it does.

This vista may be receptive to a great agreement among colors, and will charm the eye with the sweetness of its effects. It can also produce strong and abrupt ones by wise contrasts and associations made according to successive variations in the hues of the trees.

These effects are not indifferent in their selection: they are relative to the masses' general form and distance. Each should have its place, and will only look well in the scenes to which they are appropriate, and according to the class of Garden with which one is dealing.

Finally, the exterior line of a wood, whose depth can be only faintly sensed, can obtain beauties of this type if the Artist has taken care in the choice of trees that create that line.

It is by these techniques that bountiful Nature prepares enjoyments for us in every season. She varies our pleasures by features that are always fresh, and by changes that follow one another continually.

If I were unaware that man will let himself be led much less by reason and his own feeling than by established conventions (for example, those of his peers, and especially those that are habitual), I would ask, whatever the pleasures of Autumn might be, why those who live in our climate choose this season to go to the country, and on what basis this preference is founded.* It certainly has neither as many charms as the Spring, nor as many beauties as Summer. When it has barely moved toward Winter, the effects of the approach will be felt through morning mists, evening chills, and the lengthening nights. A beautiful Autumn day does not permit the hope that the one that follows must resemble it. If it does, it will be seen as an unexpected blessing, and received with this sort of understanding. Each day that follows, however, takes away a portion of the country's delights: the trees denude themselves, the leaves yellow and dry out, and greenery fades. While this change does still present us with beauties, it must be conceded that they are Nature's final efforts. The few flowers that remain, faded and unscented, dried by the cold or ruined by dampness, wither on their stalks. The woods will soon no longer be desired retreats: the small amount of shade they give is already to be feared. Water loses its charms: its coolness, so sought after in Summer, ceases to please us. The first chills, the frequent winds, the damp mists, and Nature inactive and denuded announce to us the fatal end of our enjoyments. In a word, Autumn, so different from Spring, displaying itself in bright traits and pleasing youth, and far removed from the vigor of Summer, only presents us with the wrinkles and ugliness of old age.

---

* "The earth adorned with the treasures of Autumn spreads forth a richness that the eye admires, but this admiration is not emotional: it comes more from contemplation than from sentiment. In the Spring, the nearly naked countryside is still covered by nothing. The woods provide no shadows. Greenery is only just emerging, and the heart is touched by its appearance. In seeing Nature thus reborn, we feel ourselves revived. Sweet tears, the companions of pleasure always ready to join in all delightful feeling, are already on the edge of our eyelids. The sight of the harvest may be animated, lively, pleasant, but one always views it with a dry eye.

"Why this difference? It is that the spectacle of spring is joined in the imagination with those that must follow. To the tender buds that the eye perceives are added flowers, fruit, and shades, and sometimes the mysteries that these may cover. The imagination brings together in one point in time the seasons that must follow it, and sees things not so much as they will be but as how it would wish them, since their selection depends on the imagination. In the Autumn, there is nothing to see but what is. If one is to get to Spring, Winter stops us, and the icy imagination dies on the snow and frost.["] Such is the feeling of the celebrated Citizen of Geneva [Jean-Jacques Rousseau], who has so well seen and depicted Nature. *Émile*, page 324, book II. Amst. 1762.

Of Winter

§. IV.

At the very name of Winter my imagination freezes and the pen falls from my hand. Inflexible Nature has fixed in its immutable decrees that all that has been born shall grow, decline, and die. And such is the invariable order that she has prescribed for herself—that each season will bring another to follow. But perhaps she has only established the succession of the seasons with the view to enhance one by the others.[18] If Winter precedes Spring, it is truly only to cause the experience of that season's pleasures to be still more lovely, and bring out her attractions to greater advantage. So, let us leave the singing of the praises of the charms of a perpetual Spring to the Poets. He who would desire one doubtless wishes rashly.

Despite these advantages, Winter will not appear less displeasing to my eye. Sluggish and without action, Nature has lost all that she had of interest. Let others contemplate the austere beauties of this hard season; they are without appeal for me. The most beautiful vistas, then, if any such exist, offer us no shelter against Winter's rigors. We know not how to enjoy them without a painful feeling that causes us to abandon them. All this season produces that is admirable, such as the chance occurrence of ice and frost, does not depend at all upon our efforts. Their most striking effects are due only to extreme inclemency. It would be difficult, perhaps impossible, to compose scenes for such effects. The cold of our Winter is, in addition, neither so violent nor long as to give these much vaunted incidents of which the North alone provides examples. Sometimes a beautiful sunny day entices us to go out, and provides us with a few bearable hours, but in our northern climate, these short days are rare. Heavy rains, violent winds, and a dark cold follow them all quickly, and forces us to remain idle beneath our roofs.

But when the snow covers the surface of the earth, then we must flee the fields. They are without resource for our pleasures. Its dazzling whiteness is as tiring in its brilliance as it is unfortunate in the uniformity which it spills out over all of Nature. The gray and unshaded tone that reigns everywhere, and the equally weak day that barely lights the atmosphere makes objects look the same, confuses distances, and annihilates all relationships.

You!—who nonetheless travel to the country in this disagreeable season, do you wish to obtain some enjoyment that comes from the Art of Gardens? Choose for the surroundings of your dwelling a ground with a south-facing view, where you may go with nothing in between. Cover this with grass. If it is well cared for, and the kind is well chosen, it will conserve its green. Make paths there that are solid and always clean. Plant in this area thus prepared a grove whose light masses are spaced in such a manner that the sun will penetrate them in all parts. The trees should be chosen from those that are always green and never lose their leaves. Ornament the grove with shrubs and bushes that grow with the least rays of the first sun, and with those that withstand and even flower in the frost. Through high and close plantings, always of green trees, place this grove in the shelter of the north winds and the frequent western rains. You will have prepared for yourself a very agreeable green grouping, and you will have the only Winter Garden to which our climate is susceptible. In the middle of the rigors of the season, there will be few days that will not allow you some hours of enjoyment, during which you will be able to give yourself over to the useful exercise of walking.

He who has placed a premium on possessing the most complete Winter Garden, and for whom the cultivation of delights placed within view may please, will obtain it through discernment and some expense. He should seek in the same grove a spot carefully sheltered from the north, but placed in such a way to receive the weak influences of the sun without impediment. Then, following the form of the open area that he prefers, he should place iron posts linked by crosspieces to support the [glass] frames. This structure should be arranged so that it is lost in the masses that surround it, so that it is disguised by and mingled with the plants: this will be difficult if it is created on a regular plan. Under this transparent roof, he will delight in the sight of his grove, which will present him with a pleasant view if it is arranged with intelligence and designed with taste. In Gardens of this type exterior viewpoints are not required, and indeed are even hardly desirable. This greenhouse, when warmed by artificial heat introduced by hidden plumbing, will provide him with the favors and moderate temperatures of Spring. There, he will cultivate the most delicate plants, the most delightful exotics, and the earliest blooming native plants. A thin thread of water, running but never freezing, will animate this small, pleasing, if artificial scene. If he has discovered how to plant the entrance in a deceptive manner, he will enjoy the surprise of the curious who have entered there without realizing it. Finally, this glass enclosure, strewn with plants in full growth and trees that are green and flowering, surrounded outside by constant greenery, can contain birds that, tricked by the temperature, will delight him with concerts and even early egg-laying.

With the return of good weather, and the removal of the posts and framework, the trees, whose beauty and rarity are always sought after, will seem, planted out in the earth, to have overcome the obstacles a too-rigorous climate presents for their tenderness. In this state, this grove may not be disdained, if it is laid out in such a way that the part that was enclosed blends with the plantings that surround it. By this precaution, it will even be visited in the seasons when we cease to stay shut in our homes.

OF TERRAIN

Of Its General Effects

§.I.

The pictures which we have just reviewed in brief present only ephemeral features. Although their effects may be quite palpable, and however great some may be in energy, time, which in its rapid flight gives and destroys all things, will, no sooner has it drawn them, erase their traces in order to replace them with others no less fleeting. The precepts themselves, to which each season gives rise, are but for the most part rules of detail susceptible to an infinite number of exceptions. They are also subject to local conditions that cause them to be accepted or rejected due to difficulties, and in addition, and more or less to the ease with which they can be put into practice.

Such is not the case with the large tableau, called the general *Site*, which receives a specific character from the whole of the terrain. The succession of the seasons changes nothing in its arrangement. Time will only be capable of altering its principal masses after a long succession of centuries, and even then its mark is imperceptible. It is from the combination of the undulations and play of its various parts that the terrain takes its expression. It may receive some modifications by the aid of other materials that join with it and vary its surface. Yet, despite these accessories, its contours and its framing,[†] if I may put it thus, will always be its principal feature.

While, by their immutability, sites seen from the same point present themselves in the same form, it is rare that man, this active being, remains in the same place very long. Moreover, in a fortunate site, the details are so multiplied, and the effects so contrasting, that the most habituated eye always discovers new beauties there that had escaped it. But, what richness and magnificence there is in the infinite variety of scenes produced by all the combinations of terrain, when, divided into mountains, valleys, hills, and dales mixed with flatland, spreading out in all

---

† TRANSLATOR'S NOTE: Morel here refers specifically to the timber framing structure of a building.

directions, and placed at every distance, a new site and pictures are given at each stopping place! With the help of the effects of perspective, joined with optical illusions, the slightest movements of the viewer reveal objects in different and often unforeseen forms and relationships. These relationships recede and vanish; others take their place. Situations vary endlessly. Scenes follow on each other at each step and these transitions work sometimes by simple and prepared pathways, and sometimes by sudden and unexpected changes.

When we climb or descend, the horizon appears to rise or lower itself through a comparable movement, and move away or approach in the same proportion. From the most elevated spots, the open and azure vault of the Skies crowns an immense country that has no limit other than this same Sky and mingles with it. The discovery of this vast openness, when it is the effect of a sudden and unexpected transition, always causes a feeling of surprise mixed with admiration. In low places, in contrast, the site narrows and the sky shrinks and is partially concealed behind the heights. The closest broad summits trace strong and defined lines, and by their dull hue and opacity stand out against the diaphanous color of the firmament. This contrast makes the incalculable distance between them felt all the more.

Elsewhere the eye discovers an immense flatland that ends in mountain chains colored variously according to the materials of which they are composed and which cover them, and because of the angle by which the sun illuminates them and the thickness of the atmosphere and mists between.

More circumscribed and intimate, a rich valley that the eye delights in traversing presents itself not far beyond. Pleasant hills with mild and uneven slopes define and enclose it. The happy mixture of outcroppings and hollows varies their contours in a thousand ways and begets the vales that intersect them in every direction. This interplay excites the curiosity by continual changes, and sustains attention by repeated surprises.

Transport yourself to another side, and only with admiration will you behold the imposing majesty of the mountains. From afar they make themselves known only by barely perceived outlines, and their distance and *misty*† tones merge with the horizon, but considered from close up they are enormous masses that compress and crush the very entrails of the earth. A succession of heights accumulated one atop the other is lost in the clouds, and their bluish summits meld with the skies. Deep and narrow valleys, whose harsh and steep sides form continual precipices, divide the mountains and separate them. In their rough and frequent windings, these valleys form angles that project and return, almost always correspondingly.[19] Their varied aspects present all climates and seasons at the same time. Perpetual snows crown the highest summits, and a strong and constant cold is maintained there. Lower down reign the cool and charms of Spring,[20] while the

---

† TRANSLATOR'S NOTE: Morel italicizes this term to emphasize its visual significance.

depths are burned by the sun's fires enclosed within the gorges; its rays, reflected a hundred times by the nearly vertical surfaces of the terrain, maintain a heat only rarely tempered by the west wind. On one side the soil is fertile and enlivened by the most active vegetation, on the other are only barren boulders and heathers sprinkled with a few wild and creeping bushes. Here, overhanging masses appear detached from the general one, as if barely sitting on the slender and narrow bases that support them, surrounded as these masses are surrounded by deep chasms that even the steadiest eye does not dare probe. The boldness of their protrusions and their inaccessible heights inspire terror,[21] and they impress themselves upon the astonished spectator. There we find marvelous crags, noisy waterfalls, and rushing torrents. It is in places of this type that we encounter singular and almost supernatural circumstances, such as wild caves, shadowy caverns, and frightening precipices. There, Nature, both audacious and in a tumult, seeks to lift herself above the laws of Physics, which, however, she cannot avoid. Proud of her seeming independence, it appears as if she disdains her usual workings in these divergent places, and that she recognizes no limits beyond those of capriciousness; or that, leaving her work unfinished, she wishes only to produce an incomplete rough sketch in order to show us, in her sublime disorder, the rare and striking spectacle of a beautiful horror.

All of these effects of terrain are embellished by woods, boulders, and water, and are modified by the hues of areas associated with the green of lawns, with the green of the most beautiful grasses, and with the velvet of mosses that brings out the brown and unattractive tone of the heathers, by plants of all sorts, and by the garlands formed by clinging and rambling bushes interlaced and distributed by the hand of Nature with the grace and certain and easy taste of which she alone knows the secret. To these features you must add those of the seasons, the air, and the light inseparable from shadow. You will thus have all the types of views imaginable, from the sublime to the simple, from the cultivated to the wild, and, finally, the harshest and most austere aspects as well as the most happy and gay.

It is, however, to the composition, the play, and the expansiveness of terrain that all great character owes its principal qualities. The inexhaustible variety of the terrain is such that, despite the wide variety of sites of all sorts it presents to us, and the still greater quantity of possible combinations among their vast numbers, it would be miraculous if two sites were exactly the same.

In the impossibility of showing all the advantages and detailing all the uses to be made of the slope of terrain and its invaluable unevenness, I will only add this observation: without these, water would neither fall nor flow, and it would cover level surfaces and create an unusable and unhealthy bog. There would be no pools in which to contain it to supply our needs and pleasures. Its sound and movement would no longer animate the scenes of Nature. In this state, the earth would exist neither for the delight of its inhabitants, nor for their use.[22]

Principles for Shaping the Terrain

§.II.

The infinite variety in which Nature's features present themselves will mislead every small-minded man in the Art of Gardens. Whoever has not pursued modification and not attentively examined the forms of the terrain convinces himself by an error too common that, since they are irregular and of a great variety, all of these forms are random, and that he cannot fail to imitate them by haphazard if he avoids straight lines and parallels, and outlines that are too symmetrical. In giving over to arbitrary fancy what is a necessary outcome of constant and known causes, only bizarre effects will result, as well as ones that are unbelievable and ill-conceived, since irregular forms are not without their own rules.

If these rules were arbitrary, it would be much more convenient for Artists, who have only to imitate Nature, to let themselves be guided by their imagination, and to give themselves up to all that Nature suggests to them. But they know only too well that without the constant pursuit of the study of this beautiful model, they cannot hope for success. If someone were to disdain this model, or, lacking taste, surrender himself excessively to the genre known as the caprice, he might perhaps, by the grace of the fashion of the moment, obtain a brief success. Those few times when he produces mediocre work, however, will quickly disabuse the artist and cause him to perceive his error. By contrast, he who is goaded by glory, who aspires to celebrity, will, at the feet of Nature, contemplate her, interrogate her, examine her with curiosity, and follow her step-by-step unceasingly. He will not be satisfied with himself until he has grasped the purity of her outlines, copied her forms with the most scrupulous precision, and rendered her effects in all their truth. What subtleties and beauties in her contours escape the common eye! The Artist sees and imitates them; the man of taste senses them. They are almost nonexistent for everyone else. I dare to predict that, whoever gives himself over to the study of Gardens without the doggedness that alone can initiate the Artist into Nature's most hidden secrets and unveil her beauties, will never attain perfection. Of all the Arts, his must be the least removed from the truth; he does not study Nature to imitate her, but to support her.

It would be difficult to know all the techniques by which Nature achieves her work, to follow her in all her steps, to cause her to be seen in all her forms, and to understand all her combinations. I will confine myself to several general observations on the principal causes that determine the form of the terrain: these will nonetheless be sufficient to rouse the attention of those who devote themselves to the Art of Gardens.

The perpetual circulation of water (which is endlessly reduced to vapor and pumped off by the sun's action),[23] a universal principle of activity and movement, is a physical effect well known and remarked by even the least attentive men. Light mists, which are transformed into clouds by the force of the winds that raise them above our heads, condense, fall as rain, and are distributed to all the points of the globe's surface. As the water falls, it moves and washes away all that gives way to its repeated efforts. The softest and least attached parts flow with it from the highest places to the lowest, while the hardest and strongest resist the water's impact. The terrain, when pyramidal in form and supported on a broad base, is less altered by the rain's action than when it is narrower: that is, all other things being equal, the impressions made by the rains' descent are stronger and more discernible on the lands whose slopes are steeper. Water gives more or less weight and importance to masses through the quality, grandeur, and direction of the divisions it creates. It gives these shapes more or less flexibility according to the way that dynamic forces act on passive ones. It is water that molds the mountains and rounds off their angles; it obtains harmony for their forms and softness for their outlines. It is water that ties together, by an imperceptible union, all the different slopes between its courses and all the parts of a given level. It is water still, that, in detaching the earth that surrounds it, leaves enormous groups of elevated and suspended rock formations to be discovered, against which all the water's efforts are powerless.

When, by its descent, water has fashioned convex parts that inclined planes have brought together, it flows in torrents, streams, and rivers in the concave places that contain and direct it. Ravines and gorges pour water precipitously into small dales, which conduct it into large valleys. These are as many channels that, like the vessels of the human body, divide and subdivide, and branch and bifurcate,[24] to carry freshness and life, and to perfect forms everywhere.

In the beginning, the slopes are steeper and the lateral elevations that represent the walls of these channels are closer together. But, to the extent to which these channels become more distant from the point of their origin, the hills become mountains and move farther apart. This is undoubtedly to proportion the space between them to the volume of the water that grows as much through the streams that meet it from the smaller vales as from the lessening slopes, whose steepness is generally inversely proportioned to the width of the valley.

The direction of the smaller vales is rarely contrary to that of the principal valley from which they branch, particularly at the point of juncture. Some of them draw a sinuous line in their progress, according to the quality and slope of the soils and the other types of obstacles water encounters in its flow. Without these factors, water would travel in straight lines. One may note that these meanderings are that much greater and multiplied, and that the corresponding sides of the inclined planes become more nearly parallel when these valleys are narrower and confined.

Such is the general progress of Nature in the forming of terrain, and such is the rule that the Artist must follow when he sets out to make changes to it. He will, however, never successfully apply the irregularity of mountainous terrain to a flatland. By hollowing out here, and raising up there, he will succeed in rendering it uneven, but he will not have established the general tendencies that Nature observes in her slopes. The eye, despite all this Art and expense, will quickly discern the outline and relationship of level to the areas that have not been subjected to work. It is this relationship, so easy to see, calling out man's efforts rather than Nature's, that makes manifest the inabilities of the Gardener. It also offends the viewer, who sees only hollows and mounds in these excavations where he believes he should find hills and dales.

Water is indisputably one of the principal agents by which the terrain receives almost all its modifications, and reciprocally, the terrain determines water's progress and meander. All of the forms that the Gardener sets out to impose on the terrain must bear the imprint of its action, or at the very least, he must not present effects that are contrary to this action, should he wish to give them a sense of verisimilitude, to have them adopted by good taste, and satisfy reason and please the eye. In the end, Nature must recognize them.

It is not as if the terrain does not sometimes go against these general principles in unusual forms, even if they are, in reality, the consequence of these principles. Their uniqueness only strikes us because we are ignorant of all the combinations that Nature can produce, and because we do not know some of her resources. All that we consider phenomenal proves this point. Yet, he who seeks to reproduce her should not fixate on a preference for things that seem too obviously foreign to her usual workings. He must choose the plausible over the true. For, if he were to take as model those surprising conditions that appear to be outside of her sphere to us, they will declare the weak hand of the maker in his methods or in the awkwardness of his execution seeking to render them, since they are always removed from their original context, or copied in a shabby or overly fussy way. Where the illusion is not perfect, there will be nothing more than the wonder of the first glimpse. Boredom and disgust will follow: in brief, in imitation, the forms of the terrain will satisfy us only to the extent that the Art that presents them to us has the appearance of the unequivocal truth.

I am an observer of effects only as an Artist, and I leave it to Physics to decide if valleys and mountains are born by the causes that I assign them. I am, however, entitled to believe that these causes have much contributed to their form; that they have created the greatest part of their uneven ground; that they subject these places to imperceptible, yet constant alterations; that it is by these causes that in some places the slopes rise steeply, and in others they diminish; that they fill up or hollow out the vales; that they raise or lower the flatland; and that all variations occur by rainfall and water's movement, and that it is particularly these two factors to which the correspondence of two slopes are due. Undoubtedly, violent winds, hard frosts, the powerful rays of the sun, the action of endlessly moving mists, subterranean shaking, volcanoes, and other forces in operation acting together or separately, work in concert to change the terrain. The effects that result, however, diverge but little from those that we have just depicted, and they are neither as discernible nor as general.

Conclusion[25]

If the forms of terrain are not a matter of accident, if they are not born of caprice, if, on the contrary, they are the result of the action and reaction of certain agents,[26] it follows from this that choice must not be abandoned to fantasy. These forms are subject to rules, and despite their diversity and variety, those that do not appear to be the effect of a physical cause should be rejected.

Two difficulties present themselves here that have often stopped the skillful and scrupulous Artist wishing for and seeking perfection: one regards execution, and the other composition. Here is the first.

In all the tasteful Arts, there are two distinct parts: the liberal and the mechanical. In less technical terms, one part depends on taste and feeling while the other belongs to manual labor. Some bring these two together, as in Painting and Sculpture. In other Arts, these parts are forced to assist each other and to employ foreign hands in part of the execution: such are Architecture and Music. Happy are the Artists who, able to forego others' help, or, finding experienced men, succeed in executing their composition with the most exacting precision! But, to whom will the Gardener who wishes to shape a terrain entrust the execution of his works? Where will he find workers prepared to listen to him? Does he imagine that he will win over those crude men destined to shift the earth to the taste his Art requires? Or, perhaps, tool in hand, will he go work the soil himself? Would that he had, at the very least, the resources of the Architect, who can render his ideas in a precise manner, and cause the intelligent worker to read his soul, so to speak. A mason, with the help of overalls and a plan, measure and level in hand, will suffice to complete the Architect's project perfectly, promptly, and without difficulty. The perfect execution of all the details essential for the exact truth—ever-changing forms, either in plan or elevation; the need for touches that are sometimes firm and sometimes delicate; contours multiplied by convex and concave parts; the imperceptible connections between slopes and levels; the general gradient of the terrain and its relationship to specific slopes—evade the resources the other Arts have procured for themselves. The only, sovereign, deciding judges of the effects are the eye and feeling.

The way of putting together a project and the techniques by which the property owner can be brought to an understanding of its effects form the second difficulty. There exists no property owner who does not ask, first of all, for a measured drawing from the Artist. A geometrical plan! And what is he going to see in that? How will he perceive the whole of the general picture, the feeling of a particular view, or the smallest perspectival effect? How will he understand the mixture of light and shadow, the varying features of the seasons, the effects of the air and those of distances, the far viewpoints which, while they are not shown on the plan, nonetheless are part of the ensemble? What line will show him the relationships and the correspondence of the parts to the whole, and show him the style? I do not blame the owner who knows neither the Art nor its difficulties, but what should we think of the Artist who imagines he can thus demonstrate his ideas, or who uses a means so unfit to provide understanding? I am not afraid to propose that, whoever dares present a measured plan for the instruction of a property owner, or whoever contents himself with one for his own understanding, gives, by this alone, an evident proof of bad faith, or of his own ignorance in the Art of Gardens. He might as well have tried to persuade a painter that he had created a portrait of his model in drawing a plan of her feet, and pretended thus to make her recognizable!

Only he who has a feeling for subtleties, and who knows the infinite variety of Nature's effects can grasp the impossibility of depicting them and rendering them in a topographical plan. He clearly sees the uselessness and insufficiency of this. At most he will add descriptions and drawings. Even so, he must beware the pencil of the Draftsman, whose *making* can seduce, and the pen of the Writer, whose style can deceive.

Of the Relationship of Terrain to the Classes of Gardens
§.III.

The site must have a relationship to the class of Garden. An awareness of this relationship depends almost as much on feeling as it does on reason: this relationship alone facilitates the means and spares expense in the work. Without proper application of one to the other, there can be no hope for an Artist's success, or for the owner's enjoyment.

Would it not be giving up these advantages, in effect, to plan a *countryside* on a cold ground without variation and character, devoid of features and variety? Or to establish a *Garden proper* on a vast site, abounding in grand vistas, contrasts, and distant views, or enclosed by mountains with their harsh and steep slopes covered by rocks and heathers, their austere appearance opposing the sweet and amiable tone that characterizes this class? Would it not be an obvious contradiction to prefer an arid place with sterile soil amenable to only meager cultivation, in establishing a *farm,* when agriculture, its sole purpose, must present abundance, and the only interests of its scenery are the rich productions of the land? Would it not, finally, be as inconsistent to place a *park* in a compressed and segmented terrain, since as a whole it would have neither the nobility of the style, nor grandeur in its effects? Its unfortunate surroundings, devoid of appeal, would provide only an uninhabitable wilderness as a perspective.

Of the four classes, however, the *countryside* is the one that absolutely requires a site made for it. If, of her own accord, Nature did not provide a grand character and arranged the principal materials in laying out the site, we must reject it: Is it in our power to create such a great machine?[27] Do we have the means to fabricate the immense vistas and produce the magnificent views that together constitute the *countryside*? One cannot recast Nature, as she is thus much lessened. It is beyond human capacity even to give her a character that opposes what the site presents. If it is pleasant and open, one might perhaps manage, by moving and shifting the earth and by planting to render it gloomy and obstructed, but never somber and mysterious. Does the site have a strong and vigorous expression? It cannot be softened; it will merely be weakened to the point where it will have lost both its effects and its harmony. Let the Composer, therefore, restrain himself from the desire to create the *countryside*, let him even fear changing the dominant character of the greater whole, and let him not say: *I will make a mountain here, and there a valley*. He who undertakes such endeavors neither knows the limits of the Art, nor has he understood its techniques. Does he imagine he will create a convincing illusion with a few wheelbarrow-loads of earth heaped up like molehills, presented as mountains? With mediocre rockwork methodically constructed from limestone rubble that he will call by the impressive term "boulder"? With a wiggling ditch, a few feet wide, which he will grace with the ostentatious title "river"? With the help of this childish and ridiculous imitation, he may persuade himself that he has made the *countryside*, and that on a couple of arpents[28] he will have created the grand vistas of Nature: let him disabuse himself of this, and not even attempt to do so.

If all human means are not sufficient to fashion a site of importance on Nature's true scale, the Artist who sets reasoned principles for himself will yield to the lay of the land on which he sets out to work. He will only consider that class of Garden which the terrain would support. If the site lends itself to the *countryside*, he will, guided by taste and truth, seek to make its effects better felt and definite, but not to change them: he will reinforce the terrain's own character, and not contradict it. Let him enrich it by similar and well-placed features, if this character is lacking. Let him establish connections, if it is disjointed, and, above all, let him embrace in the whole all that the site offers to the eye, because sight is not circumscribed, with no boundaries but the sky and the horizon. One can at most narrow the view at certain points and frame some nearer prospects. All that the eye embraces, however, must be part of the general whole, so that none of the features that appear seem foreign, disconnected, or separate. This way of proceeding will force him to treat the *countryside* as a whole, and to have it conform to Nature, whose absolute dimensions cannot lend themselves to relative proportions, since each of her objects has its fixed and invariable measure. Thanks to this method of *bringing together*† the terrain that he shapes and the objects that he associates with it, he will make nothing that does not appear true. He will set aside all unnatural ideas that will never accord with the *countryside*. Thus, he will compose a unified, harmonious whole whose parts will be in true agreement, each one in its correct proportion.

Human means are more effective and employed with greater success in the creation of the *park*. The effects that this class of Garden allows are neither as large nor varied as those of the *countryside*. The Artist may, up to a certain point, subject these effects to his views: however, the more amenable the chosen site is to the planned arrangements, the less there will be to do to accomplish them. Among the parts of the terrain to which it is important to give careful detail are the surroundings of the château, which greatly tend toward the *Garden proper*. This rule is founded on appropriateness, of which we have already spoken. In effect, the ownership of an estate presumes a man to be both important in term of property and possessed of refinement with the means to satisfy it. It is therefore a matter of decorum that what is within view around the dwelling should announce his wealth and his taste, and that propriety and an appearance of order make these evident. Because the château is a product of Art, we may choose the site on which it is placed and the soil on which it stands. It is apparent that these should be pleasing and amenable to the creation of a beautiful whole. But let us not, under this pretext, take on laborious attention to minutiae and childish details. Let us remember that, despite all possible efforts, artifice does not please for long, and that the charms of Nature alone have the privilege of keeping boredom at bay and of anticipating satisfaction. Further, in the composition of a *park*, the sweetest scenes and those most carefully tended must be followed by those that are the most rural and simple. How are these to be connected, if they are so different? The *park* must join with the *countryside* at the edges and to the *Garden proper* at the center. It is by this association that the pleasures of one will be united with the beautiful effects of the other, and the nobility of the style will be allied with Nature's graces.[29]

The arrangement of the ground in the *Garden proper* can be completely submitted to labor. It is here that man is truly the creator. The liberties to which this class lends itself—the softness of its effects, gentility of scenes, uncomplicated play of slopes, circumscribed vistas that need only grace in line and liveliness in color, water in small volume, and finally, a confined boundary and tight limits—all this requires neither immense labor nor considerable moving of earth, provided that one has paid attention in the choice. It is the costly trees, well-maintained lawns, the studied care, the neatness, the daily maintenance, and all the beauties of detail that, multiplied through fantasy and imagination, occasion great expense. The true purpose of the *Garden proper*, beyond the pleasure of the general view,

---

† TRANSLATOR'S NOTE: Italics are original here, indicating a particular point of emphasis on Morel's part.

is that each object be seen up close; so that, in his calm and leisurely strolls, the property owner may traverse it without fatigue, on gentle slopes and convenient walks, in order to examine all its parts at his leisure, so that each point, in a word, should offer him a simple pleasure. For these reasons everything must be precise and refined in detail, sweet and inviting in the general view, and elegant and well cared for in each specific detail.

The *farm*, which is more accommodating, lends itself to all sorts of situations, and does not require regrading for its arrangement. The most ornamental *farm* should have only a few obviously studied details: simple and domestic, it makes do with all. In whatever circumstances it is found, the *farm* will not appear separated from what surrounds it, because it must conform to the character and disposition of the terrain that determines its type. The *farm* is never misplaced, provided that the soil is amenable to cultivation. The *farm's* indifference with respect to site, rather than leading to a lack of discrimination, instead requires discretion to make it a success. Since the *farm* derives its charm and type from its situation, even more intelligence, taste, and feeling are required to determine where it is to be established. Although the plain is not to be excluded, if one were to prefer an absolutely flat terrain as its location, the *farm* would lack variety in its productions, and this variety is one of its greatest beauties. The *farm* would, in effect, be deprived of the cultivations reserved for the hillsides and dales, and without these, its surroundings would have neither stream nor meadow: two things that agree with it so well.

Water is undoubtedly desirable in all classes of Gardens, but for the *farm* it is indispensable, since dryness does not conform with the principal aim of its creation. This class must tie rural pleasures to the bounty of the fruits of the earth, and cultivation fertilized by this great agent of growth must be assured.

OF WATER

General Effects

§.I.

Water is to the landscape what the soul is to the body:[30] it animates a scene, gives radiance to a prospect, and spreads freshness and life in all the places it is found. By its charm it attracts our eye and fixes our attention. Everywhere it is the most interesting item and the first to be noticed. Whether it is still or flows slowly, proceeds rapidly or falls with a roar, its effect is neither equivocal nor uncertain. The polish of its surface reflects and duplicates objects. The mirror of calm water draws pictures that the viewer may vary at will. Its noise and movement, its own color and that which it takes from what is around it, and its property of reflecting light in almost all its liveliness give water its great attraction and diversity of character. By these it gives us the means and infinite resources to enrich the scenes of Nature and vary her expression.

But it is, above all, by its noise and movement that water acts forcefully on our senses, because it has the advantage of producing both effects simultaneously. Even when its agitation is most felt, the movement of the air does not make the same impression. This fluid,[31] which does not act positively on the sense that judges its movement, does not speak to the soul. Moving air is more pleasant for the refreshment it brings us than for the changes it causes. When its movement is violent, it is inconvenient and tiring, and forces us to seek shelter when it becomes intolerably excessive.

The strongest winds are not capable of rendering Nature more animated than their own movement and the commotion they create; the imperceptible workings of vegetation produce even less of this effect.

It is thus to its continual action and its uninterrupted sound that one must attribute the power water holds over our senses. Sometimes slow and flexible, it accedes without protest to the weakest obstacle, and turns from the least hindrance. Sometime lively and sprightly, it breaks down the strongest dam with a roar and violence, and it carries away all that stands in the way of its passage. Sometimes enclosed in its channels, it seems to proportion its volume to their capacity, and never exceeds their limits. Other times, by its abundance, it escapes and spreads out far and wide. In its meandering course it inundates entire plains, and the speed of its current forms islands through the multiple courses it hollows out for itself.

How can so much action, so much obvious, perceived movement not give a sense of liveliness to Nature when we see the traces water has left in places it has moved through, vividly recalled in its impression in dry riverbeds, and in ravines and their devastation? When, even in its state of stagnation, water is seen to tremble, through its extreme mobility, at the slightest impulse of the air?

These striking effects are not unique: water inspires many varied feelings in us, and such is its sway that, aided by the site that surrounds it, it gives a soul to the most contrary situations. Pleasant or importunate, calm or agitated, silent or noisy, it causes our feelings, in its different states, to range from the most perfect calm to the liveliest emotion, even horror.

It is water that imposes silence upon us and sends us into reverie, when, in the form of a stream more lively than rapid, it murmurs sweetly and snakes its way among grass and flowers. It is again water that rouses us when, by a more animated movement, its murmur changes to babbling that is less equal and stronger. Does it bubble around the obstacles that stand against it and torment it? Does it become more agitated and noisy? It cheers us and inspires us to activity. Does it roll in torrents? Does it tumble in cascades? Either it gladdens us by its brilliance and sprightliness, or it causes alarm in all our senses by its noise and rage.

This is not all. The tranquil surface of a lake heightens the calm of a peaceful scene, and its vast extent imposes this calm upon us. A broad river is majestic, if it runs rapidly but without fury, if its banks are high without being rough or deserted and form a basin of great proportion. A river that crosses a rich and furnished flatland, whose clear and limpid water make visible the clean and sandy bottom over which it flows, offers us a beautiful prospect. Its banks provide us with pleasant walks. We can dare to approach its gently sloped edges and rely on the security of its calm waves. But, is its course swifter, and is the wave angry and deep? It will inspire horror when we imagine the dangers it might make us undergo.

Beyond the effects that result from its mass, noise, and movement, water acquires still more characters through its color and situation. It may render a view darker and more mysterious when it flows with neither noise nor effort between the thick trees that shade it. Its transparency lends a lightness and brilliance to a landscape. Its clarity charms the eye. A previously excavated ravine becomes more disastrous each day by the damage occasioned by water's prodigious activities. A shadowy abyss is made to appear more horrible by the lusterless water it encloses in its breast, and by the muffled roar the falling water makes when its echoes, redoubled by deep cavities, carry into the distance.

The sight of a lake, whose water is thick and muddy, adds to the melancholy of a wild prospect. Finally, a river, indolent in its progress, enveloped in its course by cliffs bristling with barren rocks, and barely seen through the crude and unhealthy mists that it exhales, presents us with a melancholy and ghastly sight that repulses us.

If we measure the immense distance separating the tiresome feeling that such a prospect produces in us from the pleasant gaiety inspired by the vivacity of a pretty stream whose crystalline waters flow over silver sand between pleasant banks and, free in their course, seem to turn endlessly only to bring abundance and liveliness everywhere, we will understand the effect that Nature's materials happily combined may have on the soul. We will feel their power and the sway they hold over our sentiments, since this power alone affects us in so many ways and moves us so forcefully.

While water may be omitted from the composition of a Garden and is not absolutely necessary, it must be confessed that it will always be missed, and that the Garden without water loses not only the variety it provides, but is also deprived of one of its most beautiful objects and the most refined effects of Nature. There are no scenes so small where water would be misplaced, and to which it would not bring favor. There are none so large wherein water will not figure to its advantage and not embellish, or where its expression fails to lend and receive more strength and liveliness. There are no places so brilliant to which water will not add more radiance. Finally, aside from the impressions it engenders in us, water pleases us in and of itself. We enjoy the sight of it. We seek places where it is found. It brings a luxurious sweetness to all that surrounds it when it is well placed. But, it has grace only when free: that is, when, without any constraints (at least those that are apparent), it is found in places where the slope of the terrain would have led it, since freedom is the first pleasure of water after its clarity.

Specific Characters of Water
§.II.

Water presents itself to our eyes in three different states: still, flowing, or falling. In its first state, water forms lakes, ponds, fountain basins, and in general all that is understood as a water feature. In its second state are streams, rivers, and torrents. The third state is that of falling water, which takes the names of waterfall, cataract, and cascade.

The first impression to which flowing water gives rise, after that of movement, is of continuity. The imagination neither seeks nor locates the beginning or the end: these two terms are as invalid for water as they must be for the eye. What is immediately clear is that water divides a site. Rather than separating it in two parts, however, it ties a site together when the two parallel lines between which water is enclosed conform more or less to the winding of the valleys and dales in which it flows. This is not the case when the water's edges are drawn in straight lines contrary to the contour of the terrain. Then, water not only divides it, but also it visually breaks the whole into two parts because of the lack of correspondence from one to the other. This is a vice that destroys even the idea of continuity, which is characteristic of flowing water, because, clearly, alignments of this sort belong more to Art than Nature, and Art is limited in its dimensions.

Streams and rivers differ only in their breadth, with the distinction, nonetheless, that streams are generally faster because the dales in which they flow, being narrower and more meandering, subject them to frequent turns, not counting the effects of such phenomena as the trees that border their banks, or the boulders they encounter in their passage.

Streams, however, growing in volume as they progress through widening dales, begin to trace lines that are more nearly straight, because the greater mass of their waters has more power to overcome the obstacles that turn them. The direction of the hillsides and mountains, being farther away, holds less true and even less apparent sway over the water's course.

A relatively general rule may be derived from these observations: that is, that the broader the river, the less it will turn, and the more the undulating lines of its edges will be slackened. Thus, when the river finally arrives at a considerable width, its course will not be perceptibly far from a straight line. Despite vast turns, its continuity will always be perceptible.

A broad river, whose turns are frequent and whose angles are acute, would be neither natural nor pleasing. It would only present detached basins that destroy the idea of continuity. I have said, and I repeat, that this continuity is essential.

A little stream escapes this inconvenience. Its course is very much determined by the lively flow of its water, and by the ease with which its small space may be seen in a greater expanse. The frequency of its turnings even leads it along a line that the eye can follow nearly the whole length of the valley it irrigates.

It is doubtless unnecessary to point out that between a small stream and a great river there are many intermediary sizes that conform to the rules that we have just established, depending on whether their dimensions are closer to the one or the other.

It is flowing water's uninterrupted continuity that has inspired the art of communication: it gave rise to the invention of bridges. It can be seen from this why bridges appear so fittingly on rivers and never interrupt them, despite the fact that they almost always cross a river at a right angle. By the same reason it may be grasped why bridges make such a poor effect over still water, which, confined on all sides, does not prevent communication in any way, since one may go around to get from one side to its opposite. It is thus always a mistake merely to build a bridge over a lake and allow the far sides of this body of water to present the idea of a river: because, although still, the water must take on a flowing character. By this character, the water could thus even obtain much appeal, and in this imitation the illusion would be complete if the line the water traces follows true contours, if the two ends are thus ingeniously hidden, and, in particular if the breadth is more like a river than a stream. For, the latter, which is normally very lively, finds itself deprived in the state of stillness of this liveliness which is one of the principal traits that characterize it, and the river, more moderate in its flow, does not require a current that is so perceptible. In addition, on a wider surface, exposing itself more to the winds, the slightest zephyr will suffice to obtain a trembling that will imitate the waves of flowing water, a sleight of hand that the eye allows itself to be tricked easily.

Flowing water produces islands,[32] a feature that ornaments its flow and diversifies its often overly uniform progress. In general, an island, by its position amid the water, its plantings, edges, and even its solitude, is always a pleasant object either as a view or a site. It is in part from the difficulty in getting to it that it derives its charms: it piques the curiosity and gives rise to the desire to visit.

Those few who have paid attention to the causes that produce islands will deduce the form they must take. Water, in its course, encountering obstacles that parts it, separates in two or more narrower branches in the common streambed, and reunites in a single channel at the point where the obstacle stops. This gives all islands a form that is more or less elongated, more or less pointed at the two ends, and bulbous in the middle. Sometimes an island is convex on one side and concave on the other when found at a turning. Such is, in regard to islands formed by rivers, Nature's procedure and the face that she gives them. Art must create them according to this model when one wishes them to appear as the result of the natural causes that collaborate in their formation. The necessity for Garden features creates them. Taste fixes their location and the length, and adorns them with simple or rich ornaments relative to circumstance and to the effect to be produced, such as the view and the site.

As for the torrent, other than what it shares with the stream and the river, it is characterized most specifically by the speed of its progress. Its rugged, uneven, harsh banks must thoroughly feel the steepness of its fall and the liveliness of its course, and their disorder must show how the torrent is subjected to abundant and sudden floods. Its bed, ordinarily too wide because it often holds little water, is filled with protrusions, stones, and pebbles, over which the water gambols. Impetuous, the torrent detaches and rolls boulders, pulls up and drags along trees, and brings from afar its sands and disasters. Its frequent turns must be justified by boldly marked obstacles. If the flow encounters impediments strong enough to resist it, it stops for a moment, then it broaches the obstacle with havoc, fleeing violently and producing falls and cataracts, whose effects, at once pleasant and terrible, are never seen without emotion.

The lake, like all types of standing water, has no movement of its own, but the least action of the air causes the surface to tremble, and when the winds are unleashed, they agitate its waves, and cut them into deep and mobile furrows. The freedom that still waters have in varying their banks in many ways is equivalent to the attractiveness that rivers obtain from their uninterrupted course. The lake encompasses bays that go deep into the earth, advancing points that form headlands and promontories, sandbanks, and sometimes islands. These features, when they are brought in by the arrangement of the terrain, are as familiar in lakes as they are unsuited to rivers, for the reason that running water does not seek to spread out in all directions like still water that is pushed everywhere.

Sometimes in steep or sheer slopes, the shores of a lake oppose and resist the multiple efforts of the angry waves that break there and whiten them with their foam. Sometimes its edges are flat or slightly inclined to offer a softer prospect, when less furious if still agitated waves advance and retreat by alternating movement, drawing an undulating and mobile line on their shore and rendering it firm and even with the sand and gravel they deposit there. This allows an approach to the indefinite line they trace and invites one to follow it. From there the eye loves to stroll about a moving surface ending at the varied, and richly and agreeably furnished shorelines. When the calm has polished the lake's surface and it shines with all the light's brilliance, it is also pleasing to contemplate the reflection of a beautiful sky adorned with light clouds. The surrounding objects are painted reversed and trembling there, but we note with pleasure the precision of their contours and truth in their colors.

The unevenness in the height of a lake's shores and their protrusions and low-lying spots constitute the essential variety in the outline that circumscribes it, while the rise and fall of the terrain in which it is enclosed prescribes its general form and specific features. This form, in order to be subject to the whole, is no less given to grace and even elegance.

But if the lake takes its beauty from its expansion in all directions, and from the variety of its edges, this extension must have limits and this variety must not degenerate into disorder. The lake's surface must be proportioned to the site in which it figures, and must not be so vast that its limits are lost, even when the locale is accommodating. The eye must always encounter objects that attract it; if it finds nothing that it can seize upon, it will wander and grow weary. An immense expanse that imposes itself upon us will not be pleasing for long. Its monotony will soon bore us and end by tiring us. In regard to the lake's shores, shabby details must be avoided, and the contours must not be broken up into a multitude of little promontories that do not produce variety, but rather confusion. One must know how properly to break up large protrusions with pleasant features and interesting details.

Without actually diminishing the expanse of a lake that is too vast, one can manage to bring the shore that is too far away closer by elevating its edges, and raising them still further with pyramidal objects and by plantings of large and strongly massed trees; the dark color they receive from their thick foliage diminishes the distance. By countermeasures one may give a lake greater extent by flattening the edges down to the level of the water and razing the objects that elevate them. When the shore recedes, it blends with the horizon. The surface of the water, less perceptibly circumscribed, will appear vaster.

It is thus, by fixing boundaries that are too indistinct and rendering less precise those that are too strongly pronounced, that one may, without lengthening or shortening the distances of a lake, trick the eye by its intervals. It is thus, by appropriately placing strong foreground features that cause objects to recede that one wishes to push back, or, by interposing light and hazy ones in the opposing locations, the lake's surfaces will be lengthened or shortened. It is by using similar, well-understood means that we will thus arrive at separating points that are too close, without obliterating open spaces and confusedly placing objects one on top of another. But these techniques, which can be deployed on more than one occasion, are the most difficult and delicate part of the Art. They require great understanding of the effects of aerial and linear perspective, and an extended study of what painters call *planes*.

The lake as a type also includes islands, but their overuse should be feared. One must know how to forego them when they contribute nothing to the enrichment of the scene, since they are harmful if they do not contribute to the perfection of the vista. As they arise more from the disposition of the terrain than the action of water, they may be infinitely varied in their form. Taste and reason must act in concert in their placement and their design, and in determining their plantings, features, and extent.

The lake sometimes takes its origin from a river, when, by the disposition of the terrain, its waters find a basin large enough to contain them in their route. They then discharge themselves there, filling the basin by the effect of leveling. Then, by the effect of slope, the water continues on its way, recovering the character of a river. This is undoubtedly the most interesting way to present water, because, the entry and the exit of a river at a lake, permitting rapids, allow water to be shown very naturally in one scene in its three different states.

It is rare, however, that water and terrain lend themselves to so fortunate an arrangement, and that all the circumstances appropriate to produce a desired effect are found together. To seek to subjugate them in these difficult circumstances is often an impossible undertaking and always one that is very delicate. The clear evidence of the effort to surmount the least obstacle on the part of one or the other may erase all the charm of one of the most beautiful features of Nature. I foresee, however, he who will decide to try to create such an effect at a favorable location. He must pay great attention to the way in which he designs the water's entrance and exit, and, above all, to the way in which he places it. These two points are essential. And, if, in the execution of this project it is necessary to work the terrain, he must seek to excavate the area in which to make the lake, and not raise its edges, because the embankments will corrupt the natural progress of the terrain much more than the excavations. In addition, rapids can be fittingly placed at the entrance or with a stream at the exit. They can even be foregone if too much difficulty or expense or too many obstacles are anticipated.

Falling water is perhaps the most difficult to treat in the right way. In order to obtain rapids and cascades, artificial means, which are always dangerous to substitute for those that Nature would make use of in a similar case, are required. If it is necessary to oppose the efforts of water falling in cascades with forces capable of resisting its continual action and to prevent erosion, how are we to disguise the regularity required by solid construction, which, however, must present only the rough effects of the water's work and the disorder that its fall occasions?

Other difficulties: Will the cascades fall in a single sheet, or will they be divided into several chutes? Will their point of origin be presented in a level line? Is there a predetermined relationship between their height, their width, and the volume of water? Do these dimensions have a precise relationship with the site where the falls are found? Are falls appropriate for all classes of Gardens? Are chutes interrupted and broken by obstacles preferable to those with even sheets? What will the obstacles be? Here we have before us a host of questions, each of which has its own response, but they apply to so many circumstances, and depend on so many combinations, that each specific case would require a rule. For the man of taste I have said enough on this, for he who lacks it I could never say enough.

In all the effects of this type there is a constant rule: never let the means used to obtain the result be seen, for even if a small amount is visible, the appeal is destroyed. It is here, above all, that Art must hide artifice, and illusion must be perfect. If the artifice is discovered, the more these sorts of false effects betray their costliness and effort, and the less they interest us: if Nature is lost in trying to imitate her, these effects are ridiculous.[33]

The study of Nature's laws, joined with taste,[34] will show how to determine the most favorable place for water relative to the whole and to specific scenes and how to proportion it. This study will lead to knowing how to uncover water or to shade it appropriately, how to arrange its sound and movement according to the most fitting rhythm and accent, how to show only as much of its surface as will enhance it and increase its extent in the eye of the imagination, which is always generous when called into play. These are fine points which escape rules, but are very worthwhile for the Artist to employ.

In accordance with all that has just been set out, is it not superfluous to warn that it would be an unpardonable misconception not to follow the general slope of the terrain in tracing an artificial river, or to place water in high places, especially if it has the character of flowing water, and the lower areas lack water? Nature never causes rivers to flow on mountains, nor water to move in a sense that is contrary to the slope of the terrain.

As for the characters of water that are applicable to each class of Gardens: I will say in a few words that the *countryside* will admit all of them, and that it lends itself to the greatest effects of this Nature and does not disdain the smallest, but the artist need worry only about their relationship with specific sites, and the impression that they may make in the overall whole. For, this class rejects all that is not stamped with the mark of the most scrupulous truth.

The *park* prefers extensive bodies of water. If it sometimes allows for water in smaller sections, it will only accommodate it in specific scenes to enhance their attractiveness. The *park* has no ambition to make all the details of its ornament work together in the overall whole, and, unless the circumstances do not bring these in naturally, it will reject them as noxious or unsuited.

The *Garden proper* wants only small rivers that are calm in their course, with appropriately pleasing banks just above the water, and makes use of still water, because this does not always require a great expanse. The *Garden proper* does not allow for majestic or imposing waterfalls that require a terrain that is rugged and almost always strewn with boulders. Small, well-managed water chutes, however, provide cheerfulness, and do not go beyond the bounds prescribed for this class.

Finally, the *farm* is not choosy: all sorts of water go with it. If there is a preference, it is for the shady stream that animates the vegetation, and for standing water, whatever its dimensions may be. Either one, however, must be displayed in all the simple and unaffected lines of carefree Nature. The *farm* will avoid, as much as possible, water that ravages and devastates, such as torrents, and is only content with water that contributes to the fertility of its cultivations and the needs of its maintenance; for in this class, there is nothing that is pleasant if it is not useful.

OF THE EFFECTS OF VEGETATION

IX

The succession of the seasons throws variety into Nature's scenes: the play and undulation of the terrain determine their type, and constitute their character. Water activates them and spreads interest into them. It is, however, to vegetation that these scenes owe their most powerful charm and attractions. It is vegetation that furnishes the clothing that ornaments and embellishes the naked and unadorned earth. Without the soft tint, friendly to the eye, with which vegetation colors the earth, Nature would offer us only melancholy and wild perspectives, only pictures without harmony and grace. The sun, were it not tempered by the verdure that absorbs a portion of its rays and by the trees' shade that gives shelter from its brilliance and heat, would soon become tiring and even unbearable.

The diversity in hue of vegetation's different productions, the fact that it makes up for an always tedious monotony of levels: these productions divide, detail, and give boundaries to flatlands whose evenness and great extent render it too uniform. Hillsides, mountains, and all that presents itself as vertical would frequently offer us, without these productions, only heavy masses, barren forms, hard contours, and a horizon without variety. Valleys, which are so favorable to the productions of the earth, would be neither lively nor cheerful. Even water, stripped bare of this beautiful accessory, would lose its greatest appeal. Finally, without the cosmetics of its vegetation, the earth, poor and inactive, would be as it appears in uncultivated places and in dry and sandy deserts that reject all classes of production: a place with neither beauty nor utility.

An astonishing quantity of plants of all kinds, herbaceous, woody, creeping, and aquatic, are characterized by the difference in their size, the variety of their forms and leaves, the elegance of their flowers, and the diversity of their colors. They compose a magnificent collection of the productions that decorate the interesting and superb spectacle of Nature.

But in this host of productions, the tree, so distinguished in the order of vegetation, incontrovertibly takes first place. In raising itself up into the air, it enhances the pure blue of a beautiful sky that serves as its background, detailing its elegant contours and calling attention to the smallest features. Imposing in its mass, pleasing in its form and foliage, the tree is remarkable above all for its infinite variety. A tree of immense circumference abounds in strong branches leaving the enormous trunk at a right angle, extending proudly and carrying thick and bushy foliage into great distances. Another, slender and thready, its trunk in the shape of an upright cone, seems to neglect its weak and meager branches in order to soar into the clouds with the greatest lightness. Others, lacking a main trunk, display many branches coming from their root, and in this union comprises a beautiful cluster. A smooth, light, and shiny bark envelops certain species; others are covered in a hard, brown, and pebbly crust. The leaves of some, pulled by their own weight, are grouped in bundles that cause the ends of the delicate and flexible branches that hold them to bend. Straighter and stronger, the branches of others raise themselves nearly vertically, and carry their flowers, fruits, and leaves to their summit. A great number of trees grow boughs only at the top of their trunk. With some, the boughs arise from its base, and thus these trees present themselves as a pyramid with a broad base, or, sometimes narrow at the bottom, the pyramid broadens up to a middle or a third of the tree's height. Often irregular, trees take all kinds of forms and vary from the root to the summit. Here, the trunk and the branches are straight or slightly curved. There, they are gnarled and twisted in all directions. Sometimes their boughs rise almost perpendicularly, or follow a horizontal direction; sometimes they are oblique or bend down to the ground.

The way in which leaves are assembled on their branches produces yet another source of variety. Sometimes equally distributed, they cover and garnish nearly the whole of the branches' length. Other times, in the form of detached bouquets, they arise only at the branches' ends. Leaves differentiate themselves still further by their individual denticulation, their different size, and even by their mobility that subjects them more or less to the air's action. To all these features are added those of their hues, such as light green, yellow, white or silvery, brownish green, black or dark, and all that gives trees a transparent or dull tone, a heavy or light air, or a gay or sad character. Join with this the dissimilarities that arise from their proportion, from the understory to the forest tree; from their nobility, simplicity, and age; from the decorations they receive from their flowers and fruit; and from the difference between those that, so characteristically and subject to the vicissitudes of the seasons, change with them and annually lose their leaves, and those that constantly green never lose them. You will have infinite resources in this prodigious diversity, and an astonishing richness of forms that will furnish abundance to all that is fitting for each site and circumstance.

All these beauties of detail that trees present, however, are quite inferior to those that are produced by their association. From this association are formed vast forests, woods, groves, and detached clumps. It is from this point of view that trees must be envisaged, in order to conceive of all the magnificence of these effects that may be obtained from this important element of vegetation, either as an object in the view or as a site.

Nothing is unimportant in a wood: its mass, either more or less strong, its surface, greater or smaller, its placement relative to the prospect, its dry or humid soil, mounded or level, the line that ends and encloses it, its connection to what surrounds it, the clearings that break it up, and the type of trees that compose it. All these features, whose understanding and usage are so essential, require the greatest attention on the part of the Artist.

It is with the resources that woods provide him that he will give delights to the most melancholy places, that he will enrich the poorest prospects, that he will vary those that are most uniform, that he will soften the most austere. There is no perspective in which a similar relief cannot reinforce its character or correct it. There are no easier or surer techniques at hand to bring about the greatest changes, and their abundance will present no difficulty other than that of choice. One or two paintings done according to the principal characteristics of woods will render perceptible the power and diversity of the effects to which they are susceptible.

Let us enter a vast forest of old oaks, where the sun never penetrates. Here is felt an eternal coolness that captures and chills the senses at its approach. Its age, attested to by the enormous volume and prodigious height of the trees and by the mosses and parasitic plants that attach themselves and cover them, recalls a remote time, and leads us, without our perceiving it, to meditate on the instability of human things. A dark and mysterious day, a deep solitude, a silence as gloomy as it is uninterrupted—except by the lugubrious accents of the birds that flee the light—all this transports the soul to contemplation, and causes it to feel a sort of religious terror. This feeling, at this sight, is difficult to resist, and renders plausible the story of the veneration of forests that our forefathers had, and of their worship of them.[35]

Such is the magic of the great effects presented to us by the spectacle of Nature: these alone, invested with a truly imposing character, stir the soul vividly by means of the senses. The objects that compose them, however insensate and inanimate, in working on the intellectual faculty, succeed in elevating our mind to the most sublime contemplations.

From this vista we pass on to a cool and pleasing grove, where taste has brought together all of the greatest pleasures of that vegetation, where it has been grouped, where the layout of well-defined masses creates the liveliest effects of light and the most desirable shade. In this grove enlivened with flowers, we find this lovely production on which Nature has lavished refinement and elegance in all its contours, grace and suppleness in its forms, vivacity and variety in its colors, and the most pleasant scents. In this grove, I say, a tender grass, always new, covers its surface with a fine and unified lawn. Its pleasant verdure, rendering the brilliance of the flowers more vivid, invites us to walk there. A charming retreat through which we pass without fatigue, where we repose in safety, its calm and silence, the image of peace and tranquility, is entirely without monotony or melancholy! A delightful refuge that elicits only pleasant and sweet feelings, and whose objects bring serenity to the soul and pleasure to all the senses!

In these two rough sketches it may be seen that, while the scenes they present take their effects solely from the materials of vegetation, their impressions are diametrically opposed. Between the two extremes exist an immense number of possible modifications and different expressions.

Undoubtedly, were the earth left to itself, it would be entirely covered with trees and herbaceous plants. The first would take possession of the upper hillsides and the mountains, and the second would seek low places by preference, where coolness and humidity would suit them better. This distribution, shown by Nature herself, is without contradiction the most pleasant way and the most natural way to make use of the one and the other. Without trees and lawns, Gardens would be unthinkable. They are the principal materials, and in respect to them, others are truly accessories only.[36]

All the cultivations that add the pleasing to the useful—fine lawns embellished by masses of flowering shrubs and forest trees, a greensward of great extent that ends in a rich border of beautiful trees, strongly outlined by rough projections and deep recesses, the surface of a meadow enameled with flowers that carpet the base of a dale, varied woods and vast forests—these are the principal objects that vegetation presents to the Gardener's industry.

A forest that takes up a great expanse is suitable only for the *countryside*, but it may, sometimes, in the area closest to the château, be treated like a special and pleasant wood. By means of this relationship, the *park* will easily allow for its adjacency. In addition, the forest is not amenable to detailed embellishments. It takes its beauty from its immense extent, from the quality of its soil, from the greater undulation of the terrain, and from the age and diversity of the trees that make it up. All that Art may add to this is to make the forest accessible by paths and piercings. Without these it would be difficult and often impossible to enter.

In the midst of a vast assemblage, however, trees are often similar, close together, and positioned haphazardly. There, the distance cannot be seen and the sky is barely perceived. As a consequence, the way to orient oneself and to direct one's steps is lacking. Winding routes and oblique openings necessarily form an inextricable maze and create a disquieting uncertainty through the fear of getting lost. In a forest we follow a path, we traverse it, but we do not stroll there. These problems are avoided by aligned routes that through their direction shorten the way traveled and allow the view of an exit by which we may leave.

A wood of moderate extent does not present the idea of a frightening solitude. It may not, in any case, give rise to worry and similar fears: there, sinuous paths traced with intelligence incite a slight questioning that engages and makes one want to traverse them. Do not be persuaded, however, that it is sufficient to pierce a wood in all its width by narrow and contorted allées, as is too often done. Nothing is so tedious as wandering perpetually enclosed between two parallel lines that furnish only identical features. After having walked a long time in this labyrinth, we may doubt that we have progressed; without the impatience and weariness such an insipid stroll has caused, it would be tempting to believe we have not moved at all. Do you wish not to tire the feet? Amuse the eye with variety: this is a maxim that the Composer should always keep in mind.

If following a winding path is to be pleasing, it must be short, and an attractive and unexpected object should be presented to gratify the surprised walker just before the onset of boredom. Let the path sometimes take the walker under high and bushy clumps of beautiful trees, that cause him to enjoy a sweet day under their cool shade. Or, leaving a dense and dark thicket, let him find himself suddenly on a vast greensward, and pass immediately from the darkest gloom to the full brightness of the day. Let him pass through thickets intersected by oblique clearings that present him with a thousand uncertain routes. Elsewhere, let him encounter single trees, and, engaged by the soft carpet of moss on which they are planted, wander aimlessly. Let him hesitate a moment, undecided as to which side his steps will lead him, but that soon a pleasant and accommodating shelter, inviting repose, presents itself to his sight, determining and attracting him. From there, he will contemplate an innumerable assembly of trunks and branches of all kinds, crossed in every direction. He will see a few rays of the sun escaping through the leaves that shade them, which, penetrating here and there into the bark, shining in luminous points on the most polished and lightest of them, form a stimulating mixture of light and shade. Comfortably seated, sheltered from the rays' heat and brilliance, he will admire the contrast of the groups, the variety of the trees, the majesty of a vigorous oak, the beauty of a beech, the elegance of an ash, or the sometimes strange but picturesque form of an old elm esteemed by time. His eye will wander with ease through all that surrounds him. Here, a creeping plant embraces the adjacent tree, interlaces with it and festoons it with garlands. On another side, he finds a simple bush, a wildflower, and untidy plants that he believes to have been placed there at random. All, in a word, down to the smallest feature, that the Artist knows how to present to him as if it were the very play of Nature, and that will attract his attention and contribute to his amusement.

After a few moments of relaxation, if he continues on his course, and carried along only by a feeling of curiosity, he will again take on an unknown route, so that he finds himself in the middle of a neglected and wild wood—a retreat set apart, deserted all around, and abandoned to the disorder of rustic Nature. There, feeling alone, walking with slow steps, and forgetting himself, he will give in to the delightful distractions in which silence and solitude always immerse us. Then, at the first turning, a vast perspective opens itself suddenly before him, setting before his eye the lively view of a rich and populated countryside. This spectacle, as interesting as it is unexpected, suspends his tranquil meditations. It returns him to the tender reflection that Nature's true riches are accorded in profusion only through human sweat, and that the most painful yet useful work for society is done by the coarsest hands. An abundant harvest is scythed and tied in sheaves by a host of active arms. Grass newly mown is heaped in mounds, or spread out over the meadow. The air is perfumed with the pleasant odor of freshly cut hay. The frank and artless gaiety of the robust harvesters encourages the prospect of a bountiful crop: especially that of the young female haymakers unaffected by tiring work and excessive heat. The bustle of the horses and the carts; the movement of the field animals scattered on all sides, who, participating in the work, seem to share in the communal happiness. All these things taken separately and together compose the most interesting and animated scene, and this picture, so touching and so worthy of his regard, will occupy the viewer for a long time.

It is by such techniques, or by others taken from specific sites, that a wooded location may produce effects that are as interesting as they are varied. Each step offers an exciting novelty. A sequence of objects and images, either connected or contrasted, and brought to bear with skill or prepared with intelligence, will arrange enjoyments for us that are endlessly renewed. Their impressions, always vivid when those having the art to make the most of one or another of them, will enchant and conquer the senses, the heart, and the mind.

Woods offer us further essential observations as the object of a view: let us review some of these. Woods create the most advantageous limit to the horizon. A gathering of beautiful trees, by the variety in their forms and the unevenness in their height, will, in effect, define the horizon by their light and well-varied outlines. They join the sky and earth in the most pleasing manner. A wood in the form of an amphitheater, seen from below, always presents a beautiful and rich perspective. The greater the slope, the more it will appear suspended and the greater the magnificent effect. If the wood does not cover the summit, however, and allows it to be perceived, it loses almost all advantage from this position. This effect of suspended woods is sometimes so subtle that to reinforce it, the lack of elevation in terrain is supplemented by selecting the trees' sizes—placing the largest at the top and the smallest at the bottom. Trees used in such circumstances, necessarily being different species, must be placed with regard to their tone and form, so that the mixture is not too discordant, and that all connections are not destroyed. A strong unity is essential here.

One of the most important observations regarding woods relates to their outside edge. This line often composes a considerable portion of the prospect from the house. This line defines the clearings, terminates greenswards, decides their form, and almost always serves as the background of a prospect. There are few parts of the Garden that require so much taste and demand so much attention. If the outline that separates the wood from the lawn traces an unnatural form, allowing the Artist's intention to be detected, if, in a word, the hand that designed it is perceived, it will have neither grace nor attraction, however elegant it may be. The contours must have the untidiness that is so amiable in Nature. They must be varied without confusion, rich yet simple, firm without being straight or uniform, large, and not heavy. Let the greensward sometimes recede deeply into the woods and become lost there. Let the wood sometimes make a pointed projection into the lawn. This large, bold gesture will expand a green carpet in the eye of the imagination, so long as this feigned extension never seems too vast. This will give an appearance of breadth and depth to the narrowest wood. A border formed by soft and equal undulations will be too apparent. Particularly at a certain distance, it will not escape the insipid uniformity presented by a regular line, which it begins to approach.

It is thus through the aid of strong protrusions and large projections, along with variety in its plantings, that attractiveness may be injected into the exterior line of a wood and give it movement as much by the line that it draws as by its vertical effect. The combination of all these means creates marked distances that present distinct masses between the most salient parts. These masses allow the *planes* [of the landscape picture] to be noticed and to vary. The closest trees dominate the farthest away, and cause their heads to play gracefully in the sky. Similarly, the tallest and most vigorous, by the color of the leaves and the thickness of their branches, seem to approach, while the smallest and lightest retreat and distance themselves. These effects, based on the laws of perspective, gratify the gaze and charm the viewer. They offer him an astonishing variety, and show him other vistas and a new decor when he changes his position.

If a bump, a mound, or a sudden change in the slope of the terrain determines the separating line between the wood and the greensward—a separation common enough in Nature—these features will furnish yet more ways of varying the outside edge. The most beautiful and majestic trees may crown some eminences; simple bushes will barely cover others. Well-placed gorges and artistically fashioned valleys will give the mound a natural rise and will invite, by the easy slope they present, entrance into the wood. A few isolated trees, placed in the front and intending to meld, so to speak, the wood and the grass, will cross the entrance without hiding it. They will give the wood's outside line a sort of indecision allowing it to be modified without changing its major parts, and make it an object of perspective much more interesting without the harshness of precision.

There are few circumstances where one must make a clearing in a wood from one side to the other. The openings must be reserved for the clearings at its heart. These provide the wood with important features, viewpoints, and perspectives that are always attractive, because they are unexpected. There may be found the opportunity to create clearings without affectation yet with success, and a frame of the appropriate dimension best suited to the pictures presented by the openings may be given.

Finally, if because of compelling reasons, such as a field that is too closed in by a shallow wood, a valuable viewpoint, or another cause that will determine that a wood be cut through its full depth, the two lines of trees that thus arise must be contrasted in such a way that the separated parts produce the effect of two woods coming together, not moving apart. One will succeed without difficulty if the opening is found at the exact lowest spot between two slopes where the terrain's rise will assist in facilitating the illusion. When, however, the opening is on level ground, or on a single slope, or when the trees on both sides are of the same species and the same height, it is very difficult for the opening not to have the appearance of gap more notable for its awkwardness than for the reason it was created.

I would never fall silent if I were to note all the objects worthy of attention that woods present, or all the fine and useful observations which are appropriate to them. We draw help from woods to fix the extent of a perspective, to prescribe the exact limits of a site, to connect buildings and follies to a landscape. All the circumstances in which they may be used—to trace routes, design paths, and give shade to water—and all kinds of woods, from the humble and cool willow grove to the ancient forest, these constitute an immense field open to the Artist. He will find in it all that the most fertile imagination and the most refined taste may suggest.

I will, however, move on to the application of the principal uses of vegetation in the classes of Gardens in which it is fundamental. I will summarily observe that all types may have meadows and lawns, but that, in the *countryside* and the *farm*, they are as much a useful as appealing feature. In the *park* and the *Garden proper*, in contrast, the useful gives way to the pleasing. Communal fields are only appropriate for the *countryside*, and pastures for the *countryside* and the *farm*. Lawns are reserved for the *park* and, more particularly for the *Garden proper*, from which it derives its delights. Forests can be placed appropriately only in the *countryside*, but they may be adjacent to a *park* as an accessory. Woods belong, as a feature, only in a *park*, and, as a visual prospect in the *countryside* and the *park*. The latter shares groves, clumps, and all attractive plantings with the *Garden proper*. As for specimen trees, they find their place everywhere. A few scattered woods suffice for the *farm*; only willow groves are appropriate in its low, cool places, and orchards above all else are its most attractive woods. Finally, all the types of cultivation created by useful industry and directed by a taste for simplicity are the *farm's* domain. If they are also found in the *countryside*, it is when the *farm* is part of this, as a collection of all that vegetation may produce.

OF ROCKS

X

Rocks are only worthy of attention, and are only noticed, when they have a forceful expression with a strong character. Too rough and austere to pretend to have grace and elegance, they work only in the wild views in which they are the best feature; they add an element of fear to deserted sites.

If they are brought together in strong, elevated masses, they impose their majesty: such is the very impression of the large vistas of Nature. In their different combinations, their most bizarre and extraordinary forms tend either to a terrible or awesome effect. Since they are only found in very mountainous places and have a great solidity, they contribute an astonishing rise and fall to the landscape that is enhanced by the torrents and falls of water that nearly always accompany them. They are covered with moss, which gives them color, and are ornamented by creeping plants; they coif themselves in trees and shrubs, which attach themselves wherever they can, scarcely able to take root and growing only with effort. The constraints and obstacles that they encounter twist these, forcing them into singular and picturesque shapes and situations that enhance the scenic effects.

Rocks are among the materials of Nature that the Artist may seize upon, when she places them at hand; but they cannot be created and can rarely be transported and arranged with success.[37] They are but slightly amenable to his wishes. Further, any imitation of them would seem too small and thus lack interest; with some rare exceptions, these are but poor and shabby. One will never manage to make of them a majestically imposing ensemble, a terrible one that frightens us, nor a marvelous one that astonishes: all expressions which would command our attention.

Moreover, if someone were so rash, so vain as to attempt it, where would he place rocks? In the *Garden proper*? He would deny himself everything that is important, wild, or frightening. The tiny rocks, unable to elicit any of their proper effects, would certainly ensure neither grace nor gaiety. And who would, in the middle of lawns and flowers, in a territory dedicated to sweetness and softness, position some brutish stones little apt for that place? If Nature had put them there, the first responsibility of the Artist would be to destroy or hide them. What about in a *farm*, where fertile soil must lend itself to agriculture? Their sterility would be an obstacle, adding no kind of attraction. If there is a type of farm that accepts them, then—as will be shown—they must be in such quantity and distributed with such disorder that the scale of the enterprise and uncertainty of success would discourage their use. It is not by using fake rocks that we can change how a landscape looks, and give a savage character to a grand scene when Nature did not do so. Can the Gardener use rocks in a *park*? He can admit them in distant areas where the site permits it, but reject them when the effect is wrong and when the manner of treating them is not sufficiently grand to eliminate all suspicions of fallaciousness. Finally, can he place them in the *countryside*, the only class of Garden where they can be treated with proper magnificence? And then, does he imagine he will give them their proper importance? How will he pile up huge boulders one on top another? How will he, through Art, obtain those grand effects and strong characters that will capture our attention and admiration alone?

Let us agree that rocks can be fashioned in only a few cases, and that, short of a powerful illusion, all attempts to do so will always be ridiculous or ineffective. Only with great circumspection will an Artist of taste and experience attempt to make them. But if Nature has presented them to him, then he must try to reinforce their given character with the skills that he possesses. He should connect them with plantings, when the rocks are scattered. When some pieces jut out between the trees, he should cause them to appear to join with larger ones, and thus gain some importance that they would otherwise lack. Let the Artist cautiously discover the most beautiful masses, and detach those he wants to emphasize from what surrounds these. Let him sometimes ornament them with plants that break their excessive uniformity and take away the barrenness of overly even forms. Let him elsewhere augment the effects of scenery, already wild, by spreading over it a somber texture of gloomy, dark trees that are not alien to such sites. Sometimes he could enhance these by overshadowing them with large, soaring trees. Let him provide access to the least approachable places by cutting paths into the sides of steep slopes, as we see on mountains and less frequented places. Or again, clearly with precaution against peril, let him make a track along the edge of a precipice that appears more dangerous than it actually is. Let him establish a crossing over a deep torrent by boldly making, on a rocky outcrop, a rustic bridge that time and age leave half-ruined. The sight of this structure, always picturesque, has a chilling effect, and from every angle confers horror on the scene. When the occasion arises, he can decorate some out-of-the-way valleys with fresh vegetation, though without pretension or obvious care. In the midst of sterility, the contrast will be striking: an unexpected meeting with some cheerful meadow, decked with trees of radiant green, consoles and compensates for the painful sentiment of an arid desert. In the end he will, with care and taste, attach a strong and telling character to all features apt to receive them.

Does water play a role among the rocks? The Artist will give movement to the water appropriate for the scene. If the scene is majestic, the water's flow will be neither hasty nor too slow, but in great volume. The Artist will prefer, instead of many small waterfalls, a single cascade worthy of the place. Is the scene a wild one? He will separate the water into small streams moving at different speeds as if in jerks, and send it through sharp and irregular turnings. In its course, the water will spill over into marshes covered with rushes and aquatic plants that lend an air of abandon. For an astonishing or terrible type of scene, he will cause the water to leap violently out of rocky fissures, tumble in foaming and precipitous falls, or roll in impetuous and noisy torrents. Its roaring, amplified by echoes, will make the site more frightening and more extraordinary.

To enhance, to correct—that is the essence, more or less, of what the Artist must do to work with rocks. Those means, which are not always above his abilities, will produce beauties that are masculine, and vigorous effects, which he would have tried in vain to obtain in wanting to create them.

If, however, upon mature reflection, ready means will allow him to introduce an assemblage of rocks to strengthen the character of and give expression in a few of his Garden scenes, he will not forget that the terrain must be varied and unequal as well as hard, that trees, shrubs, and plants can only be of the species that grow in dry soil, and finally, that the site and its locality are organized in a manner that suggests Nature forgot them. Even slight experience will have taught him that he gains nothing by an imperfect imitation by using all kinds of stones, even when by their singularity they seem to lend themselves to his views, and even if they were shaped and arranged by the most able Sculptor. He will never produce a true effect except by transporting real rocks, distributed in the way that Nature would have done in the place from which they were taken.

To these precautions, he will add that he must assemble them with sufficient artistry so that they appear as a block of large dimensions. This is one of the great means of eliminating any sense of the artificial: this type of construction must, above all, avoid giving rise to this sense, since it destroys the illusion. He will also take care to introduce this scene with preparations that announce it naturally: a sudden transition and a different type of surroundings will suggest a contrast made by man. In short, through Art he will recover Nature.

What makes rocks so resistant to treatment is that they must never appear constructed by their arrangement or by the place they occupy. This technical difficulty, which falls short of creating grandeur of effects and cannot achieve a perfect illusion, often leads to features that are pitiable, even laughable.

To the taste that gives grace, to the feeling that spreads through interest, the Artist must also add the resources of the genius that easily enables the toughest enterprises and the approaches that will successfully execute them. The fortunate Artist who unites all these talents that direct his pencil, moves forward with assurance, and determines at a glance the relationship of each part both to the whole and to the others. He allies grand effects with small features. He imagines striking oppositions. He understands delicate, well-managed connections. He employs the most striking contrasts successfully without fearing contradictions. He does not ever sacrifice the beauties of the whole to those of detail. In a word, he puts everything in its place, rightly proportioned, and always achieves his aim by the most direct and simple means.

OF BUILDINGS

XI

Here our subject is not construction, but instead the science of Architecture, and positively not ornamentation, which is its Art. I envisage buildings through their expression and character. My undertaking is to consider those of the countryside in association with the features of Nature, to examine the effects they produce in a landscape and a Garden, and, in the end, what they add to a scene.

Appropriateness in Architecture is a fine and delicate matter of feeling. It is acquired less through the study of rules than by the deep understanding of the customs, of the usages of the period, and of the country of habitation;* appropriateness is not exactly the same in the countryside and the city. In the latter, each building type has its own characteristics, but it composes a whole that is independent and without influence on what is adjacent. Dwellings touch, and yet are distinguished by the differences in their proportions and decoration. Other than their alignment, which is dictated by the public right-of-way, their height depends completely on the condition, need, and means of the owners, and the taste of the designer. The perfect harmony of decoration and the building with purpose leads to appropriateness. This assemblage of different types of construction of every sort constitutes a city, and provides its attractiveness. Without this variety it would resemble less a city than an immense, single building. However beautiful its decoration might be, its monotony would render it gloomy and boring. This uniformity would, in addition, be impractical. The differences of state, fortune, and rank of the inhabitants, the monuments erected to its glory or for its use, and the structures required by the features of its situation necessarily vary the form, location, extent, and character of a city's buildings and give each sector its set of features. Here are

---

* Appropriateness in Architecture is like seemliness in clothing or behavior. It is a general convention that use teaches us. The forms of Architecture have nothing in themselves that determine this appropriateness, since they are pure invention. Subject to local taste and arbitrary combinations, these forms vary from age to age, country to country, and climate to climate through nations' endlessly varying customs and uses. They have no boundaries except those of stability. This truth will be more convincing if one looks at ancient monuments, at the types each nation has adopted, and at the vicissitudes of this art over time and in different places. In this, Architecture must be distinguished from Garden art, which finds its type in Nature, and which should be, in all countries and ages, as invariable as she is.

the embankments, there the plazas, and large and broad streets crossed by smaller and narrower ones are found throughout. The most lavish and elegant edifices are placed, without intermediary, next to the simplest and most ordinary houses.

In the country, however, most of the buildings are generally found at great distances from one another. They have, aside from their own character, a relationship with the site that surrounds them, and an influence that is sometimes felt far and wide. It is this relationship of character to site that I identify as *appropriateness* in Garden Art. Once I have made it clear, and have discussed the situation that is appropriate to each building type, their character, form, and mass, as well as the style and color that will place the building in harmony with the landscape in which it appears, I will have accomplished my task. The job of the Architect is to build for stability, to arrange the interior for pleasure and comfort, and to provide the Gardener with an expression on the exterior that he expects for the charm and truth of his views. This important goal will often force the Architect to sacrifice the details for the whole and precise rules for general effects.

Buildings, seen from this point of view, are what are called *constructions* in Painting: an expression I will use to denote the buildings in question and all the structures that human industry adds to Nature in order to embellish gardens. If Architecture is thus appropriated, it will become a new branch[38] added to a refined Art that already possesses so much knowledge and taste, and whose productions are as admirable as its features are useful.

As works of man, structures should only be accessory features in the landscape; since they are not works of Nature,* they presuppose a goal and an intention. This goal and intention must be made manifest at first glance through the form that structures present, and by the position they occupy. As *follies*, they ornament a perspective, but as *appropriate* features, they add to the character and effect of the scene. Buildings, in order not to be merely an accessory in the landscape, must contribute in determining its expression in many circumstances.

Indeed, do you wish a landscape to appear to be living? You will achieve this with domestic buildings. Do you want a spot to be more solitary than it already is? Place a building that advertises retreat or neglect in an isolated position. The smallest bridge will convey a crossing, despite the apparent obstacle a river presents. A site that is nothing but rural will acquire a touching attraction of rustic simplicity

---

* Despite what has been said by all the Authors who have written on the origin of Architecture, I do not think that this beautiful Art found its models in Nature. These authors repeat, one after another, that columns arose from tree trunks that formed the points of support in former buildings constructed with wood, that the entablature that surmounts them was only the beam that served to support the floor joists, and that the pediment represented the eaves of the roof. From this, they have concluded that Architecture was founded on Nature, but where did they see her intend that tree trunks carry anything other than their branches, fruits, and leaves, or receive the end of a squared piece of wood? The primitive hut, however simple and rude, was certainly the fruit of industry and reason, and not the imitation of Nature. The only rational result these Authors could take from this assertion is that improved Architecture, in using stone, has brought forward the primitive forms of wood buildings, and that is all.[39]

through a humble cottage. An understanding of structures' influence in Garden Art requires the greatest taste and reflection.

When you travel through the countryside, casting an eye on a vast landscape and examining the varied buildings that are scattered through it, you will find each has an expression proper to it, and a character that defines its purpose. At one end of a valley crossed by a stream a village appears. It is a gathering of small, simple, low buildings. Their roofs, of the same height and similar to each other, play among the trees of the Gardens belonging to each house. The only church, placed in the center and set apart, is a considerable building made into a pyramid by its clock tower.

Through the uneven trees of a neglected wood that borders a meadow, the thatched roofs of a small number of scattered huts that form a hamlet are barely glimpsed. These rustic dwellings, each placed in the middle of an orchard surrounded by weather-beaten, simple palings, are so little noticed that they do not disturb the solitary character of so rural a site. Without the little cultivated fields, herds grazing in the meadow, and the bitter sounds of the shepherd's bagpipe, one would wonder if it were inhabited.

On the slope of a hill stands an ancient château. Its appearance has a certain quality of importance that identifies it as the lordly manor. It is surrounded by large trees. Under these, the roof forms and the weather vanes on the towers that flank them still dominate. The Gothic decoration, the stability of its construction, and the hue that time has printed on it lend it nobility, and advertise the antiquity of its owner's lineage.

At the center of its vast fields, you see a group of buildings of varying forms and heights. It is a large farm, surrounded by an enclosure in the middle of which are seen the barns. The manor house stands out, and the unevenness of roofs: the round and pointed one of the dovecote dominates, mixed with the wheat hayrick. The whole presents a rustic and at the same time picturesque effect: laborers and animals people it. Through their vigilant care, the cultivated surroundings have provided stable wealth, the goods of the earth, and give the farm an air of life and above all an abundance that possesses neither the grandeur nor the luxury which do not always indicate affluence.

On the opposite side, the eye is drawn by the brilliance of a slate covering: it is the house of a parvenu. A frontispiece, crowned by a pediment carried on columns, marks the middle of the facade. The whiteness of its plaster, the vases, statues, terrace walls, and water jets assault the gaze more than they refresh it. The house seems isolated, thanks to its straight avenue, its courts and forecourts, its trimmed trees, and its symmetrical parterre without greenery. Its raked allées cut and divide the landscape that surround it. This barren and discordant assemblage, that neither pleases nor interests, is among the products of proud opulence, and is as far removed from Nature's beauties and rural graces as they are foreign to the property owner who brings his boredom there from time to time.

Turn your gaze to a charming dale. Contemplate its gentle slopes and the unified, green lawn that cover them. Admire the beautiful, ingeniously grouped masses of trees that embellish it. An elegant pavilion that crowns a balustrade can be seen only in part. Fresh plaster envelops all its sides and glows with a greater brilliance. Singular and rare trees and flowering shrubs form charming groves around it. These are traversed by a stream that, in its bending turns, appears to vanish and reappear again, casting itself in the end into a small lake surrounded by a lawn shaded by tall trees that mix with the masts, sails, and the pennants of the light boats that drift on the calm surface. A few elegant garden follies, well-placed, provide shadowy and mysterious retreats intended for repose. These crown the ornament of the Garden of this attractive country house that taste has bedecked with all that the most refined Art and Nature has that is luxurious.

At the foot of a barren and craggy hillside scattered with heather and rocks is a factory where the use of water is favored. Trees planted for pleasure, the result of the owner's care, are all the more remarkable because of the unproductive soil. The need for spillways has placed it in one of those dismal and wild spots, that, without that need, would never have been inhabited. The smoke of the furnaces, the whistling of the wheels, and the noise of the water that moves them and of the machines connected to them, render the situation all the more singular and strange.

Not far away, on a site as solitary but more amiable, one encounters a country dwelling. A path between two unaligned hedgerows mixed in with pollarded trees, knotty from frequent pruning, serves as an avenue. This is covered in fine grass, which is browsed daily by the commensal animals of the cottage. The manor is situated at the edge of a meadow planted with fruiting shrubs whose branches interlace; a stream of lively and clear water flows from a brook, crossing and watering the meadow. Willows and alders mark the free contours of the stream; some of their roots obstruct its course, rousing a slight murmur. The modest buildings, carpeted in ivy and enlivened by the creeping vine that greens its walls, are sheltered from the heat of midday by a great nut tree. Its foliage rises above the roofs, and its shadow serves as the shelter for the chicken-yard birds, whose calls and movement animate the surroundings of the dwelling, but do not ever disturb the calm. O country retreat, innocent sojourn! Who has not coveted your sweetness, and who has not drawn a sigh at the prospect of a retreat so simple and so peaceful?

These are the principal countryside manor houses, and the sites appropriate to them, which as such merit the attention of the Gardener.* In examining their effect, he will acquire knowledge of their relationship to the scenes in which they are placed, and of the appropriate character for each kind. This study will teach him to avoid misconceptions in his work. He will not construct a cottage where a

---

* One will have doubtless noticed that among those that I have just reviewed, I have excluded the symmetrical Garden.

country house is required, or a mansion where a château must figure. He will not place a ruin in the *Garden proper*, a kiosk in the *farm*, a middle-class house in the *park*, a palace in the *countryside*, nor an Italian pavilion in a rustic and wild site. He will also learn to relate follies to Nature's features. These structures are of a type so different from the materials that make up a landscape that a great deal of Art and taste is required to connect them.[*]

Before placing the manor house, the Gardener will already have fixed this first objective of appropriateness; he will even have planned the principal distribution of his Gardens, in order to place them in a favorable position, and in order to determine the mass relative to the extent of the site he has destined for the house. Is the expansiveness of the building too great? He will restrict and retrace it. Is it too small? He will make it appear indistinct and bare.

If the needs of the property owner require buildings of a greater volume than the site will allow, he will restrain himself from piling up story upon story to resolve the problem. This practice, used in the city, where the terrain is rare and precious, where height must make up for what is lacking in surface area, is not only useless and misplaced in the country, it also produces the most unpleasant prospect. In addition, it creates an obstacle to enjoyment, because it places the Gardens at a considerable distance. One is not tempted to go outside, one goes seldom for a walk when the guest rooms are on the second floor. Is there a staircase to traverse? One hesitates—it is a sort of barrier that arrests.

I would prefer to divide buildings, to detach those from the manor house that are only accessories, and I would only leave visible the mass that is in proportion to the general picture of which it is a part. Why should the baths, for example, not be a separate feature with their own Garden and specific site? This would be better than placing them in humid, unhealthy, low locations with no view, as we are often forced to do when everything is aggregated under the same roof, in the wish to have everything close.[40] Must the chapel and the stables be immediately connected to the residence? I think, on the contrary, that this way of separating secondary buildings into several courtyards can provide pleasant features in the composition and has advantages in many circumstances. Would this not facilitate interior layouts and keep guests separated from certain inconvenient and inopportune service functions? Besides, what is more austere, hard, and distant from country graces than this luxury of buildings, these artificial constructions, and this enormous pile of stone?[**]

---

[*] Architectural Art differs so much from that of Gardens that it is only habit and necessity that causes us to put up with the mixing of buildings into Nature's tableaux, and that all construction not excused by need is defective. This is why stairs, ramps, and walls intended to support earth, contain water, and hold in terrain are so repugnant to the eye and to taste, appear so misplaced in the landscape.

[**] When a rich City Dweller buys a property in the country, we might imagine that he seeks liberty and calm, and that his goal would be to give himself over to activities that are as healthy as they are amusing, to enjoy the air's purity, Nature's spectacle, and himself. One would also think that consequently Gardens are one of the important aspects with which he will occupy himself first. But no—what interests him first and almost uniquely is his

After having decided the massing of the manor house, its location must be determined—but what will be its position? Will it be placed halfway up the hillside, at the top, or the bottom? Will the soil be level or sloped? Will what is called a beautiful view be preferred; that is, an extended view with a limited aspect? Let me be permitted to pause a moment on this very interesting aspect of Garden Art. This subject is new, and its discussion here will not be amiss.

Two essential considerations must guide the position of the manor house: the prospect and the shape of the terrain. The one must serve to obtain easy circulation and engaging walks. The other must present a whole that pleases at first glance, but which is always interesting. I will add a third consideration: salubrity. The union of these three conditions forms what I would call a pleasant situation.

I would not want a very extensive view from my house, however beautiful it might be. Such a perspective surprises and enchants at first, but soon loses its value: its charms dwindle and even vanish completely from being constantly in sight. Such is the continual effect of the feeling of admiration and surprise, which lives only in the first moment and does not return, and the more vivid its impression the less it lasts. If this vast perspective brings together a great quantity of objects, it will be tiring. They will be so far away, so mixed up and confused, that they will barely be distinguished: none will attract and be of interest. If there are few objects, the view will be indistinct: the eye will look without seeing, not knowing where to rest.

An extensive view, possessing only momentary surprise, will thus be misplaced in front of the manor house. The habit of looking at it at all hours will render it dull and worthless, and perhaps even tiring. Let us consider for a moment that this view could be the most beautiful of all the ones that various positions in the Garden might offer—to deprive it of this powerful attraction would be negligent. For, with nothing interesting to present in it, why should one go there? Great perspectives and great discoveries, however, are so much more pleasant when seen less often and for less time, if Art has made them more exciting in how they are presented in the surprise they elicit, in the contrasts that show them to advantage, and if curiosity incites one to seek them out. If they are a theme of a stroll, the end point of a brisk walk, and the reward for the resulting slight fatigue, it is then appropriate

dwelling. He piles stones upon stones, he decorates its surroundings and its courtyards. He encloses the water, he fences in his land. There are so many workers and so much material in evidence it might be said that he wished to build a town. The house is never big enough, or of sufficient exterior volume. On the interior, nothing is spared. For the decor, nothing is beautiful enough, rich enough, brilliant enough. He brings greater luxury there than in the city, he wants all the comfort of softness. More pleased with his buildings, where he unfortunately shuts himself in, than his Gardens, his true place of repose, he speaks only of his gilded salon, of his sumptuous furniture. He shows his marble baths, his beautiful arrangements, he vaunts the great walls of his terrace and of his ditches. What does he get from such excess, such expense? He soon wearies of it: without the table, the gaming, the great company he has taken such care in assembling, he would not last twenty-four hours without dying of boredom. So it must be. Let us have a small house in the country. This was the advice and inclination of Socrates. Let us make this house neat and commodious, but let us obtain an agreeable and cheerful Garden, and we will enjoy ourselves.

to distance them from the house; from there they lose all these advantages. These are my reasons for distancing the manor house from views that are too wide. I would not choose a wild and barren view—it would be melancholy and afflicting. I would above all avoid placing the manor house in a wet location near a marsh, whose standing water would be subject to stagnation. This prospect is as repugnant as this situation is unhealthy.

I would prefer a familiar view, whose principal features are within my reach and together appear pleasant and cheerful, and whose moderate extent suggests that they are part of my estate, so long as my Garden is not a *countryside*. This air of propriety will add interest to my enjoyment. I would like to have a prospect that offers me the hope of an engaging stroll through the arrangement of the terrain in a gentle slope near the manor house. If it rises too steeply, the view will not be pleasant and varied, and walking will be tiring. If it descends too precipitously, the effect will be as improper. The eye, in addition, will not follow a slope that is too steep, but leap over it, and seek beyond the objects that are at the top. The interval will be only a lost void. I will not deprive myself in certain circumstances of a far distance. This feature, in providing air and a larger sky, will terminate the perspective pleasantly, bring out the foreground, and render the edges indistinct without making them indiscernible. If such a site inspires neither admiration nor surprise, it indeed refreshes, provides interest, and is never tiring. It is attractive for its ensemble, details, and the charms of variety.

In addition, each class of Garden must have its own individual character, and the perspective from the manor house must be different. For the *countryside*, an extended view is required, yet one that is furnished with features that determine its character and enrich the picturesque and varied effects: the site is given by Nature, and the lay of the land is not made, but chosen. For the *park*, the viewpoints will not be as distant, and the site will be less vast, but it will present a pleasing gathering of larger parts in relationship with the château. This relationship proclaims ownership, one of the characteristics essential to it, as it is to all Gardens.[*] If our site is the *Garden proper*, its prospect should be closer and within its own bounds, since it only rarely connects to outside features. It only requires a moderate extent: thus it will easily lend itself to the forms one wishes to give it. Its type and character depend almost entirely on the Composer: he may create all of its effects. He may ornament it with all those embellishments that combine well, including, of course, pleasant woods, unified lawns, and tranquil water associated with gentle slopes. As for the *farm*, its view will have no fixed limit; its orchard, its enclosures,

---

[*] It is good to remember that the manor house of a countryside must have its own Garden of an appropriate character in the sector in which the building is placed. This Garden, however, which is only a very small part of the general ensemble, must work with the rest to form the whole, if not by its uniformity then by its identity. This is not to say that the manor house may not have the countryside as its sole Garden: in this case, the character of the house will be subject to the general tone.

and the type of its cultivations will provide a site of constant interest, and will form its principal scenes: the other features that will come into the picture, if they are in accordance with the type, will be an ornament that will contribute to it, but otherwise are not necessary.

Rarely is the manor house well sited at a high elevation. Steep and difficult slopes make strolling tiresome and walking unpleasant. An indistinct and descending view never provides a pleasing perspective. In such a position, the house will be deprived of water, which is found more commonly in valleys. Woods, seen from above, do not provide as beautiful a sight as from below, and the building, as an object in the view, will appear isolated and detached from the landscape. If there is a manor house for which such a situation may be apt, this may sometimes be the wild *countryside*, provided, nonetheless, that the situation does not deprive it of walks, is not too far from the water or the woods that render a dwelling pleasant, and that its great remoteness is not merely poorly compensated for by its broader view.

Locating a manor house in the middle of a flatland is even more detrimental. A great plain offers only a cold evenness, a constant monotony, and a graceless horizon without variety. The expanse is immense, and it is taken in at a glance. All features and details are lost, because even the smallest obstacle hides them and obstructs large areas. If the site has water, it will be standing, and seen only when it is vast and close by. I would therefore avoid the plain in the establishment of the *park* and the location of the château. I would decisively eschew it for the *countryside*: this type pleases only in varied prospects, in great hills and valleys that give the most beautiful effects in Nature. Even the *Garden proper* and its country house will find limited resources here. Only the *farm* is fitting for a plain, but these two classes of Garden will be deprived of a number of effects and features, and will not obtain all the beauties of which they are capable.

Thus, I would not seek out a flatland in any case for the site of the manor house and the establishment of its Garden, whatever kind it may be. I would prefer the narrowest and deepest vale instead: at least it presents a few resources to the Artist, such as water and vigorous vegetation. The hillsides that enclose it provide features in their details, and often obtain effects that can exempt the pleasures of the view denied in similar situations.

Since heights, flatlands, and deep valleys all have more liabilities than advantages, sites halfway up the sides of broad valleys should be given preference: they bring together and offer, in effect, all that makes up a beautiful landscape and pleasing vistas. There, waters of all kinds are found. There, hillsides combine with vales, and woods with meadows, and their mixture gives rise to the most enticing features. There, productions are very varied, slopes are very gentle, walking is easy, and the air is neither too active nor too thick, rendering these situations very healthy.

It is not sufficient to have proportioned the building's mass for the extent of the site, and to have chosen the most appropriate spot. It is also necessary that the character, the style, and the color of the building be fitting for the scene and the class of Garden for which it is designed.

For a *park*, a château is necessary, but what form should it take? How will it be distinguished from other buildings? Its background will instruct us.

The château takes its origin from unfortunate feudal times, when, due to the state of constant warfare, might made right. A lord, powerful enough to attack, also wished to defend against being surprised by his peers. He constructed a stronghold for his safety, which enclosed vast buildings to serve as the refuge for his vassals and to defend against the sudden incursions of the enemy. He often chose an inaccessible height to form its foundation, or, if he was obliged to locate it in low areas, he surrounded it with water. From this came the vast enclosure of thick, high walls, deep moats, drawbridges, and towers with arrow slits: monuments to our former barbarity.

But today everything is changed. A château is nothing more than a country retreat, where the master may leave behind the toils of the city, and savor in peace the sweetness of rural retirement and the pleasures of the countryside. All that remains of his former might are his useful and honorific rights, and the preeminence over all that are connected to his domain. His vassals, formerly his serfs, are no more than his clients and protégés. Ah! If ever a personal taste, use, or some other motivation caused the gentry to spend more time on their lands, they would acquire a far more valuable prestige: the one acquired by making others happy. Sound Philosophy, in spreading her light, in purifying mores, has brought men together without disturbing the hierarchal order of society. It is the habit of living in the fields, however, that brings a man compassion for his fellows: he sees their needs and their misery at close range, and he does not comfort them in vain. He enjoys the happiness it brings them, and here seeks out the unfortunate soul who would have been pushed away in the city. In this relationship of beneficence and gratitude, the heart, in constantly being exercised, necessarily becomes human and sensitive. I ask forgiveness for this tangent, and I will return to my main point. The château's style must announce preeminence, which is its essential character. It will be enough in this to keep the towers that flank it, its high attics, and its virile and ancient Architecture, but its unhealthy moats must be filled in, and its grim, imprisoning walls taken down. Its frightful drawbridges, useless today, should be destroyed. Thus the château will retain the noble and sovereign character that must mark it, a character which, in this form, is much better associated with rural graces than with those we give to our modern châteaus.

A building of multiple stories, terminated in two pavilions that are only barely distinguished by an imperceptible projection and rustication or fronted by an entrance pavilion surmounted by a small pediment feebly marking the center: this ornamentation seems, by its frequent use, to have become the characteristic sign of our modern châteaus. Occasionally, columns add no nobility whatsoever to the edifice. The whole is capped by an attic story that is truncated, low, and squashed, and pierced by dormer windows that shrink it even more. Such is the style that has replaced that of ancient châteaus. It is true that this style has been supplemented by long and tiresome straight avenues that have as their sole and never-ending view this tedious front, that we have enclosed ourselves in iron grilles instead of walls, and have surrounded ourselves by courtyard after courtyard and parterres, which are types of magnificence that belong only to palaces and mansions. The château is lost in the middle of all these great voids, which are more admired when they are more spacious, although they are justified neither by necessity nor by attractiveness, and have many inconveniences. They isolate the manor house, set it at a remove, separate it from walks, and create a belt of sand and paving that tires the eye and the feet. Better still that the courtyards are not enclosed by walls and buildings! Thus the proprietor and his company are unable to go outdoors without encountering an unappealing stroll exposed to the heat of the sun and the insults of the wind. Little tempted to visit the Gardens, whose prospect is without attraction and insipidly monotonous, they pass their time in the country as they do in the city: that is, shut up indoors. It is not worth the trouble to go out.

Let us leave palaces and mansions and all that belongs to them in the cities. Let us build châteaus, pleasure-houses, and farms in the country, and not confuse the imposing style of grandeur with the ostentatious tone of luxury and riches. In addition, this form of modern châteaus is not the sole province of this tone: it has become the model for all buildings constructed in the country, and confuses the seigneurial manor with the private house. And the farmer, who will have built his establishment on a property, will rival the lord, and even surpass him in magnificence, in sumptuousness, and *appropriateness* will be annihilated.

If the *park* requires a château that proclaims distinction, the house intended for the *Garden proper* can only be a pleasure-house. For it must be reserved sweetness of finish and lightness of forms, and all that decoration has that is pleasant and cheerful. Here, nobility must be sacrificed to grace, riches to elegance, and sumptuousness to taste. Great masses will always appear heavy here, because the site of the Garden is commonly of a moderate extent. It would be a presumption on my part to enter into the detail of the decoration of the country house; the Architecture of our time, which has improved in all its types, offers us charming and numerous examples of agreeable and gracious composition.

The buildings of the *farm* will be low, simple, and without decoration, but great attention will be paid to the way in which they are sited, so that the group they present will be pleasant and rural, and, so that, if one controls their confines by the means of plantings and enclosures, they will form a picturesque composition: this will be their greatest charm. Their simplicity will arise not only from their forms, but even more from the materials of their structure. The less humble manor house, however, will distinguish itself from secondary buildings, and notably in the middle-class man's farm, where it may even become a pleasant country house, without deviating from the rural style.

As for the *countryside*, I have already said that the manor house is only one particular feature of the overall ensemble, and has the form required by the site that it occupies. To select the form for it, you will simultaneously consult the general effect and the small area assigned to it, and subject its style and decoration to the character of the specific scene to which it belongs, and above all to the *countryside* type. Build a cottage only if one or the other of these factors allows for this kind of building. What? A cottage serving as a manor house? Yes, a cottage: the *countryside* is not the Garden of a voluptuary sybarite, but instead belongs to the man of taste. To his eyes appropriateness is preferred to the misplaced exhibition of luxury.

The manor house is the principal, but not the only kind of building for Gardens, which allow many types. Some of these buildings are intended for effect, and others for need. It would be better if all of them owed their existence to both motivations. It is rare that those only meant for true utility, or at least its appearance, and those built purely for effect really embellish a scene. However pleasant, however well situated they may be, if some kind of need does not justify them, they will displease simply by showing too obviously an intention to please. As garden follies, buildings are only successful features when placed appropriately, with neither pretention nor confusion, and when the scene's character receives more expression from them. The abuse of this simple resource simultaneously announces the wealth of the owner who has paid for them and indicates the insufficiency of the Gardener who has set them in place.

What is there of interest, in fact, in a collection of ostentatious buildings, especially in those imitation monuments that always lack either the scale or expression of those they are supposed to represent? What is more nonsensical than the association of all the types—ancient and modern, Greek and Gothic, Turkish and Chinese—in a single Garden? How does one claim to bring together, without offending common sense, the four corners of the earth in one small space, and all the centuries in one moment? Can a bridge only be Chinese? Does the elegance of a pavilion consist in its Gothic form and ornaments? Must a resting place be presented in the elegant form of a porch? This is not all: if the Composer subjugates himself to the rules of Architecture he will often affect a severity that does not always accord with the graces and even less with the effect he sets out for himself. If it should happen, on the contrary, that he mistrusts and neglects these rules, and, abandoning himself to the delirium of a free imagination and knowing neither restraint nor measure, he will make an uncouth mixture of all the types without worrying that he is gathering them in a single design scheme. Such follies make, and will appear in all circumstances to be, a monstrous composite and a barbarous production. If one makes use of what I have just said, that often the precise rules of Architecture must yield to the effect, I will have been thoroughly misunderstood.

And, finally, what if the question of siting were added to this absurdity? If, in the middle of a lawn, or on the slope of a hillside, a methodically rounded mound were erected, placed there with the express purpose to isolate and to emphasize a folly that is often without correspondence to or harmony with the expression of the scene? If, on the edges of a cool stream that ornaments an elegant Garden, a ruined tower or a boulder were to be constructed? If, in a wild site, a pavilion decorated with Architecture's richest ornaments were planted? Or if an Egyptian pyramid were erected in the middle of a grove devoted to flowers and the graces of Spring? Does one imagine to thus produce contrasts? Contrasts, however, are not contradictions: Is the project to create an illusion? This crude artifice does not even assume this intention.[41]

The *countryside*, which alone may give itself to a great variety of effects and be open to a great diversity of character, will never permit liberties so contrary to all verisimilitude. If the character is pastoral, only buildings and *follies* scattered equally through the country and the fields will be fitting. If wild, rustic buildings only will be required. If deserted and abandoned, ruins that are the vestiges of its former state will be permissible, but these should not be shapeless, piled-up heaps[42] of debris. Ruins will enrich the site only when their grandeur impresses, and will only capture the gaze when they are picturesque. They will only be as interesting when, venerable due to their antiquity, the surviving parts will cause the general form and intended purpose of the monument of which they are the remains to be recognized without great effort, when trees grow from their foundations, when ivy covers their walls, and when the moss and grass that covers them validates their disrepair. If these are the conditions of this type of *folly*, who would dare attempt to build one and imagine successfully obtaining the most perfect illusion?

I will avoid reviewing all the building types, and their application to each class of Garden. Were I to depict all their characters and effects; to distinguish all that taste approves and rejects; to enter into the details of the refuges, retreats, and resting places; to speak of all the kinds of enclosures and barriers; to prescribe the way in which they must be placed not to interrupt the flow of the terrain and not restrict the views; to describe all the kinds of bridges, fix their proportions relative to viewpoint and distance, and determine the agreement between their width and that of the river they cross and their height with the banks on which they sit, I would go beyond the limits of theory. I will only observe, regarding these points, that, depending on the circumstances, the more rustic as well as the more magnificent buildings will suit the *countryside*, the more elegant and lighter ones suit the *park* and *Garden proper*, and the simpler will suit the *farm*. In general, stone bridges are more masculine and severe, but those of wood are lighter and gayer, and obstruct water less and are better linked to the effects of a landscape. Because of their grace and variety, they are often preferable.

I could fill an ample volume with all the subjects that could be discussed, and undoubtedly even then I would not have said everything. It is enough, though, to awaken genius, to stir feeling. It is enough to achieve the goal that I have set for myself, to have demonstrated that structures and follies are subject to the rules of taste and the laws of reasoning, and not to caprice and fantasy; that in all cases the most exact verisimilitude must be attained and appropriateness observed; that it is a fundamental failure to erect gaudy buildings in the country; that magnificence is contrary and puts flight to the rural graces that please only in their simplicity; and that, finally, buildings, as accessories only, must conform to the site, and not the site to the buildings.

But where will one place the temples, the Gothic churches, the cemeteries, the tombs, the verses, the inscriptions, the allegorical and emblematic monuments, and all the imitation and capricious buildings that fill up the modern Gardens that gain favor under the name of *English Garden*? What is the site, finally, that is appropriate for them? I beg my Readers to suspend their eagerness until the chapter intended to discuss the *types*, wherein these matters will be discussed.

XII

OF THE COUNTRYSIDE

*Description of Ermenonville** 43

The *countryside* is a great machine that demands imagination and superior talents: it is the equivalent of the epic Poem in the Art of Poetry. The Artist, who gives himself to this particular class of Garden, is superior to those who dedicate themselves to other types, just as the History painter is superior to the genre painter.

I have already observed that the distinctive character of the *countryside* is variety: in effect, it offers all the tableaux of Nature; it admits all her circumstances and lends itself to the beautiful disorder that characterizes it. It pleases in its bold transitions and contrasts. Like Nature, it is disposed to an infinite multitude of modifications and combinations. Open or dense, hilly or level, dry or watery, deserted or peopled, the *countryside* can be sweet and amiable, or somber and barren, grand and important, or simple and naive, or productive and rich. It is from these qualities that it draws different expressions, and according to what predominates, it assumes a character that is either rural, cultivated, or wild. These are the three principal types.

The *rural* is more or less rustic, but it always assumes sweetness and simplicity in its prospects. Its features have nothing of the surprising or extraordinary. Its slopes are gentle, its greenery cheerful and animated. Its waters flow without violence, and are agitated only by small obstacles. It delights in valleys of open ground with shady sides. It likes willows, poplars, and trees that are gay and light. It requires few follies, because it is somewhat solitary. If it accepts a few, they will be small hamlets, cottages, or scattered cabins: this type is the most interesting of the three. We all feel its charms, and the gentleness of its effects and simple pleasures are generally pleasing.

---

* I thought I should apply my principles through examples: this is why I provide the description of the Gardens of Ermenonville and Guiscard.

Agriculture, fields, villages, and farms compose the *cultivated* type of landscape. Its hillsides are graced with vines and fruit trees, its level areas are fields divided by hedges and separated by fences. Its valleys are pastures covered with flocks. Its water—streams and tranquil rivers—carry fertility to all parts. Its rich and populated aspect presents everywhere the fruits of work, activity, and industry.

The *wild* type is recognized by its broken terrain, its sinuous and deep valleys, its high mountains cut through frequently by gorges and ravines. It abounds in rocks, and has vast and dark forests. Its arid sands produce only heather and are covered with moss. Its waters are furious torrents or noisy waterfalls, and also large lakes, majestic rivers, and uncultivated marshlands. Its buildings are simple, rustic hamlets, blackened and smoky smithies, and old, abandoned châteaus, ruined towers, and ancient monuments that have resisted time.

All of these types may be further modified, one by the other, and in this mixture, they produce new characters and acquire very different expressions, according to the manner in which they are associated and the reasons for their combinations.

I have said that a *countryside* <u>cannot be made</u>, but it can be perfected. It is Nature that organizes its principal effects and sketches its main forms. All Art consists in grasping the whole and carefully distinguishing and strengthening the traits that shape its expression. If the Artist dares to invent features, he will allow himself only what Nature herself could have placed there, and these will be proportionate to the site and similar to its scenery. He will reject all that alters, weakens, or is contrary to the general character.

The gardens at *Ermenonville* offer a *countryside* that is partly rural and partly wild. Its beautiful valley, the river that waters it and the slopes that define it, the plantings that embellish it and the meadows that cover it, have a truly rural character. Mountains and gorges, the species of trees it produces, the barren sands, vast stretches of heather, rocks, and a large lake make another area of the *countryside* very wild.

The valley facing the northern facade of the château was, a few years ago, a repellant marsh incapable of any improvement. Its peaty soil retained the water from a thousand springs that fed it. Four or five muddy channels could not drain it. Day and night, thick vapors arose to engulf it and cover its surface. Symmetrical allées confined the views on every side, rendering it as boring as it was gloomy. Plantings contributed to the unhealthy situation by restricting the free movement of air, while, hiding the slopes, they disrupted the flow of the terrain and turned an agreeable valley into a cold, featureless flatland. On the right and the left, the hillsides and charming dales were ignored or neglected. A fine forest close to the house was so cut off that it provided neither embellishment for the site nor walking enjoyment. As for the rest, a swampy parterre, deep canals holding dirty water that was always covered with reeds and grass, and a hornbeam labyrinth on each side where one dared not enter on account of their extreme humidity, made up the Garden's insipid decoration. To the south, a courtyard surrounded by buildings saddened the view. An old and heavy door opened on to a road between two walls: the gutter of the landscape. This road, the only route to the château, was necessary for connecting one part of the village to the other. Beyond, a sodden vegetable garden, enclosed by walls, was terminated by a stone-faced embankment intended to contain the waters of a pond and topped by two lines of linden trees, confining the view and constricting the sky. Finally, everything was separate and unconnected. The lay of the land was everywhere unnatural. Views were blocked on all sides. Every part was unrelated, without linkage and without cohesion, and there was neither character nor expression. That was Ermenonville at the time it was entrusted to my care.

Today, to the north, a sweet and cheerful valley has replaced the monotonous and symmetrical flatland. The drained marsh has become an excellent and agreeable meadow. A wide river has been substituted for the fetid canals. The flowing water is constantly stirred by breezes and remains clean and pure. The majority of items that embellish this prospect, all naturally positioned, awaited only the removal of some plantings that hid or isolated them. The felled trees have revealed a delightful site that is terminated, two leagues distant, by a mountain with a village at its summit, below which is the tall, half-ruined tower of Mount Epiloy. This beautiful feature makes the background of the view, and appears always to be colored in blue and misty tones, which, because of the distance, gently bind the sky and the horizon.

With the walls of the enclosure destroyed, along with the Gothic courtyard entrance building, the continuation of the valley from the south can now be seen. It forms the perspective at the rear of the château. The river that has its source on that same side now waters and crosses a lawn once occupied by the vegetable garden. This lawn connects on the right with the forest and becomes lost under a growth of tall trees hanging over a steep slope; to its left, it ends with the river. The embankment that crossed the valley has been disguised by a combination of earthmoving and planting, and, no longer cutting across it, now provides this spot with a projection just as natural as it is positive, and its east and west sides appear to come together. A cascading sheet of water overflowing from the pond justifies the projection and animates the scene with its movement and sound. This perspective, as agreeable as but less extensive than the other, looks completely different, although it is equally rustic. The more enclosed site is neither vague nor indecisive, its items are both nearer and more united. With the noonday sun, our sight traverses them happily, as it delights to wander at all times of the day in the northern valley.

The road, which serves to connect one part of the village with the other, now takes a new direction, and is seen only because it is frequented. Freed of the walls that closed it in, it has been moved to a sufficient distance so as not to be bothersome, yet it is close enough to make out the details of the château perfectly. The perpetual motion to which this road gives rise populates and enlivens the area around the manor house. Crossing the road as it does, the river necessitated the establishment of a *wooden* bridge. This structure contributes to the embellishment of the composition, creating the foreground of the picture.

Of the two sides that enclose this valley, the one on the right is prolonged and appears, by a perspectival effect, to descend as it moves away. Against the sky, the tops of the trees covering this side sketch a fugitive line that marks the land's contour and gives a sense of the continuation of the valley veiled by the rise. On the opposite side, a less steep slope that is planted with well-spaced nut trees, is covered with green grass from top to bottom. The pond, seen only when one has climbed to the top of the rise, has now become a well-formed lake that, like the valley, becomes lost behind the trees and among the windings of the wooded slopes.

The river, after returning around the lawn, passes under the bridge over the road and soon afterward empties itself into channels, from which it eventually emerges to spread itself freely on the lawn in front of the north side of the château, where it forms an irregular and extended basin. At the end of this, it reacquires the character of a river and runs down the valley. In its course, some islands divide it into several branches and vary its flow, its banks, and width, justifying its detours. Profiting from the difference in height between the body of water and the river, a lock was constructed to allow boats to pass between the levels, a maneuver that has invited curiosity and permits embarking directly from the château.

The valley is embellished by the course of the river that waters the whole length of an immense meadow, and it is ornamented with various features that contribute to its variety without lessening the sweetness of the picture. To the left, and close to the château, is a strong, high mass of Italian poplars whose gentle shade invites an evening promenade but does not spoil the grass where they are planted. Beyond, at the head of the woodland, appears a mill surrounded by trees: altogether an agreeable grouping. In the same direction appears the tower of the abbey of Chailly and, though somewhat distant, seems to belong to the place.

Some distance away, the valley is cut in two unequal parts by a robust clump of alders that shade the course of a stream. This well-positioned mass contributes to perfecting the composition by dividing the valley that would otherwise appear too wide for its length. This narrowing creates a considerable depth on the left side while serving as a *foreground* for the mountain and the tower that terminate the prospect. The other side is bounded by a wood that crosses and terminates it without forming an obstruction.

The line of plantings that shape the form of the eastern valley begins immediately after one of the two bridges that cross the ditches and link the château with the Gardens. At a short distance, the edge of this wood projects forcefully into the lawn and sets a foreground. Beyond it, a small rise planted with trees makes a middle ground. Finally, the wood that marks the end of the less dense section of the valley forms the background. This exterior line has sufficient sense of movement to provide a graceful effect, and it is not so busy as to destroy the gentle harmony of the whole; this gentleness and tranquility make the true expression of the landscape when seen from the château. It is especially at sunset, or on a beautiful, bright summer night when the moon is reflected in the river, that this harmony makes itself particularly felt, and the picture acquires new charms.

The wood to the right, whose outer line has just been traced, provides meandering walks and paths, along which clearings that open upon a pretty valley are encountered. A wooden bridge across a stream coming from the valley leads to a less open scene, where a sandy slope is partly covered with trees. These pleasing changes in the terrain make a highly varied play of hillocks and small dales. Slopes that begin steeply are softened and covered with grass as they descend gradually and imperceptibly toward the river. This hillside turns back to the east and disappears in the depth of the valley. The opposing slope presents an amphitheater of village houses intermixed with trees; its summit is notable for the church and bell tower that crown it. This beautifully composed prospect creates an effect that is always lovely from the various points from which it is seen, and offers a view that is always new and always pleasing.

Retracing our steps and crossing the valley and river near the clump of alders, we find the château ahead, and farther away to the right we see the forest and the slope before they descend sharply to the southern lawn. The other part of the village is located at the bottom of this slope where it turns, but its effect is very different: simpler, more scattered houses are almost all covered in thatch, with gardens and meadow in front and the forest behind, and give the sense of a charming hamlet in the midst of the woods. The only building that stands out slightly is the gable of a chapel, with its little bell. If this prospect does not play a role as important in the scene as the other, its more rural effect is more in keeping with the general tone.

To reach the wild sector, we must take the southern lawn that leads toward the forest, and find some paths on the right that wander up to a dry and mossy lawn. From there, the wild part is visible. A large lake is enclosed in a vast basin formed by a circle of mountains broken by deep gorges, covered with heath and clumps of many sorts of trees. Among them are superb junipers with no shared species or size. Their branches and stems rise up, creep, and bend to make an extraordinary picture. Behind one of these mountains, which descend abruptly, are the church and abbey of Chailly, and a vista beyond. These two features do not go against the effect of this very wild scenery at all: the view acquires even more character through the effect of pines and the evergreens of all kinds planted there.

The gentle slopes and charming lawn continue to be seen down this hillside as it descends to a lake that waters its base. The forms, plantings, and edges of this vast body of water are strongly contrasted. On one side, the brow of a high mountain, covered with large rocks piled one on top of the other, creates a point that pushes forward boldly to the lake, leaving but a narrow passage between itself and the water. On the opposite shore, an isolated, relatively steeply sloped mound completely planted with trees from top to bottom creates a circular projection that extends into the lake, forcing it to take its outline. The rise of the surrounding heights is bold, dismal heather covers the soil, groups of creeping junipers abound on the hillsides, and the dark green alders grow on one of the banks. The bulrushes and reeds take up others, painting the water brown. These surrounding elements infuse the picture with a somber tone, and stamp it with a character of great austerity: this character is so different from the two valleys of the château that it might be imagined that they are separated by an immense space. These two sites, however, do touch, and only a moment suffices to pass from one to the other, yet by their position the eye cannot perceive them together except from a few points, and from these they do not harm each other.

Beyond the lake, the ground is more broken up, even overturned. The water pours into low spots and forms marshes covered by all sorts of trees. The sand is more evident, the soil is drier, and the mountains are higher and barer, making a barren and very wild land. Despite this, the view is anything but repugnant. There is a great variety of effects, and the trees are of so many different species and forms and in so many situations—here willows and alders, there oaks, and on the heights birches are found. The shape of the terrain is extraordinary. Green lawn appears on the small hills, and the fresh grass of the sunken dales is sown with rocks and heathers. Mixed together, all these items offer a disorder lacking neither beauty nor appeal.

This was the state of the Gardens of Ermenonville when I ceased working there. Thus, a disagreeable location became a charming landscape, a marshy and unhealthy site was changed into a cheerful and airy valley, and an unfortunate place was transformed into one of the most interesting situations. Yet, although its vistas are very picturesque, its scenery very varied, and its overall expression responds perfectly to the definition I have given for the class of Garden I call the *countryside,* I must warn the Reader, since I use this site as an example, that the form and modern construction of the château amid a landscape that is wholly rural is a major defect that disturbs the harmony of the whole. Fortunately, it has nothing to do with the wild sector, which would have been quite a pity.

If the Gardens' only objective were to please at a glance when seen from the manor house, those at Ermenonville leave nothing to be desired, but since the château is part of them, from whatever point it is seen, its style, color, mass, and location spoil and upset both the general effect and particular scenes, since it must be included in the composition in which it plays a part.[*] Thus, it is isolated in the middle of fields, unrelated to its surroundings; there is, in the end, absolutely no

---

[*] In the countryside, not presupposing a single property but instead a gathering of different ones, the château cannot have an immediate relationship with it. This notion is central to my principles and confirms what I have advocated for manor houses and notably for châteaus, when I have said that they must have, within the estate, a section that is particularly suited to their character. See also the note on the manor house in the *countryside,* page 111.

congruence between this type of landscape and the building and scenery in which it is placed.

Independent of this sin against appropriateness, its position, crossing and cutting the valley in two, is unfortunate, since it interrupts it. This obstruction is all the more striking since a small view from the west prompts a fervent desire to have it undivided. Beyond the fact that its style has nothing of the rural, its character is itself weak. From the north, it presents only a huge, white, monotonous facade with nothing to enliven it beyond its flanking towers. If it offers a more favorable southern prospect through its projecting wings, it can still be criticized for the large number of buildings that surround it—too voluminous a cluster for the extent of the site, which, in addition, provides no sense of the rural. As for the side elevations, they cannot be seen, since the château is hemmed in on the sides.

It must be acknowledged, on the one hand, that it would have been difficult if not impossible to alter the character of this large building, and more difficult still to correct the defects of its situation. On the other hand, the layout and local features accord only with the *countryside* and would never be suitable to the establishment of a *park*.

The Artist who must create Gardens for a manor house already built will too often confront insurmountable obstacles of form and situation. He will find it difficult to provide both a suitable ornamentation for the site and a position well chosen relative to the lay of the land and the nature of the effects it requires. Here, it might be a large building in a small space, there, brilliant ornamentation and a poor site. Often, the placement will isolate the manor house and detach it from the landscape, or the soil will be unusable, and the situation will be disagreeable and without any interesting aspect. The arrangement of symmetrical Gardens always corresponds to the form of the buildings and is subject to their ornamentation and aspect, since they are always regarded as the principal object, but in the country they are mere accessories. Regular gardens work on principles that are so different from what I propose as my theory, that rarely does it happen that what is fit for some can be appropriate for the others. But let us return to the Gardens of Ermenonville.

It was not enough to have conceived a design for land whose primitive state seemed unable to provide harmony and was contrary to any pleasing result. The site, at first glance, offered few resources and many difficulties. It was definitely not enough to have determined the principal masses and the main effects, because the great part of the details still remained to be attended to in order to bring this enterprise to a conclusion. The work has since been continued. Although I have certainly earned the right to say what I think of it, and although in submitting this further work to a just critique I might shed some light on the principles of the Art, I think I must leave it to the judgment of people of taste. Those who will visit the Gardens of Ermenonville, having read this work, will readily appreciate that these details have not been made in the same spirit that governed the whole.

Yet there is room to hope that the person who has been so affected by the beauties of Nature will defy received opinion and give them preference. It is to be hoped that the person who has dared to give his nation a foremost example of a type whose charms and advantages should have arisen earlier, wanting to justify to the curious that his Gardens attract in great number by the reputation they have earned, will not allow them to be lightly handled and that, by confiding them to expert hands, he will bring them to the state of perfection of which they are capable.

OF THE PARK

Description of Guiscard[44]

The *park*, unlike the *countryside*, cannot be subdivided by type. To give a correct idea of this, I would add to what I wrote above, that it must be envisaged as a large Garden that embraces in its totality both rural and wild features. By admitting masculine beauties from the one, however, it avoids what is too austere, and in utilizing simple graces from the other, sets apart what is rustic in it. The *park* holds a middle place between the *countryside* and the *Garden proper*. It is distinguished from the latter by its extent and by the dimensions of its individual parts, by its ability to ally itself with all the scenes of Nature outside its boundaries, and above all by the formal exclusion of all the productions that arise from capriciousness and that are born of personal taste, with affected ornament and coquetry in its details. Even in the composition of a *Garden proper*, these are allowed only with reservation. The *park* is distinguished from the *countryside* by the connection of the manor house to its Gardens, and by the manor house itself, which can only be a château. Although the park can and must align itself with objects outside and bring them into the composition of its views, it does not merge with them to the extent that this relationship eliminates the edges of the propriety. This character stops it from being mistaken for the *countryside*. Finally, it differs in that the *countryside*, a product of Nature, scrupulously excludes everything that allows the perception of it as a formal arrangement; so that, in the union of its parts, the *park* does not avoid showing that it is the product of Art, and that it owes its charms to a combination of taste that seeks to assemble the beautiful effects of Nature, to place them in the most advantageous light, and to render them agreeable and their enjoyment easy.*

---

* The Artist, a man of taste who devotes himself to the Art of Gardens, is not insensitive to the ridiculous pretension of embellishing Nature and doing better than she; happy to be able to assist her, he avoids contradicting her by submitting her to alien forms and substituting effects that she would not acknowledge. His aim is to put in an agreeable order every interesting thing that she offers; to associate, in the same place, in the same manner, and by the same means as she does, the scattered beauties that she seems to have only randomly dispersed. Art then resolves to place them well, to give worth to some by the means of others, to vary the ensemble, without destroying the harmony or unity, without diminishing their character and expression, making intelligent use of contrasts and managing oppositions; to establish natural liaisons and to produce favorable transitions; from which

Independently of Nature's charms, the *park*, as a specific kind of prospect, requires a composition of a noble style. This comes not from the sumptuous decorations that ornament the surroundings of a palace and announce wealth and magnificence, but rather from the beautiful masses and grand prospects, extensive property, majestic trees, beautiful forests, large water effects, vast lawns, and above all from a certain informality in its design that suits it grandeur so well.

The Gardens of Guiscard, which unite some of these advantages, seem to me in addition to fulfill the conditions that constitute a *park*. Although these gardens have not yet been finished, I will not omit giving a description. I can do it all the better since they are well advanced and the most recent work has been invariably stopped.

The old park, about four hundred arpents, was entirely regular. In front of the château, there was an avenue by which no one ever arrived. It owed its existence, not to need, but to the convention that considered a long allée of trees directed at the middle of the château as essential, even if it was useless. The allée terminated in courtyards and forecourts, and, in a layout more ordinary than pleasant, the château was placed between them and the parterre. To the right and left were planted groves where all geometrical figures had been exhausted. Straight allées cut through the woodland in all directions. Tall hornbeams bordered and enveloped the masses of woodland so precisely that, with the exception of the outside of the allées, the remainder of the *park*, that is, more than five-sixths of it, was absolutely useless for enjoyment. Large, deep moats surrounded the manor house and its dependencies and contributed neither gaiety nor salubriousness to the place. In the *park*, stagnant water confined in regular, though vast basins were perceived only as the crest of a tall, steep embankment that enclosed them. It was doubtful that the waters were free of those plants that defile, spoil, and lend them an unpleasant aspect.

All of the land sloped toward the château and offered, in terms of view, only a symmetrical parterre bordered by parallel allées of trees shaped in squares on all sides; beyond, a wide opening in the woods terminated the perspective. The sky, cut by a level line at the highest part of the terrain, made for a poor, barren, and featureless horizon. The hard and compact ground made walking at all times impractical. Dampness turned it into a thick mud, and when dry, the raked surfaces, the only places where one could walk, provided only uninteresting earth with little hard bumps that were tiring for the feet.

In giving a sense of the former Guiscard Gardens, which in their symmetry united all the beauties of a regular type,[*] I had in mind not to criticize it, but to

one sees that the Art of Gardens does not aim to produce an artificial representation, that I'd call the Garden of Art, but rather to order them in conformity with the rules indicated by Nature herself.

[*] The Duke of Aumont, owner of this land, originally planted the gardens of this park, which were deemed the most beautiful of this province. Beyond prejudice, neither the reputation of these Gardens nor his natural affection for his own work prevented the owner from seeing that there was a more interesting type. It was his taste for the Arts, his desire to contribute to their perfection, rather than the continually agitating restlessness that leads to frequent changes by those who have the unfortunate ability to enjoy everything, that engaged him in trying a new type and to sacrifice his park.

show the resources that the Artist can find in parks of this sort, where the plantings have matured, when he has the chance to organize them according to the principles I have set out in this theory. For the more or less five years I have been working on this project, the finished parts create the effect that can only be obtained after thirty years. As I write, none of the previous forms remain. All the straight lines have disappeared, all the artificial contours have been erased. There are no vestiges of the straight allées, inasmuch as the woods have infiltrated them, and the lay of the land, completely altered, has regained its natural slope.

This park, the extent of which is now more than doubled, presents three large parts at first glance whose totality is imposing: a vast lawn is in front of the château, a very large lake waters its edges, and substantial woods border it. The château, whose moat has been filled in, stands now on the edge of the lawn and right in the middle of the Gardens. Formerly located in the lowest part of the terrain, it appears now at the middle of its rise, through the manner in which the slopes were constructed. It dominates the west side of the *park*, and benefits from the lawn at its base and the line of the woods that enclose it. Glimpses of part of the large lake can be caught here, beyond which the plantings on the opposite side open toward a pretty valley.

Although it is of modern construction, the château does not lack the nobility befitting a seigneurial manor; its general mass has a grandeur that allows for considerable unfolding of views, since, as it presents one of its corners toward the Gardens, there is little chance of not seeing two of its elevations.* It is also well proportioned to the site where it is placed. The coloring it receives from the bricks, of which it is partly constructed, allies its tones with the landscape much better than stucco. In addition, the forceful projections of its pavilions, the play of the uneven height of its roofline and its varied forms give it an importance that proclaims unequivocally the habitation of the lord of the manor.

The large lawn spans the two principal facades. On the southern side, where the parterre had been, the grass comes up to the building on a very gentle slope. On the west, the lawn returns and descends on an even gentler slope to the lake, where it disappears to the north. Not far from the château and on the same side is a pool formed by the abundant springs that emerge from a group of rocks and give rise to a pretty stream whose limpid waters reveal the sandy bottom over which it flows; it is ornamented with a few new tree plantings of the kind that like to grow near running water; it follows the slope of the western lawn, and after negotiating its detours, which force it to meander through the little valley through which it winds, it flows into the lake opposite the farther valley.

---

* This manner of presenting buildings gives them a more substantial appearance and greater expansiveness than when they are seen head-on and from the same direction; the receding lines increase them, so to speak, through perspective, and vary their forms by virtue of the spectator's position, allowing them to be seen in different views.

Immediately at the end of each of the château's facades are plantings and shady walks. On the left, a terrace connects the building to a copse with a path through an agreeable grove of trees and the flowing shrubs, the scents of which are wafted on the morning breezes. In this grove we have sought to assemble all that vegetation possesses that is pleasant and cheerful in the most interesting forms, and it is precisely as it is described in the chapter on Spring in [James Thomson's] *The Seasons*.

The outer edge of the grove defines the left side of the large southern lawn with a contour that is gentle at first. This line allows the radiance of the flowers, abundantly supplied, to be perceived through several openings, as well as the play of the light and varied masses that compose it. A pleasing shaft of light strikes the principal clearing, and the shadows of the trees project enjoyable effects on to the grass that carpets it.

This edge then projects abruptly and vigorously by means of a thick planting of linden trees that push back and distance the wood beyond, and this allows one to suspect that behind the planting is a large recess where the lawn is in effect extended; this is where it connects to a large road through part of the wood. The line then turns back on itself in a great contour, and completes the frame of the southern lawn. In this return, the line merges with a very natural break that serves as an intermediary between it and the wood. As soon as this break is discovered, it reveals all its liveliness and modulations, and then it disappears from sight behind the plantings that conceal it. The light clumps masses and detached trees, pushed forward, contribute further to breaking up the continuity. In some places, this break lowers and separates like a little dale to ease the entry into the wood, which, in opening, seems to serve the same purpose.

Arriving close to the high ground and facing the corner of the château, the line abruptly turns and determines the form of the left side of the western lawn. Here the break fades imperceptibly; it is lost in the slope of the ground, which, becoming steeper as it advances, forms a slight incline upon which the lawn rises. The lawn then becomes hidden beneath groups of widely spaced trees that imperceptibly grow closer as they recede. In front of these woody clumps, freestanding trees and scattered shrubs blur the line and merge with the lawn. All these plantings descend, in a rambling fashion, to the edges of the lake.

The other facade of the château is flanked by a broad pavilion. From its base, a sequence of widely spaced, freestanding trees extends for a considerable depth, and as they advance they enclose the right side of the western lawn. At the center of this planting, a wide road leads as far as the head of the lake. There, it joins an allée of elms which terminated the former park on this side. The trees of the allée were allowed to remain because, since they are quite tall, they hide a ground with no interesting view, and shade the lake agreeably. As I noted above, those facing the valley were felled to open a view toward it and to enjoy a pretty meadow almost completely covered with willows which rise gradually as they extend further, and continue up to a wood on top of the hillside a fairly large distance away, pleasantly bounding the horizon. This charming feature places a fresh and rural picture beneath the château when it is seen from the other side of the lake, and gives the park, too uniformly terminated on this side, some rise and fall and a considerable extent, appearing to be part of it through the care taken to integrate the plantings on the inside with those on the outside.

The mass of freestanding trees that extends from the broad pavilion not only supports the château but also serves to connect it to the gardens. Without these, it would appear too detached.*

Another lawn, or rather the continuation of the western lawn, continuing to the right below the freestanding trees, occupies the site of the forecourt, and in this state can pass as such for those who cling to this mania; it is set off with a border of thicket divided into two or three large sections. The outline of these masses is linked to the end of the scattered trees and to the plantings that grace the head of the lake.

If we climb the southern lawn beyond the large mass of linden trees, we encounter on the left the entrance to the road that crosses part of the woodland; it is covered its full length by a green lawn. A wooden bridge, soon glimpsed, makes clear where it leads; it is situated over a small stream at the place where it flows into a body of water forming a small, oblong lake under the shadow of tall trees. The water of this stream comes from several springs and was formerly brought from some distance and at great expense to embellish the grand parterre with three small jets. This stream, although small, in winding down a small valley in the middle of the woodland makes for a pleasant feature in the sweetness it gives it, in the liveliness of its flow, and in the murmurs occasioned by little waterfalls and the trees that work against its course by often setting themselves against its passage. I think that the effect produced by these waters will not allow anyone ever to miss the purpose for which they were first intended.

From the bridge, the green road crosses the left-hand wood in varying width. It proceeds with turns that always present a great unfolding: it leads to an old forest at the extreme edge of the park that is pierced by various paths. The one that is directly ahead crosses it from end to end and finishes on a plateau precisely at an angle to the forest and at the point where the hillside reaches a rounded summit, from which we gain a view of a very beautiful countryside, crowned by a broad horizon. At the bottom of the slope, we see a valley covered with irregularly planted trees in a meadow watered by a stream. Villages and scattered houses embellish and populate the prospect: mountains, their summits covered in woods, extend into the distance and merge with the valley that loses itself in windings.

---

* Large trees near buildings provide an excellent means of creating this linkage, and places them in an intimate relationship with the Gardens. This association gives them value and offers an interesting situation in the prospect which is not available to those deprived of them.

Below the woods are fertile fields, diversified by their cultivation. On the left, the scenery changes; the lay of the land only allows one to see an enclosure of mountains that draw the sky into a line more or less in a half circle. They have a somber appearance, since they are covered with thick forests, and they are close together and continuous, allowing no opening to the distance. On the right, we glimpse part of a lake, beyond which we imagine enclosures and buildings of an agrarian farm in construction.[*]

In order to enjoy at leisure this beautiful view that embraces two horizons and that one encounters with surprise after having crossed through the wood, the construction of an open pavilion is proposed for this flat platform provided by Nature. She has happily shaded it with vigorous and dense oaks that divide the view into several tableaux.

To the right, this hillside turns and descends a steeper slope than those previously followed. The soil is covered with an excellent pasture dotted with tall, superb oak trees at some distance from each other; trimmed periodically, their straight and even trunks sprout only small branches from the base to the crown. This pasture descends into a sweet valley that widens as it enters the wood and forms a kind of basin that ends in a steep hillside; the prairie that carpets its bottom makes a slight turn, passes below the projected farm buildings, and continues to the lake.

So not to interrupt the progression of the green road, I have neglected to bring attention to the three branching paths encountered along the way. One leads to a very large clearing, enclosed by a wood contrasted as much by the lines it traces as by the variety of its trees; we arrive there through a dark thicket at the point where it is at its densest. The effect of this transition is all the more striking because this vast clearing leads to another seen in a hollow beyond a few trees; this provides much more depth to an imperceptible slope that the eye constantly scans.

On the left, a pastoral and rustic farm must present construction proper to the place, which is itself very rural. The buildings, of earth and wood and thatch-covered, are set against the old forest and enclosed by neglected hedges and rude palings, and are glimpsed through a few masses of tall trees. This site of this scene, that relates to nothing outside itself and is just a vast pasture filled with livestock in the midst of the woodland, would lend the picture the rustic character suitable for a farm of this type.

If one crosses the two clearings, one reaches groves composed of masses of forest trees of different sorts, shapes, and sizes; the green lawn where they are planted offers the walker a number of routes by which to traverse and leave it. Though detached, these masses make a continual shade under which we eventually reach the grounds of the agricultural farm on a slope that descends to the lake.

---

[*] Below, in the chapter on the farm, the difference between the agricultural farm and the pastoral will be seen.

It is from the top of this slope that the extent of this superb piece of extensive water can be judged as to its shape, the contours at its edges, and the features that vary and embellish its banks.

The second branch from the green road leaves a crossroads made agreeable by the way the trees compose it; to the left, it leads to the high road through a thicket. There, a wooden fence leaning against a very simple pavilion clearly indicates the entrance to the *park* and the avenue to the château. On the other side of the route, a barrier closes off the road that leads toward a considerable wood, cut through with paths to facilitate hunting pleasures. One could also, by another route, reach this wood that is more neglected than those already discussed. The third branch leaves from the bridge, and has, for its aim, not simply to link more closely this wood to the park, but also to obtain a much longer road intended for travel either on horseback or in a carriage, which I will soon describe while explaining both its route and the principles according to which it is conceived.

This quantity of woodland would be tedious if attention had not been paid to giving it the greatest variety; if care had not been taken to divide it with clearings that break up its continuity or to nuance its effects with a great diversity of character by vistas and points of view, by the nature of plantings and the way the masses are composed. In fact, this diversity in the large masses of individual trees shows off the play of their trunks in all their depth, and even the objects beyond; by their spacing, they provide a light, uninterrupted shade that neither harms the grass nor prevents the free circulation of air. This diversity is also in the thickets of different widths and ages, and in some of these tall trees are scattered, and in others small clearings and agreeable paths are mixed. Elsewhere, one encounters an old grove whose shade and constant coolness are sought out in the heat of summer. Soaring up through the effect of their proximity, the trees make lofty and somber vaults that are imposing in their height and obscurity. Further off, one wanders through sequences of groves of all sorts, some light and open, others crowded and clumped. One finds everywhere either the open sky and brightness of day, or a perpetual shade and somber shelters because the interval between the masses draws either paths that go in all directions or extended clearings. Finally, the woods form a sequence of groves of different types that offer new and unexpected effects at every step.

In several years all these effects will be more marked, because the trees, previously crowded together and airless, were only branchless trunks and now, thinned out and separate, are free to spread and stretch out and to produce branches and leaves. What they have acquired, in the short time since this healthy operation was made, announces what they will become and all that must be expected as a result.

What makes woods more agreeable still is the attention given to varying and softening the slopes of these grounds in which they are planted, making a surface commodious and easy for pleasant walking. Beautiful lawns should generally cover the surface, such as the sort seen in the parts already completed. Many well-made pathways, practical in all seasons and at every hour of the day, circulate and connect to one another and take the walker into all of the areas of the park worth seeing. By means of all these facilities, anyone can wander at will in all the parts of this vast area, in the uninterrupted shade of a succession of woodland and groves that connect, with continual variety, all the most admirable and attractive scenery that this type can offer.

I said that the fence and the pavilion on the large road announce the entry to the park and château. This road leads there in effect by the green route, by the wooden bridge over the small stream, and by the southern lawn. This avenue, which is a part of the Gardens and reveals them to the extent one travels it, is undoubtedly preferable for the objects and sites met in its meanderings to the straight and even lines of trees that are all alike, as dismal as they are beautiful (that is to say, longer); as soon as one strings these trees together, they present us nothing until we arrive, other than the door in the middle of the manor house closing the vista. I always wonder what could be found so pleasant and interesting in these endless alignments: Is it the similarity of the trees? Or their equal spacing? Is it the propriety of closing in the view between two parallel lines and only ever presenting the same subject? I find in that only an unbearable monotony. If these long lines along the public roads bore us and are far from pleasing to us, it seems that after having traveled on them for a long time we would become weary and wish for the moment when they are no longer seen.[*] Yet the smallest shack in the country is thought not to be able to do without perpetuating these lines in an avenue.[**]

Avenues have still other problems: they cut the terrain in two, and spoil the most beautiful site; for it is rare, that given the two end points of a straight line, you can find level ground.[***] To obtain this level, the land is excavated here and filled up there, and then only across the width of the allée, so that sometimes it is buried between two stiff, harsh embankments where all irregularity is rejected, and sometimes it is raised on embankments, without any connection to the adjacent land, or at least completely separated from it by two ditches. For, to thus cut into the terrain is to alter its form, thereby committing the most serious of mistakes. Besides, because it is subjected to making a right angle to the front of the château, the avenue requires turns that frequently lengthen the route it takes from its start.

---

[*] The reasons for preferring straight lines on major roads can serve as neither excuse nor authority for using such avenues in a Garden.

[**] A lord has spent a fortune on making an avenue in front of his château. Delighted to arrive by a straight line, I was pressured to go see this masterpiece of taste and invention. What route leads to you, Monsieur le Comte? The St. Denis road, he tells me; is your avenue, I reply, longer than that at St. Denis? Oh, no. Is it wider? No. Is it straighter? Why all these questions, what do you mean? I mean that it is a misfortune for your beautiful avenue that it is necessary, in going to see it, to pass by the St. Denis road, which is longer, wider, and probably just as straight. I, who know the St. Denis avenue, whose length and monotony have annoyed me more than once, am not tempted to go and admire that of M. le Comte.

[***] Or even a gentle slope. But however steep it may be, changing direction is never considered. It is impracticable, as this often happens: Is there nothing so irrational?

So, in whatever circumstances they are built, such avenues have inconveniences. The least of these is boredom, which is inseparable from uniformity.

The lake merits some attention for the role it plays in the Gardens. This large body of water, with a surface of more than sixty arpents, will soon be finished. Originally, it consisted of two ponds at different levels, one in the park, the other outside it, separated by a large embankment. The two, now enclosed within the *park*, will be completely united to form an irregular and elongated lake whose outline follows the uneven undulation of the ground that surrounds it. The bank on the side of the great east lawn has a very gentle slope, especially in front of the château, which makes the water easily seen. Continually stirred by the winds, this is always clean and neat: large, differently proportioned inlets push into the land, while the land moves forward to push the water back. On the opposite side, the higher banks, partly covered with plantings, are more uniform. In some places, the plantings come right down into and are reflected on the water's surface. Others are more set back, and permit the unevenness and variety of the banks to be discovered. Everywhere the plantings trace lines that contrast or unite with the embankments. The play of these plantings is not the least of the beauties that make them valuable.

In the depth of these plantings, we encounter rural groves, their paths covered by willows. Shadows of all kinds of trees mix on the carpet of lawn. Sheltered from the dying rays of the setting sun, this place makes a cool and pleasant evening stroll. From there, besides, a view can be had of the lake and of the part of the *park* that provides many prospects from this side. The château will be seen as well as the lawn on which it sits, the large mass of isolated trees that support it, what is glimpsed beyond this. One will be pleased by the beautiful expanse that is offered on the opposite side, which is crowned with tall trees that give it greater elevation without letting us see the steeper slopes. One easily sees how much the waterbirds, the small and large boats, the mast and flags mixed in with the trees, give the scene a sense of movement and make this body of water so pleasing.

Extending from the south, the lake touches a part of the terrain of the agricultural farm. This scene, of a different type from that of a pastoral farm, is placed deliberately at the end of the park in a place that suits it best, and, linked to it, will become a feature that injects variety by a new ordering of things. The buildings and their surroundings, if well composed, will furnish pictures of another kind, without clashing. The work that agriculture requires, and the animals and livestock that must furnish this area, will enliven it: the intelligent owner, too much a friend to what is good to disdain what is useful, will from time to time cast an eye toward the interesting occupations of the country and find in this association of the agreeable and the productive a new resource to amuse and distract him, to which he will not be insensitive.*

---

* The charms of Nature, the variety of views, pleasing perspectives, inviting walks, and salubrity, in a word all that make natural Gardens interesting, are not the only advantages to take from this. There is another that contributes more than one imagines to this amenity—its productivity. There are few segments at Guiscard that do not yield

I promised to designate where there would be places for racing. This exercise, reserved for major large landowners, has its natural place in the *park*, which is their Garden. The ancients, who made a strong case for bodily exercise, and who gave themselves to it through taste and reason, dedicated a place in their Gardens especially for this: the Romans called the area for gymnastics *Kystus* and that for horseracing *hypodromus*.* These words, borrowed from the Greek, show that this custom goes back as far as they. We have kept horse and carriage racing; but we never worry ourselves about what might make them pleasant. The English, who number it among their delights, were among the first to insert into their gardens paths specifically designed for it that they called "*Riding*," a term from a writer of taste who translated *bridle path* that I am happy to adopt.**[45] Here are the principles that have guided me in what I outlined for Guiscard.

It seemed to me that the great pleasure of a riding course consists in the variety of sites, tableaux, and viewpoints that are encountered along it. Its slopes must be gentle and easy, and its ground practicable in all weathers for horses and carriages. I believed that nobody should have to pass the same place twice, so it is appropriate that the route leave one point and arrive at another, and be, consequently, of some length. Since, however, one is not always disposed to take a long ride, I thought it would be good to arrange it so that a person could cut short the ride at will without having to double back. I felt that despite all these precautions, the route would soon be tiresome if it were so circumscribed that it was impossible to leave it, and that it should be clearly marked so as not to get lost, yet that it must not be separated like a path between two hedges or a road between two ditches. For in any circumstance and especially here, there should be no obstacle, nor hindering of liberty of movement. You embark on an easy way, and you hope for pleasure. You are tempted by the beautiful effects of Nature, and spread attractions and variety along the route: these are the only boundaries for a riding course, but never fear. Constraint upsets and uniformity is boring; there is no grace without freedom, as there is no pleasure without variety.

There is one further observation I have believed to be essential: not to make a riding course something that is always distinct or detached from the Gardens through which it passes. It may sometimes be separate from them, if the location allows and variety requires; but when it is part of the Gardens, it must blend with them so that one does not notice the course except when riding along it. Finally, it occurs to me that if, in the most interesting spots, resting places were to be

---

revenue. The great lawn is an excellent meadow. All the groves are regularly cut. The waters hold fish. In the woodland there are very extensive pastures to feed livestock while they are being raised. They are at the same time the Gardeners for the grass, for, in grazing, they will maintain it. The park is moreover a modest enterprise, since it requires no pruning, mowing, or raking, and all flowers that require daily attention have been proscribed. There are no fountains, terrace walls, or walled enclosures. The roads and walks are of solid construction.

* See the letters of Pliny the Younger for descriptions of his Gardens in his Tuscan and Laurentine villas.
** See the excellent translation on the art of modern garden-making [François-de-Paule Latapie's 1771 translation of Thomas Whately's *Observation on Modern Gardening*].

established where those who participate in this useful exercise may stop with pleasure and relax; if shelters were to be constructed for when the weather is bad, no
enjoyment will be lacking.

These are the conditions I discerned in making the riding course at Guiscard.
It is linked intimately to the Gardens, or, to put it better, it is part and parcel of
them. It has much variety in the sites that are met along its way, whether it is part of
the Gardens or leaves them. Everywhere its slopes are gentle. It starts immediately
at the château, crosses the southern lawn to reach the bridge over the small stream
in the wood, then continues to the large woodland, beyond the public road, by
a route with a thicket on one side and single trees on the other, to enable one to
enjoy the view to the left. This wood, which is vast, provides a lengthy route for the
riding course by the different directions that it takes. This length can be shortened
according to one's fancy. We sought, however, to distinguish the rest of the riding
course through the wood by circular routes, which lead to an exit and return to the
park by a third connection of one with the other. On this path a large range of the
countryside presents various and very pleasing views. Farther on, one soon rejoins
the old forest, crossed now by the road that leads from the pavilion at its end. Not
far beyond, an opening leads to an embankment descending to the bottom of the
valley below the big lake, and then climbs the opposing hillside though tree-lined
paths across the cultivated fields. From there, on the right are seen the eastern
mountains in the distance completely covered with forests. Ahead is a glimpse
of part of the lake, above which is the old forest that, once it is crossed, reveals on
the top of the hillside a line of beautifully developed woodland that descends and
loses itself in the deep vale, already described. Finally, these paths end at an iron
gate at the head of an allée of elms. Going along the side of the lake through the
plantings, one arrives at a road made through the middle of the large masses of
scattered trees that leads to the château on the side opposite the one where the
ride first began.

The rider will encounter shelters distributed along the riding course. There
will be sufficient resting spots of all sorts at places that present the most beautiful
prospects, or the most inviting retreats.

This riding course, which we have just followed, furnishes an excursion of more
than four thousand toises. It enjoys the variety of different features that the countryside can provide, crossing through woods, cultivated land, meadows, and lawns; it
has levels and varying, yet easy slopes. It can be shortened in various ways by leaving
the wood and continuing along the grassy road, or by avoiding the pathways across
the cultivated fields; one can even take a ride that does not leave the park by following the green road, reaching and crossing through the old forest and descending
below the farm to the lake side that leads toward the château on the western lawn.

I omit many interesting details that embellish this *park*. These would take me
too far: what I have said can suffice to make known the style that constitutes this

class of Garden, to make clear the benefit taken from its location, its various situations, and its former state, in order to give an idea of its effects and to indicate the spirit in which it is designed; to bear witness to the efforts to return the terrain to its natural configuration, to give the waters a grand character, and finally, that special importance was given to obtaining all that is pleasing and varied for the woodland, this important segment of the Gardens, both as a site and prospect. And although this *park* offers no singular features, no extraordinary effects, such as imposing rocks, astonishing waterfalls, or massive landforms, they are little missed, because its great variety leaves nothing to be desired.

OF THE FARM

XIV

There are few establishments that, having true utility as their purpose, bring together as many pleasures as does the *farm*. This Garden is perhaps the only place where the former and the latter join without detriment but instead lend mutual support to each other and take advantage of their association. In effect, in a well-ordered farm, all the plantings and cultivations intended for pleasure must be productive, and all those with a useful purpose must and can be pleasing.

Fortunate is he who sets himself loose from his main ties, disdaining more respected work and occupations that are more tiresome than well considered. By fleeing the cities' troubles and preoccupations, giving himself over to the sweetness of rural life and the innocent occupations of the country, and contemplating Nature in its effects and productions, he enjoys the peace of her beauties and benefits! All that she offers him are gifts and causes for pleasure. Each season and each moment provide him with more. What heart would feel nothing at the spectacle of Nature being reborn in the beautiful days of Spring, seeing the first movement of the sap that gives us tender greenery and makes the flowers bloom along with the hope of the grower? Who remains unmoved at the sight of the riches that cover the earth in midsummer, and the abundant harvest approaching maturity? Who can look with indifference at the hillsides and orchards with grapevines and trees laden with mellow and ripe fruit? And who has never been witness to the innocent pleasures and not sometimes shared the open gaiety that reigns during the time of the Autumn harvest, making it a holiday?

And Winter, a season that we find so distressing in the city and see as so gloomy in the country—Winter also has its pleasures. It is truly a time of enjoyment. The inhabitants of the fields enjoy the abundance and well-being provided by attics and cellars; plentiful company is all about, which is very different from social life in cities, where one is visited far more than seen. The next harvests require preparation; this is the necessary outcome of those completed. Beautiful days that in our climate are not rare in Winter allow for exercise and healthy walking. A thousand other resources,* in a word, agreeably fill up one's leisure, and render a stay in the country in this season more bearable than it is imagined.

When the places where all these interesting scenes occur offer an amiable site and a cheerful view through their organization, then the country unites all that is pleasing. The farm admits all situations and takes advantage of earth, woods, and water; it rejects no hillside, valley, or flatland. It only requires soil amenable to cultivation. The farm, I say, alone procures a combination of the pleasurable and the useful, and all that is required to obtain this is a man of taste to arrange it and an intelligent grower to direct it.**

The precepts of agriculture, not being my subject, do not enter the plan for this work. Thus, I do not envision the farm except through the pleasures that taste may add. I warn the Artist, who is but poorly informed about rural economy, however, that he will succeed with difficulty in the organization of this class of Garden whatever other talents he may have, because in his plans he will often sacrifice the useful for the pleasing, while he should cause them to collaborate.

There are two kinds of farms, with very different purposes. Consequently, they require a specific form and method in their composition, and because of this difference, I distinguish them as *pastoral* and *agricultural*. The first type is primarily occupied with livestock, taking milk from some and wool from others, and raising their young. It requires abundant pasture, good grazing, and large meadows. Field cultivation is secondary. The second type, in contrast, is principally concerned with all types of cultivation, and requires enormous fields, workable flatlands, and fertile hillsides. It only has the pastures and livestock that the need of its maintenance requires.

---

* I do not speak of the hunt. This amusement is not allowed to the field-worker; those for whom it is reserved do not see the disorder that it causes. The tyranny practiced by gamekeepers often entails crop destruction, and disgusts the growers and is their curse.

** If one sets aside the insane prejudice that has placed the state of the grower in the lowest social class, doubtless because he is subject to painful work carried out by crude hands, one would derive a just opinion, and one will almost always find a man worthy of esteem if one is open to it. It seems to me that the Minister who directs a great State, the merchant who conducts a vast business, and the property owner who directs a large cultivation all contribute to the common good, albeit on different paths, and should be equal in the eyes of reason. The man of the State seeks to master events by foresight, the merchant, fortune through industriousness, the grower, Nature through his work. The first takes care of the prosperity of his citizens, the second makes them rich, and the third clothes and feeds them. Thus, he who procures the things of primary necessity, creating basic materials, should be without contradiction the most considered, if the consideration accorded by the State were not nearly always the inverse of utility.[46]

The Grower does not confine his work to manual labor. To the extensive science of agriculture, he lays combinations of the finances and work of commerce: his operations are open to the deepest speculations. To complete them fruitfully and successfully, he must have extensive knowledge, especially in physical science founded on observation and experiment; this alone does not lead to error. Always joining reason with practice, his wise economy takes advantage of all. Nothing in his hands is useless. In the same look he takes in the whole and penetrates to the smallest detail. In a word, the man of the fields at the head of a great operation, independent of the talents needed to conduct it well, ordinarily has solid virtues. He is simple without being crude. He has more customs than manners. He is humane and hospitable. He does good without ostentation. He enjoys abundance without luxury. He lives in ease without softness, and the interest that animates him is neither base nor sordid. Such is he that in almost all countries is placed below the City Dweller through blind prejudice.

Since neither of these two types excludes the other, it follows that the farm that brings them together in the same proportion will be mixed and thereby make a third type.

If I envisage these three types by their variety, each can be categorized as a simple, more or less rustic farm, or a middle-class man's farm that is more or less ornate. This farm, without exceeding the limits of country character, is open to embellishments. It may, by a fortunate composition, obtain a pleasant arrangement by the hand of the Artist, and receive tasteful details from his care that inject liveliness and interest. The graces with which he will adorn it will seem to be a necessary result of the features of the site, linked to those of cultivation. The simple farm will take its charm from its situation. Its pictures must be agrarian. All the care taken to ornament it, if too conspicuous, will disfigure rather than make it appealing. The farm should sometimes even present the unrefined effects of Nature in all her carelessness. However, subjected to the industrious hand of man that it may be, the farm will accommodate uncultivated land well, and wild sites mixed in with pastures and crop fields. These will help to give character to the rustic type of landscape.

All farms must bear the imprint of the work required by cultivation. This is its purpose and what distinguishes it from other Gardens. The pastoral farm, however, being less subject to this than the agricultural kind, must be more restricted in its embellishments. Especially when ornamentation is obvious in the rustic farm, the site will have no more than an equivocal expression, and will infallibly lose its true character. It is certain that the more adornment is added, the less pleasing the result.

From this, it may be seen that the agricultural farm, being only what a man has made of it through labor above all, lends itself more willingly to all the attractions that rustic effects may provide. The pastoral farm, in contrast, having less need of this aid since its productions depend less on work, affects a more rural and neglected air. The mixed farm, which is merely a blend of the two other types, takes part in all that is appropriate for each of the others.

If someone were to confer upon me a ground intended for the establishment of some kind of farm, after having walked it and examined it carefully, I would take account of what I could hope from it by the impression it made upon me. I would recognize the class to which its character and totality may lend themselves, because it would be a mistake not to follow the site's indications and to imagine deciding the type of farm without consulting the site. I would start by determining the most appropriate place for the buildings, as much for the appeal and salubrity of the setting and the effect they must produce as objects in the view, as for the ease of their use. That being said, I would then look at the grounds, having understood, for example, if their layout and features are favorable for establishing a middle-class man's farm. I would divide its larger flatlands intended for cultivation with enclosures: they commonly present a cold monotony, because worked lands never seem pleasing at first glance. I would furnish the areas that are too bare, and also provide a terminus to spaces that are too vague. Through the diversity of their form and extent, these barriers would make each enclosure a site with its own specific crop and character, and together they would embellish the general whole. The well-massed hedgerows, trees, and shrubs, set out intelligently and excluding those that are not pleasing, would enclose my fields, and define the circulation paths. These paths will be more or less tended and decorated according to the type of farm, and will themselves become Gardens and charming walkways through the elegance of their contours, the variety of their forms, and their features. They could be covered with beautiful grass shaded by plantings that may be varied and contrasted. Sometimes a clean and sandy path might cross the lawn and plantings. I would arrange all the effects that may arise from the viewpoints mixed with the prospect of the fields. I will profit from the features that present themselves along the route, such as pastures, a small wood, springs, or a fountain. I would even create some of these, if grace and variety require, provided that they are justified by the nature of the locality, and when encountered offer more charm than surprise. Finally, I would establish resting spots, making refuges analogous to the scenes wherever the latter would gain by them, and others where they would be desired.

Independent of the embellishments they procure for the landscape, these enclosures have the additional advantage of safeguarding the rich productions they surround. They are a shelter against violent winds, which, after heavy rain, turn over and knock down the plants. Without this barrier the unfortunate Cultivator would often see the fruit of his labor lost, and the hope for an abundant harvest would vanish on the eve of its enjoyment.

If one might object that the shade these plantings cast on the edge of the ground is perhaps counter to good cultivation, I would respond that this is a disadvantage only for those who do not know that artificial lawns and meadows succeed perfectly in light shade, which gives the ground a coolness favorable to this sort of growth. Therefore, I would frame each enclosure with greenery in the width of its shade. This will be a useful feature, and a new means of embellishment. Barren fields, which look so barren when fallow, will be made pleasant by this border, and will remain so when they are being worked.

Meadows that provide fodder, pastures that fatten the herds, the orchard that gives fruit, and the kitchen garden that furnishes vegetables will also be separated by enclosures. This variety in production will add to the views. There is no country so monotonous or flatland so boring that it cannot acquire a diverting variety by this manner of division. This device, so simple in itself and practical everywhere, can render the most insipid property the most cheerful, and make a gloomy farm—like those that in fact exist—a delightful country landscape, without diminishing revenue or departing from the rural character that befits it.

There are two kinds of orchards: one is rustic and the other cultivated. The latter has its place in a vegetable garden: it requires daily attention and meticulous care. As for the former, it will fill in one of my enclosed areas, as I have already said. If it is situated conveniently and set out with taste, it may become a feature as interesting in its effect as in its production. By the pleasing mixture of forms and volumes of fruit trees of all kinds of species, and by distributing groups well and enhancing them by planting them on a green lawn, a charming grove can always be made of a rustic orchard. It is not necessary to believe that an orchard favors only a symmetrical quincunx arrangement. I know that there are some fruit trees that must be isolated to thrive, but I also know that there are many that produce well in groups. These require only slight attention on the part of the Cultivator to render them prolific, and in addition they only need it in the first years.

These fruiting groves, if I may so name them, have beauties specific to each season. In the Spring, the flowers they provide in excessive profusion present a dazzling show in their variety and effect beyond the perfume they exhale. This effect is even more ravishing when the clumps are better composed, and the groups more industriously arranged. The Summer fruit that follows the blossoms pleases the eye as much by the variety of their form, the liveliness of their colors, and the way they are distributed on the trees that nourish them as they gratify taste. Autumn fruit is no less pleasing or tasty.

There are some fruit trees that get along with vines and fruiting plants with runners, and happily provide support for them. One may, in bringing them together, obtain shady and useful nurseries. The vine branches and garlands that festoon the trees, decorated with their hanging fruit, vary the trees' effects and provide pretty features.

The appearance of the vegetable garden is so cold and its arrangement is always so methodical that it is admired only for its usefulness. It has no visual attraction, but a well-organized vegetable garden may also present an interesting tableau. What spoils this type of cultivation, independent of the lack of taste that presides over its composition, are the high walls that always surround it and give it a depressing aspect, making it a completely separated place without connection to what is around it. This naturally leads to an observation that is quite essential:[47] although I have not neglected to mention it in the course of this work that, whenever it was a question of the ensemble, agreement, and appropriateness, a more detailed explanation is nonetheless required. It is this: in vain will an individual scene have been composed with all possible elegance, and all the beauties of Art and all the graces of Nature lavished on it uselessly; it will lack something, not give a pure pleasure, and not have an appealing charm, if the frame is not made for the picture, that is, if the spot where it is placed, if the features in the middle of which it is found and which complete it in making the entirety, have no relationship with that particular scene, or one appropriate for it. The general whole determines the first impression, continuing and renewing it each moment. As is said, the first impression is always the strongest. The whole almost always determines the pleasure or repulsion we feel at the sight of a specific scene, a garden folly, or effect, however often they have nothing in and of themselves that is appealing or displeasing. It is that ensemble that brings together what contributes to that picture, and that sets in place the most advantageous extent of the sky. The frame, which is part of the ensemble, links the objects that enhance one another, and separates those that are detrimental to each other. It veils what should not be shown, but often allows a suggestion of the depths, the backgrounds, and the spaces that the imagination fills and adorns, reconciling what the eye sees in the happiest manner, and arranging with greatest attention what the most intelligent Artist could not have made, had he supplied it there. In a word, it extends or closes in, and interrupts and breaks as is needed and according to the demands of taste and circumstances.

I am imagining a delightful wood that is naturally connected with the parts that precede and follow it, and now, transport it to an isolated spot that leaves nothing to imagine beyond its edges. In a word, you thicken and close in its frame exactly, and at that moment all charm vanishes. You move a rustic orchard that is so fresh, a stream so lovely, and choose another site for the one and different surroundings for the other: they will not make the same impression. The former will have the same extent and the same trees, the latter the same water and course, yet the effect will be completely different. You will believe they had taken on other forms. It will be the same if, instead of moving the picture, you change what is around it, if you substitute another setting. What causes this? It is that the frame is no longer the same; nothing is perfectly isolated in Nature's scenes. Each effect, each feature depends on what is around it, and affects us differently by what accompanies it. Everything that presents itself to our eye has a kind of connection to what we have just seen, and even with what we assume we must see. Let us note in passing that when it is tricked this foresight is the source of contrasts and exciting transitions. Finally, objects trace a sequence of simultaneous and successive images in the head according to their association, bringing worth to one another, and strengthening the present impressions and preparing for the effects of those that must follow. It should be noted, however, that there are some sites and prospects that leave nothing to the imagination beyond what they present. These do not need assistance of this kind. These are the largest and sometimes the smallest, because in the first the immensity of the frame is nullified, and in the second it uses all its power: in other words, it totally isolates.

These ideas may appear slightly metaphysical, and for many people my frame will be merely a dream. Its existence and effects, however, are very real, and the Artist who misunderstands them will often give birth to compositions that are incoherent, disjointed, and without a sense of the whole or harmony.[*]

---

[*] This is why Gardens, wherein one makes a different scene of each grove independent of what follows and precedes it are so cold and say nothing to the soul. This is why those wherein one associates disparate, dissimilar objects will appear vague, and tiring, and cause fluttering of the eyelids.[48] They will leave the disorder of which they are the image in the head.

Let me return to vegetable gardens, and say that this part of our Gardens always sins by virtue of its frame. In effect, it becomes separated, isolated, and poorly connected. It is not simply that its walls are an unfortunate enclosure that disconnects it from its surroundings, but also that the forms and systematic arrangement, always insipidly monotonous, to which we subject it, render it merely a boring feature, and give it an air of barrenness that should not be expected from the perpetual verdure of the plantings that grow there, and the activity of such painstaking cultivation.

Why not, for example, enclose the vegetable garden with ditches in the parts where it can be allied with everything in proximity to it in the direction of the midday and rising sun? Why not substitute hedges, wood palisades, or even straw for these unbearable walls? Finally, why not prefer dense plantings of large trees that would provide the Garden with protection against the destructive north wind? It is thus that the vegetable garden will obtain grace, participate in the attractiveness of other cultivations, and cease to be a sadly neglected object.

Let us not be persuaded that this arrangement and these layouts, in order to be different from those generally practiced, are unfavorable to the vegetable garden. Dutch Gardeners, who are just as curious as we with respect to this type of cultivation, and perhaps more intelligent, prefer them because they have the obstacles of climate to overcome. They use no enclosures other than fences and only trees for shelter.

The layout of the vegetable garden, I know, necessarily demands order and consequently a kind of regularity. The same kinds of crops must be brought together and placed in a location that is suitable for them, with the most advantageous exposure for ease and success in cultivation. But these factors do not require the Garden to be cut into squares surrounded by flower beds in which shrubs and flowers are placed in too-small quantities, always at equal distance. Neither do they require that wide, raked allées take up the most useful areas elsewhere: their dry and bare soil is lost to all benefit.

The vegetable garden of my farm would not be laid out so. Taste would decide its form, and the quality of soil and the right exposure of its location. The difference between cultivations would put variety into the effects. The grove of bush-form dwarf and low fruit trees,[†] which I call the cultivated orchard, would be at the head of the most protected part. This would also be where I would lay out my fences to support espaliered fruit trees. I would still plan a section for

---

† TRANSLATOR'S NOTE: Morel here refers to pruning practices relevant to fruit tree cultivation of the period. This "grove" is a *buissonnier*, which has no modern English equivalent. Here, fruit trees were pruned in bush form—that is, they were allowed to grow in a multibranch, bushy form above the main stem, but with the center pruned out of the circle of branches. Of the two sizes of fruit tree Morel discusses, dwarf is easily understood. The other is the "mi-vent" which is the modern French equivalent of *demi-vent* or *demi-tige*. In this size, the main stem or trunk from which the fruiting branches emerge is usually between approximately three and four-and-one-half feet high.

fruiting bushes, and below or in a separate place would be the larger vegetables that can forego watering. The more delicate and green vegetable plants will be placed in the lowest part, laid out in rows and separated by small paths to facilitate access and cultivation.* All the ground would be covered, and I would lose none for tiresome compartments in useless pathways. This gathering of greenery, whose general form will not be a square between four walls, will instead be given to me by the features and form of the terrain, and will please the eye and abundantly provide what is needed, because, without forgetting the effect of the composition, I will have attended more to the advantages of cultivation and its position than to regularity.

Finally, I will neglect no part of the ground that will be given to me, because there is none that must not, through my care, contribute to the profit and appeal. Economical vistas everywhere, associated with rural graces, will be the base of my projects and goal of my work. If I have a low and wet ground, I will make a willow grove of it. If I want willows, poplars, alders, and all sorts of trees that like damp soil, they will be laid out so as to embellish the general picture and the specific site where they are planted. I would like them to provide cool walks in Summer, and arbors in the Winter. Near the manor house, I would like to set apart a specific place for a rustic wood if the general order does not oppose it. I will seek out the species of trees that would succeed best there. It will serve as a retreat for men and animals in overwhelming moments of strong heat.

Finally, if Nature has given me a stream, I will restrain myself from decorating the edges with methodical plantings that are repellant to good taste. I will refrain from smoothing out the uneven outlines and substituting elegant forms, or the dreary, straight line. I will keep its irregular turnings, and seek only to make the approach easy. I will make sure that the edges are covered with fine grass, and that too much damp does not keep curious strollers from walking there. Finally, here silent and tranquil, there agitated and bubbling, shaded on one side and open on the other, free everywhere, I will add only features that Nature, in her lovely disorder, could have given rise to and placed there herself.

After having arranged all the grounds in the most productive way, and giving it the most appealing form, I should turn my attentions to the buildings. It is in the ornamented farm that the manor house can distinguish itself with a kind of elegance. I would like it to have a ground and second floor only to give it less height and less importance. I would prefer the gaiety of tiles to the dark color of slate. I would permit it to have fresh plaster. I would above all avoid a symmetry too exact in the ornamentation, and an over-expansive prospect would cause it to lose its characteristic unpretentious air: the middle-class man's farm, however ornamented

---

* One can get an idea of this layout by casting an eye on the marshes around Paris. They present a gathering of verdure whose regularity is nothing less than disagreeable.

it may be, is neither a grand retreat nor an opulent refuge. It is either the country house of the city dweller of ease, or the domain of the Cultivator whose extensive property places it above the level of simple need. It must be commodious and not luxurious, appropriate and not magnificent, cheerful and not ornamented.

It would be appropriate for one of the facades of the manor house to have a view of the farmyard. A farmyard is indispensable: it characterizes the farm. When it is arranged and laid out well, it comes very close to being an unpleasant feature, but its movement gives it a lively and animated air that provides recreation and amusement. It requires a space proportioned to the buildings that its maintenance necessitates. It is also important to lay it out well for ease of service. With these useful precautions observed, one can occupy oneself with what will bring it cheerfulness and cleanliness. One should shade it with several trees, leaving views out to the countryside. These methods used appropriately divide the always unfortunate, excessive continuity of buildings, and make an effect that is also healthy, and inwardly pleasing, as well as cheerful for the exterior view. Finally, the buildings can be composed, and the farmyard arranged so that, from wherever they are seen, they present a refuge that one would be pleased to inhabit. I would indeed be clumsy if, with the roofs playing between the trees and the country surroundings, I were not to obtain some picturesque effects.

I would prefer the rustic orchard to the vegetable garden as a pleasure Garden in front of the manor house. But if, in the general form neither one nor the other may be found to be appropriately placed for this use, I would substitute a lawn on a gentle slope maintained by sheep who would be its Gardeners. I would scatter some groups of trees for shade there, and also distribute some flowering shrubs to spread liveliness in the vicinity, and place an engaging walk before the owner's sight. To make it practicable for him, I would make a few walkways circulating through the masses that would cover them with their shade, and thus lead him into his holdings by the paths that go around them. I would, however, pay little for these sorts of Gardens: for, if I have measured correctly, the whole will form a promenade, and one will encounter amusing features on all sides that will attract, and useful objects that will interest.

Such will be the plan more or less, on which I would form a middle-class man's agricultural farm. I would only place ornamentation where its character permits: I would want that this ornamentation be only the necessary result of what is proposed for this establishment. Undoubtedly, only similar arrangements will have true charms. The general harmony of all the parts and their connection to a common goal, rural economy, will gratify equally both the property owner, who, finding in his patrimony the pleasing and the useful, will own and enjoy it at the same time, which is relatively rare, and the simple viewer, who, certain of the efforts that the Creator has made to please him, will believe he owes the pleasure he feels only to unexpected yet fortunate combinations.

This is but a brief sketch—I only present a review of the principal features, and have spoken only of the most ordinary cultivations. I have said nothing of these that are specific to each climate. Every situation, having its own character, may supply other resources to an Artist sensitive to the charms of the country and Nature's seductive graces. In the quantity of features that Gardens embrace, however, all can neither be known nor predicted. I would simply add that it is difficult to imagine a type of Garden more interesting than the farm. There is perhaps nothing so attractive as the spectacle of a country in a fortunate setting, whose fertile soil is embellished by the collaboration of diverse rural scenes linked one with another, when they spread out before our eyes all the wealth of vigorous vegetation, the fruit of careful and well-conducted cultivation.

The pastoral farm offers tableaux that are more rustic than the agricultural farm. Pastures and meadows are amenable to valleys and their slopes, but rarely great flatlands and high mountains. It happens, in addition, that slopes and valleys associate well with woods and water. Are these not, in effect, the sites and materials that ordinarily make up rural scenes?

There are very perceptible differences between the pastoral and agricultural type. The earth of the agricultural farm is often barren and constantly worked, carries the imprint of the hand of man, and presents the changing of the seasons from one to the next. The principal and nearly unique production of the pastoral farm, however, appears more like a gift, the pure generosity of Nature, than the fruit of the Cultivator's industry. The earth there is always hidden under a carpet of greenery that is renewed by itself alone. For this reason, the care given to its embellishment, however necessary, is less apparent. The line that its enclosures draw is more uncertain, less decided than the enclosures of the agricultural farm, which is more precise in its outlines. In addition, the frame of the latter is more detached and distinct: the furrowed earth, different in tone from lawns, could not be confused with the continued greenery of the paths that surround it. Unlike its pastures, the grazing fields of the pastoral farm ally themselves in an imperceptible way with the grass that carpets its paths. Also, ground that is worked requires, in order to facilitate cultivation, a certain extensiveness, a kind of regularity, and often an evenness of division, but the divisions of grazing fields, which are freer in their proportions, lend themselves more easily to those that taste would like to instill. The enclosures of the pastoral farm closely resemble the openings made in a wood, because of the diversity of their forms and dimensions, and especially by the freedom that they allow in the distribution of the surrounding plantings. These, which can be thicker or thinner, and combined in more ways, are made up of groves and small woods, the sum of which always provides the opportunity for charming effects.

One of the things specific to the pastoral farm that signals its purpose and distinguishes it from the rustic *countryside* is its palings and barriers, which, dividing the grazing fields, serve to form parks for the separation of animals. However simple their construction, they can have a sort of propriety in the middle-class man's farm, and the division lines they trace can be arranged with a certain order. This is one precise indication of this class of farm.

Cultivated fields, which it cannot go without, will not be united in a single sector. It would be appropriate for them to be dispersed and interposed between the pastures and grazing fields. Too many large areas in cultivation would destroy its character and signal a mixed farm. Thus, when a dominant pastoral character is sought, they must be broken up, for fear that the type risks remaining unclear.

This farm has, like the agricultural one, its orchards and vegetable garden. They are treated more or less the same, but the manner of distributing the buildings differs. The pastoral farm does not seek to bring them together, far from it: it scatters them to one side and the other, and hides them sometimes in the depth of the woods. The ones that are most used, such as the barns, stables, cowsheds, and sheep pens, are commonly very large. Their gathering would form an overbearing volume, and would not be in harmony with the rural character. It is enough that the manor house be surrounded by the buildings most necessary to daily maintenance. Among these the dairy counts as one of the most essential. Its interior will be at once an appealing and useful feature.

I will not weigh myself down with the details: I will content myself with noting the characteristic differences between one type and another, indicating the distinctive traits. In effect, after what I have said about the farm in general, and what I have observed about each in particular, I do not need to stop to observe the particulars of the mixed farm, however amenable it may be to a great variety, since it brings together the two types.

As for simple or rustic farms, the particulars can be predicted: for example, a site that is very uneven, with harsh and rough terrain, and rocks, water, and rustic woods mixed with the features of cultivation appropriate for each class. The enclosures will be more contrasted, the paths more unkempt, and the buildings and folly structures, built with more ordinary materials and in a simpler form, will be placed randomly and as if by accident. Everywhere will be the ever-interesting disorder of Nature left to itself. In general, this type takes its expression from its singular location and from a country made strange through the composition of its sites. All this will be perfected by the accessories that Artist's talent and taste can add without altering the character of simplicity and rusticity of its tableaux. All fabrication and construction that has some pretension and is not rustic will be shocking and will infallibly weaken the strong and vigorous expression of this type of composition.

I doubt, however, that a type so rough in appearance will find many partisans, few people like the great effects of Nature enough to choose it by preference, even when the character of the site lends itself to it. The property owner has undertaken expenses, and the Artist has taken pains and care: they want these to be obvious and to strike the spectator at first sight, and believe them to be lost if they don't call out the talents of the latter and the opulence of the former. Nonetheless, it is less the case here than everywhere else of making a show of difficulty over-come. The wisest and most sensible Artist decides only painfully to hide himself behind Nature, I realize, but let him guard himself carefully against the desire to show himself. This misplaced pride will cause him to commit the gravest errors. To the property owner who is insensitive to Nature's effects I have nothing to say. If there happens to be someone who owns a place appropriate for the estab-lishment of a rustic farm, who has sufficient taste to lend himself to the views of the Artist, it would be easy to make him understand the charms that this kind of Garden has in the spectacle of Nature in all her truth and liberty, and success will be achieved only in appearing to have done nothing, and in persuading that every-thing is owed to the fortunate features and to the layout of the locale. I do not know if I am fooling myself, but I believe that the rustic farm is harder to treat than the most elegant Garden. It is not a question of fresh views, of delicate touches, of soft contours, and of imperceptible transitions that everywhere else are met with pleasure: here bold lines must be drawn with firmness, and energetic effects, sudden and wise contrasts, and strong oppositions are needed. The greater whole must be embraced. All the vistas, even those of the same type, must be different in tone, and the most astonishing scenes must be intermingled with the simplest features, and the most ordinary cultivations must sometimes be surprising, even magnificent, without ever appearing elegant, let alone artificial.

If, however, an excess of delicacy were to cause this type to be rejected as the principal [Garden] subject, it may find its place in a setting where greater opposi-tions of class and type are sought. The *park* and even the *Garden proper*, with its light graces, can be connected to the farm, in order to obtain a change of scene and to make a contrast. Well managed, the passage from one to the other can enhance both, and produce a lively surprise and a very exciting effect. It will, how-ever, always be dangerous and often impracticable to try to make this association with neither intermediary nor preparation: only a superior talent can find the right connection. It is one of the most vigorous efforts of the Art of Gardens.

OF THE GARDEN PROPER

XV

I n the great scenes of Nature, in the prodigious variety of her pictures, I have presented to the man of taste a Garden that I have called the *countryside*. The *park*, through the nobility of its whole and the beauty of its details, has furnished a Garden to the proprietor of a lord's[49] estate. He who devotes himself to cultivation, the well-off City Dweller who has managed to obtain an estate in the country, has found his Garden in a *farm*, where the pleasant is joined with the useful. For the rich man who may, by dint of his savings, indulge his fantasies, and for he who needs to multiply his holdings to vary his amusements, I have reserved the *Garden proper*, in which pleasure alone is the goal. For very different reasons, this class of Garden may also be that of the respectable citizen who, devoting himself to the public good, owes almost all his time to society. He would not be able to abandon for long the difficult occupations imposed on him by the state without failing in his duties. He nonetheless needs relaxation and distraction.[*]

The *Garden proper* offers fewer resources than the other classes because it lacks variety and utility, and is only imagined to provide the enjoyment of a few moments in a beautiful season. It is appropriate that it should be located at only a little distance from the city where the property owner resides. This proximity is much more convenient, because the functionary, due to his work, and the rich man, for another reason, both make only short visits there.

When the Artist sets out to compose the *countryside*, the *park*, or the *farm*, he consults the site, which absolutely decides the type, the character, and the principal effects: he is forced to subject his plans to the shape of the terrain and to the general masses that it presents to him. In the *Garden proper*, however, he creates almost all the features, and he fabricates all the views. He gives it almost all the character that he wishes, especially if its terrain is of middling extent, because when it is enclosed within its boundaries, the small amount of the *Garden proper's* surface excludes the

---

[*] Is this difference between owners not required in the character of the Garden? I think so. Appropriateness, it seems to me, asks that one should be more magnificent and sumptuous, and the other more elegant and noble.

multiplicity of its scenes, the effects of a certain vigor, and large tableaux. All this facilitates the choice of the right location for its establishment.

The *Garden proper*, which is required to take all its pleasures from its own sources, obtains them through the grace in its efforts, the elegance in the whole, and the sweetness in its details. To arrive at this end, however, the Composer is forced sometimes to distance himself from this precise truth that is so praise-worthy elsewhere. Let him not, nonetheless, indulge in the too-common mania of creating tableaux from pure fantasy under this pretext. He should restrain himself against the false taste that distributes and heaps up a multitude of structures and follies in the *Garden proper*. These run counter to the type, and they cause Nature to disappear. It often happens that, placed randomly and deprived of analogy with the scene, they are disproportionate and without verisimilitude. This is an abuse that reveals an impoverished imagination, complete ignorance of the principles of Art and taste, and consequently, a very mediocre talent. With these pointless means, he will believe he has made a *Garden proper*, and has only fabricated at most a bad decoration without interest—a tedious assemblage of incoherent parts that might be visited once out of curiosity, but never tempts a return.[*][50]

Thus, although divergence is permissible in the *Garden proper*, and although a more obvious combined arrangement, more delicate forms, and a stylized order-liness reveals artistry, Nature must not be so abandoned that it is completely foreign. Attractive trees should be intermixed with flowering shrubs, grouped and distributed with taste to provide cool shade and delightful groves. Manicured and well-tended lawns whose color is friendly to the eye should cover the soil with an even and unified carpet of greenery. Limpid and transparent water, calm or lightly agitated, is sometimes in the open, sometimes shaded, presented in appealing and varied forms, juxtaposed with flowers and grass, and surrounded by features that lend it added grace and receive it in return. A certain softness is in the play of the terrain. The gradual and almost imperceptible slopes please the eye by following them. The walkways and paths, bordered by attractive plantings, are appropriate to all weather and constructed with care, traced with precision, followed by our feet without fatigue, and direct us to the effects in the most favorable view. They are laid out to enjoy all the moments of the day, and lead to well-chosen scenes or to rest-ing places dedicated to the charms of solitude and the sweetness of retreat. Finally, dark and mysterious refuges, situated advantageously, are appropriate to embellish the areas where they are placed. For them, elegance and lightness of form is pre-ferred to the richness of materials and the severity of rules. These are the principal features that must enter into the composition of the *Garden proper*.

---

[*] One day I accompanied a woman in one of these modern Gardens where we see a numerous collection of follies of all types and buildings of all sorts, crowded together in a small space—marble temples, thatched cottages, windmills, statues, towers, churches—where one finds many stones, few trees, and even less greenery. When she had traversed it, and she saw that we were about to leave it, she said innocently, "let us go see the Garden."

Does it not circumscribe this Garden too much to restrict it only to these simple means? Should we not fear that these objects, so ordinary and so common, are too weak a resource to obtain the attractions that this class assumes? Limited to the use of these materials alone, will only cold and monotonous compositions be produced? This poorly founded opinion has certainly given rise to those Gardens in which so many productions of Art and Nature have been brought together in such profusion, and where all types are confused and all characters are juxtaposed. I strongly doubt, in a country so fertile in great Artists, that in a century in which taste has made so much progress, this novelty that at first dazzled, can survive for long. I return to my objection, and claim that, if *Gardens* wherein only the proposed materials admitted have failed to obtain the approval of people of taste, and if they have presented neither charm nor interest, it is because most often, when mannered in his compositions, the Gardener gives them neither character nor expression. Or when, bereft of means and lacking imagination, he repeats himself in his designs, knowing only a small number of combinations which he uses everywhere indifferently. Or when he copies mechanically in thoughtless imitation, transporting to his grounds what he has seen elsewhere, without considering what would be appropriate; he is ignorant of the Art of associating effects with the Garden type and of taking advantage of the circumstances.

It is therefore less the insufficiency of materials than the incapacity of he who uses them that must be blamed. These materials offer resources like the colors on the painter's palette to the Gardener: the result depends on talent and not what is put into the work. It is genius alone that gives birth to masterpieces that delight us. Ah! What is impossible for he who brings exquisite taste and the profound secrets of his Art to this divine gift? If he is simple in his means, his combinations are infinite. Through his astonishing productions he captivates the heart and mind. He stirs them and bends them to his will. He gives feeling and warmth to all he touches: he animates stone, he causes canvas to breathe, and he communicates movement and life to all of Nature: this is his magic wand.

Does he take command of the *Garden proper*? Immediately, everything is embellished and colored with the most brilliant hues. The sorriest and most austere sites present pleasing and cheerful perspectives. The most uniform become tinted, the most drab become varied, and the most unprepossessing and unruly are transformed into a delightful place to visit. The water that he directs will seem more voluptuous. The shaded areas he creates will seem cooler. The resting places that he prepares will be more inviting. From each touch of the paintbrush a new grace is born. If he composes a group, he causes his judiciously chosen trees, shrubs, and flowers to give picturesque forms that enhance the beauty of some and the effect of others. Finally, natural and simultaneously refined in his compositions, he creates interest through amusing details and charms through an elegant ensemble.

Rarely is the *Garden proper*, so sweet and elegant at first glance, connected well to the sites that surround it. The simple features of the country are too rough; this juxtaposition causes the *Garden proper* to lose its grace, and would unfailingly destroy its expression. It must therefore be given a frame: it must be enclosed by plantings that hide everything outside that could be detrimental to it. Failure to observe this precaution becomes a fault that is graver when the *Garden proper* is smaller, because a small *Garden proper* requires still more care and sweetness, and consequently less relationship with what is outside its enclosure.

Independent of the lack of similarity between the *Garden proper* and the ordinary objects of the country, connections to it that are too immediate and openings that are too large will overwhelm it. It will be drowned in vagueness and count for nothing. If, however, its size is such that it accommodates several scenes and admits a variety of pictures, if, in the end, it plays the role of a small *park*, being thus able by well-kept passages to arrive at wilder scenes, it will be possible to obtain a few well-chosen exits. In coming closer to Nature, it will ally itself easily with the features that compose her. For it is a general maxim that the larger the site, the more its effects must be true and natural. This gradation takes place not only from the small *Garden proper* to the large, but also must be observed from the *Garden proper* to the *countryside*, where the truth in its vistas must be rigorous.

All cultivation, other than what contributes to cleanliness and maintenance, is misplaced in the *Garden proper*. Its delicacy flees all that evinces pain and heralds work, when either one or the other lack pleasure as its cause. From this, it follows that all idea of economy and finance must be excluded. In effect, small pieces of worked ground, small mounds planted with grapevines, and little sectors of meadow and garden herbs, however they are arranged and from whatever point of view they are seen, are features that do not properly figure gracefully in the *Garden proper*. Their home is not in the place destined to charm the eye and provide agreeable strolls: they would at the very least run counter to this. I would have neglected this negative precept if I had not seen several *Gardens* that were thought to be embellished by small samples of all kinds of production, where all the least interesting plants and herbs were made to sprout in little circumscribed spaces, mixed with the sweetest flowers and most elegant trees, with the pretense of presenting attractive effects in this chaos. The obvious uselessness of such a cultivation makes it childish as well as tasteless. Cultivation is undoubtedly interesting, when, treated seriously, it presents a real usefulness. But does it enter into the composition of a Garden? It will only appear well in the *countryside*, where it makes a tableau, or in the *farm*, where it is the principal feature.

The exclusion of purely economic cultivation from the *Garden proper* is not made in order to introduce items of luxury and magnificence. What only announces opulence and is intended only for ostentation may well satisfy vanity and produce a feeling of admiration in the first instance, but never makes up for the taste that brings out the most attractive effects, much as the skillful Sculptor draws a masterpiece out of the most common material. Those of little talent seek wealth in materials, and believe that its sparkle adds merit to their small productions.

I have only one more word to say on the Garden's manor house—the country house. It is felt that it must match the Garden by the graces of its decoration, and that it must be all the more elegant as the *Garden proper* is smaller. A very major feature in the ensemble, it is very important that its ornamentation, its mass, its hue, and its character be perfectly in accord with the *Garden proper*. If any one of these proprieties is neglected it would be sufficient to disrupt the general harmony on which the true beauty of the type depends, because the least fault is a stain on the finish of the whole. Because the *Garden proper* has only a small number of sites, the most advantageous position for the manor house will be easy to find. But if it appears detached from the *Garden proper*, if it is not surrounded by lawns, flowers, and trees, and if, in a word, their union is not intimate, its location will be a failure, both as a feature of the view and as an effect.

From the observations that we have just made in this chapter, it follows that the essence of the *Garden proper* is to please through its neatness and maintenance, that it requires elegance in its composition, grace in its forms, and sweetness in its views. Its effects must be mild and voluptuous and its prospect must be cheerful. By its refined details and selected features, it offers varied and interesting amusements and easy strolls to the property owner. When these conditions are best observed, the *Garden proper* will bring together all the charms and beauties to which this type of composition may receive.

OF THE TYPES[51]

The theory that I have just given is entirely based on Nature: it alone has furnished the precepts, examples, and materials. These, although small in number, have furnished combinations so immense, nuances so different, that they have sufficed in composing views and scenes of all kinds in order to produce all sorts of characters, and to obtain the greatest variety of expressions. With talent, the Gardener will always know how to bring out the most magnificent and majestic effects as well as the simplest and the most rustic, the most cheerful and freshest perspectives as well as the most somber and wild. In bringing together only the features that are needed in the Garden, and rendering their use familiar, he will obtain, without separating himself from the rules of Nature, everything that must give his compositions grace, attractiveness, and variety. He will obtain all the effects and features appropriate to embellish Gardens and to make them interesting. Are these, however, the only ones of which this Art consists? Should I have excluded all those productions, all the fictions that imitation takes pleasure in bringing to life? This is what remains for me to examine.

If I knew how objects outside of man acted upon him, how insensate and often immobile beings put his senses in motion, and how, then, pure sensations produce feelings; if I could calculate the point to which the education and habits that form general mores and determine specific opinions, influence taste and judgments, and modify affections, I would easily deduce the causes of propriety and impropriety from these physical and moral understandings, according to the way in which they are presented to him. I would understand attraction and repulsion, what is cheering or depressing: in a word, what pleases or displeases. Surely, developed well and applied to the Art of Gardens, these principles would enlighten the material that I have addressed, but this task is beyond my strength. It belongs only to that part of Philosophy that sounds the depths of Metaphysics to arrive at these first elements. I will confine myself to comparing those Gardens, which, such as those that I propose, have followed the route of Nature and have taken her as model, to those which, by opposition, I call genre Gardens. The result of these comparisons will perhaps not be entirely fruitless.

In the number of Artists and amateurs who have created Gardens, some have used only artificial ornamentation. Others have believed that the representation of an action that recalls an event must be included. Some are happy to copy Nature more or less faithfully, but the greatest number have introduced ornamentation, fictions, and all sorts of imitations in their compositions into Nature. Almost all, groping their way forward, have attached themselves to the genre without regard to the [Garden] class. This absolutely essential distinction, which should have served as a guide, was misunderstood or neglected, and fantasy, given free reign, has distanced the search for the principles of the Art, cast uncertainty upon its true goal, and, finally, led to ridiculous compositions that have outraged people of taste and disgusted people with good sense. However, despite these digressions, it has been understood that the Art of Gardens is open to great beauties and many attractions, and that, reduced to its principles and brought back to its objective, it can occupy an honorable place among the liberal arts created for our pleasures. Thus, those who are more careful have taken the position, before deciding, to expect that more reasoned productions and more successful attempts will offer examples to follow.

From these Gardens of imitation and whim, directed by personal taste, arose different types, such as the *poetic*, the *romantic*, the *pastoral*, and the *imitative.* I will not cite the symmetrical type here that preceded them—I devoted the first chapter of this work to this*—nor the picturesque,[52] which, envisioned as a type, is nothing other than Nature's. If, by picturesque is understood the choice of objects, their form, arrangement, and the combination of effects to which the Landscape Artist gives preference, when he wishes to present pleasing sites, this expression is only a qualification that belongs equally to the Art of the Painter and the Gardener,** because the two Arts have things in common, and each takes Nature as its model, because they seek almost the same effects, and because in many circumstances they utilize the same skills to achieve their goal. But, if they conform somewhat in their aim, they have still more differences in their procedures.*** One creates Nature, so to speak, since it uses the same materials that it lays out in the same order, and makes use of the same means. The other imitates the truth by means and

---

* Devoid of character, expression, invention, or nuance, its altogether mechanical pace excluded it from the ranks of liberal arts. Its cold monotony, its rigid uniformity inseparable from boredom left it almost without champions; to speak of it again would be unkind: you do not fight a defeated enemy.

** According to this point of view, the picturesque belongs so equally to the two Arts that this expression was incontrovertibly taken from that of Gardens, as it was of painting, if the latter had not gone ahead of the other.

*** What these two Arts have in common may mislead the young Gardener, and send him in false directions. I do not make this remark for no reason: I have seen some seek models for composition in prints, I have seen others imitate the paintings that they had in front of them. This is a source of error, as shall be seen. One will admit that wanting to make the original from the copy is at the very least to invert the order of things. In addition, the kind of pleasure that one expects from the two Arts, not being the same, the means of each must be different.

procedures that are absolutely foreign to Nature. One makes the reality and the other represents it. Both are admired, but the enjoyments they offer are not the same.

By these distinctions I do not claim to decide the merit of the two Arts[*]— I compare and simply note the differences. There are a thousand circumstances in which what has worked in a landscape painting would only be a bad effect in a real site, and could not be placed successfully in the same positions, however one might want to suppose them to be similar. This is because often an object that pleases in a representation displeases in reality. I will go further, and emphasize that what is necessary and advantageous to the one is useless and sometimes harmful to the other. Look at the Painter's work—he only presents the same site: from whatever point it is viewed, the various objects in its composition are always shown in the same order. All the effects of perspective are the same. The light always falls on the objects on the same side and constantly at the same angle. Finally, the painting offers only one single moment of the day, a single season of the year, and a unique point of view.

On the ground, the various positions of the Viewer give nuance to the effects and vary the perspectives. To be sure, from the same position, the Viewer only sees the same things and in the same order. Let this Viewer, however, take several steps, climb, and descend: immediately, as if the objects could move, the scene changes, and offers new vistas and presents with new combinations. This ability to vary the effects, denied the Painter, gives great advantages to the Gardener, but if it provides abundant resources for his compositions, it can sometimes also set insurmountable difficulties in his path. He must present all the variations and combinations. He must, in composing, foresee the effects occasioned by the daily revolution of the sun. He must work for those of the morning, midday, evening, and night, which influence the character of his perspectives astonishingly through the continual changing of shadow and light, and by the variety in tone and color. Finally, he must consider the succession of the seasons that modify and tint the tableaux of Nature so variously.

In painting, it is less the beauty of the objects represented that makes the beauty of the painting than the Art with which they are rendered. Beyond genius in composition, liberty in *making* is admired, as well as the audacity and elegance of the touch, the perfection and subtlety of the design, the truth and vigor of the colors, and the intelligence of the chiaroscuro. In the Garden, the composition that consists in the order, arrangement, and disposition of the features makes up all the merit of the work; it is in the composition alone that the real talent of the Artist

---

[*] When one casts an eye on the sublime productions of the Claude Lorrains, the Wouwermans, the Vernets, when one sees the truth with which these Painters have rendered Nature and the astonishing illusion that they have placed in their paintings; when one imagines the magic of this art that has subjugated the sky and its immense vault, the vacant air, the clouds, the sea, the vapors, the light, even the night to the power of the paintbrush; when one considers that a small space holds a vast country, that a flat plane presents depth, projections, and distances lost to view; when one realizes that all this magic operates through a few colors mixed on a simple canvas, and that the manipulation is nothing, and that genius does all—who could refuse one of the highest places for this divine Art, whose marvels I have only touched on?[53]

resides. The touch and the making are nothing for him.* Nature, whom he has, so to speak, subjected to his orders, willingly complies, and shares the toil with him halfway, completing and perfecting the work. Under his direction, it shows herself in all its graces, and deploys all her advantages, but he alone chooses, places, combines, and mixes. He alone prescribes the forms, assigns the proprieties, fixes the degree of expression, and determines the character of the Garden.

In the imitative Arts, an image that is too lifelike or too perfect does not elicit our admiration, if the Art that produces it does not reveal itself, because there is no imitation without Art, and the work's merit could not be felt without recalling that of the craftsman. These two ideas must be simultaneous and intimately linked. If a statue, for example, should be so exactly lifelike that at first glance it would be taken not for an imitation, but for the object represented, and the Art is not noticed, we would pay no attention to it. It is only at the moment when we perceive that it is a representation that we like to consider it. For this reason, the Sculptor always refrains from disguising his material with the natural color of what is represented, which would add too much to the illusion. He wishes to show that he knows how to give the softness of flesh to stone, the lightness of hair to bronze, and the suppleness of fabric to marble. If I have preferred the Sculptor's work to the Painter's to give a sense of my idea, it is because a painting, not having the advantage of true relief, need not fear a misunderstanding engendered by the illusion of color.

Thus, to truth in representation combined with the idea of worth and difficulty overcome we owe the pleasure caused by the productions of the imitative Arts. In Nature's Gardens, however, the viewer's pleasure and admiration do not come from the merit of the Art brought together with the perfection of imitation. Nature's beauties have no need, in pleasing us, to recall the talents of the Artist, because it is not in imitation, but in themselves that reside the interest and pleasure to which they give rise. They must, on the contrary, carefully hide the Art that has produced them. In the entire course of this work I have proved that when the means are apparent, they destroy pleasure and interest, whatever merit they might announce in the Artist who has put them to use. In great Art, these means are never suspected, and in no case should the strings and machines be seen, but should instead be veiled with the most scrupulous attention and the greatest skill. I could cite many other differences between the two Arts that are equally obvious, but these are enough, I think, to demonstrate on the one hand that, if the picturesque is a genre, it is Nature's, or, by the same token, it is the type proposed in this theory. On the other hand, the Art of the Landscape Painter differs greatly from

---

* Although, in speaking of Gardens, I have sometimes made use of the expressions touch, making, and color, and while I admit that they are nothing in this art, nonetheless what I say here entails no contradiction, because these expressions, that properly belong to painting, can also belong to the figurative in the art of Gardens.

the Art of the Gardener, despite the fact that these two have Nature as master and its effects as goal.

I end this perhaps overlong digression here, despite having much abridged it, but it seemed necessary to me. I will return to genre Gardens. Let us start with the poetic, which chooses its subjects from Mythology and ancient fables. It sets out to present us either with some event from heroic times or some pagan mystery. To achieve all these fictions, sites analogous to the scenes are planned for representation. The viewer must be transported to Egypt, Greece, or ancient Rome. To this end, temples are built, statues of the divinities are set in place, and sacred groves are planted. Does one wish to present the Elysian Fields? Shadows are introduced, and demigods and heroes are shown. Are these the Gardens of Flora, or Pomona? Satyrs and Nymphs will be found there, and Dryads and Hamadryads will be caused to converse with Fauns. Who knows, however, how far such representations have gone to produce the effects the Composer had in mind? He tries by calling in costumes and ancient buildings to his aid, and puts to use a thousand other means, but they are so little known and so ambiguous that rarely do they recall the ideas that have been associated with them. Have hieroglyphic figures, verses, and inscriptions been added? Is there a need for recourse to Greek or Latin? Learned people can deal with these, but when they have seen and gone through it all, their interest will wane and never be renewed. As for other people, who make up the majority, they will barely glance at these enigmatic constructions and at this assemblage that says nothing to their imagination and even less to their soul. In addition, events without action and actors without movement cannot sustain the attention of the viewer for long: once curiosity is satisfied and all is said, there is nothing of interest that can be recalled. Such is the effect of every representation of action without pantomime.[*]

I suppose that, in their execution, these Gardens have a certain truth that creates an illusion. If, however, all this Art can attain only very imperfectly this degree of perfection, as it is easy to demonstrate; if the buildings do not have an imposing magnificence, grandeur, and antiquity; if the sites lack the expression and character that is proper to the site where the scene takes place; if the proportions are mean and the relationships missed—then the effect will not correspond to the enterprise, and will only present a ridiculous assemblage. In addition, the more pretentiousness in the project, the more the representation will appear pitiful.

Nature's Gardens have none of these improprieties. The features that make them up are always in their just proportion and true relationship. Their appeal can be seen at first glance, and their charm manifests itself at first inspection. To

---

[*] Despite their astonishing illusion, the famous shows that Servandony gave at the Tuileries would not have sustained the attention of the viewers for two hours if they had not presented a succession of effects and if there had been no action involved.[54]

feel these, the viewer needs no explanations to understand what they mean. The pleasure they provide requires neither erudition nor preliminary reflection. The impressions they make are at everyone's disposal. They please the learned as well as the ignorant. The degree of sensitivity that Nature has accorded nearly all men is enough to find some attraction, because the expression is unequivocal. Whether it is sweet or sour, informal or imposing, gay or sad, cheerful or wild, it is clear and precise, and no one will hesitate over the character presented.

In addition, Nature's scenes have all the movement they require: in the water, air, and vegetation, and in those occasioned by work in the countryside and the animals that populate it. The periodic return of days and seasons is sufficient, because no one expects more from natural effects. It is human to enjoy the future as much as the present. To the pleasure a beautiful morning brings us is combined that of the beautiful evening and the beautiful night that must follow. Thus, the attractions presented by a beautiful season are often united with those of a following season. If we add utility to all these considerations, and if we keep in mind the astonishing variety of effects and characters that this type offers, its ease of execution, and the small expense it requires, it will be understood why the country has so much charm, and why Nature's spectacle pleases generally and never bores. All this suffices to account for the preference given to her.

The goal of the romantic genre is to realize what the imagination can give birth to and Art can execute. This liberty, which seems at first glance to provide great advantages, facilitate means, and enrich the composition, is precisely what should cause it to be rejected. It has almost all the defects for which the poetic is reproached and none of the resources. The subjects that it permits are limited by and confined to a certain number of facts on which literature, theater, and the imitative Arts instruct us. In their representation, costumes recall events that a certain number of people have made familiar. The romantic, however, encompasses enchantments, fairies' dreams, and the wonders of magic in the enormity of subjects it embraces. It claims to realize the most fanciful ideas, the most extravagant creations, and only presents bizarre facts or events known to no one except whoever conceived them, or to whomever the inventor has bothered to explain them. In order to give the scene the character appropriate for such representations, sites of an analogous expression must be found: deserts, lairs, caverns, and old dungeons. Recourse to extraordinary means and expensive machinery are required. In supposing, however, that Art and Nature have collaborated to give character to these views, anticipating a perfection that they always lack, this type will, necessarily, always have a great defect: these figments of the imagination are always beyond representation, however perfect the latter may be, because it never corresponds to the idea formed for it and always remains well below what has been conceived. This is what marks these representations with a character of childishness and immaturity that always disgusts in this genre.

There is another type that appears to adhere more closely to Nature. This is the pastoral, whose scenes are entirely rural. Its goal is to recall the time when men, knowing no cares other than guarding their flocks, lived dispersed in the countryside in a fortunate atmosphere. These times, however, are no more, and these customs no longer exist. Shepherds of today do not at all resemble those of the times of the patriarchs. If by pastoral we understand those scenes and figures that the Poets have painted for us in their eclogues and songs, then according to this hypothesis the location of the scene will have only a weak expression, since the human figures are the essential objects. Without them, the most rustic country will proclaim nothing of the pastoral, at least according to the ideas that have been formed of this type. Shepherds and shepherdesses must be introduced, and decked out with ribbons and garlands. Then this genre will fall under the category of poetic, and in addition it will have all the improprieties of the romantic, since all these images are attractive when made by the Poet's pen or the Painter's brush, but make a very mediocre effect in representation. Stone and marble actors are very cold and very inappropriate to animate the scene.

If there is a pastoral type that is admissible as a Garden, it is, it seems to me, what I have given as an example in the pastoral *farm*. This is the only interesting and reasonable way to use it. There, the shepherd, who is not an unmoving statue, takes care of the herds, and the unornamented but neat shepherdess occupies herself with the useful details of the creamery from which she draws a profit.

It remains for me to speak of the imitative. In this, the other genre Gardens should be included, since they all have imitation as a goal, but I restrict this to the imitation of places. The Artist seeks to represent a foreign country, to transport to the site what he knows of the uses, forms, and constructions of another country or another century, without adapting either the actors, facts, or events. Does he wish to have the viewer walk in Egypt? He erects pyramids, and makes Lake Mæris. He separates the river in three branches to make the Nile delta, and wants to populate it with hippopotamuses and crocodiles. If he can, he grows papyrus. If the site is China, he builds porcelain towers, kiosks, and pagodas. His bridges and rowboats and all his garden follies will have Chinese ornamentation, and everything will bear the mark of the foreign down to the plants and fruit. All these imitations, however, are always incomplete and fool no one, and appeal only at first glance: that is, through novelty and singularity.

This genre is, through the abuse it has undergone, perhaps the most dangerous of all, and will not survive for long. In rejecting symmetrical Gardens, bizarre compositions have been substituted for them. They have been filled with a multitude of follies placed without order, laid out without taste, principle, or intention. Costumes and buildings of all periods and countries have been brought together without selection or discernment. Mythology and history have been mixed together; Greek temples have been put with churches, and palaces are placed next to cottages. Asia is confused with America. Contrary to Nature, we have been creating sites denied by the location: mountains have been raised, valleys hollowed out, rivers built, and stones fabricated.* Contrary to taste, these features have been given arbitrary proportions, and imitations made without verisimilitude. Marvels have been thought to be made by filling up the picture with disparate objects, as if this were a way to create Nature, perhaps even imagining she is thus embellished. All of this has produced nothing but repulsive and costly childishness. From these observations it follows that all imitation presented as such does not belong to the Art of Gardens, but instead to ornamentation, spectacle, or whatever one wants, but not a Garden.

The simplicity of Nature is only reached after having exhausted all these combinations, just as the truth is only met after having traveled a long circuit of errors. Such are the workings of the human mind. Genre Gardens have been, wherever the reformation in this Art has operated and wherever the revolution[55] has taken place, the first step in a new career that has begun. The Art of Gardens in these first moments appears as a new earth that produces abundantly, but that at first provides only wild plants and coarse grasses. It is up to the true Artists to cultivate it, and it is time to improve it. The taste that perfects and good works that hasten progress, in furnishing good models, will return us to the proper type, will determine the development that must be followed, and will establish the principles that are yet uncertain of this beautiful Art.

Yet, I foresee many obstacles to its advancement. It is commonly believed that there is nothing so simple as to create Nature, and that nothing is easier than to make up a Garden. There are few people who do not believe themselves capable of doing this, or at least of giving good advice. According to this opinion, the wisdom of the Artist is negligible, or, if he is consulted, his plans are not followed, or only partially completed: they are truncated, mutilated, taken apart, and dispersed. What Artist has never experienced this contradiction? The powerful individual, who ought to protect him, imposes his own ideas and hinders his genius. The rich man subjects him to his fantasies, and far from using his wealth to take part in the perfection of the Art, it becomes a means of corruption. The half-wise man, the worst of all, causes the Artist to experience disgusting humiliations: misled by common understandings and proud of his small successes, he disdains advice, and does not suspect that even the errors of an experienced Artist are worth more than his so-called masterpieces. In a word, each believes himself capable, and all want to realize their ideas, or, rather, the extravagant dreams of their imagination. From this arise ridiculous, weird, and sometimes even monstrous productions, that are seen to hatch everywhere, and from this arise implausible imitations. From this,

---

* We can discern what are supposed to be mountains, valleys, rivers, and rocks that are made artificially, and what kind of illusion a site composed of them is capable of producing.

finally, come Gardens without principles or character, devoid of expression and interest, where all is confused—types and classes, and the natural and the artificial. Should it not be feared that these examples of a type so frivolous, so opposed to good taste, in multiplying with impunity before the eyes of a Nation enlightened by the truth but in love with novelty, should prolong the infancy of an Art that is still in the cradle?

Notes to the Translation

1   Morel follows Whately's lead in elevating gardening to the ranks of the liberal arts. Whately writes: "Gardening . . . is entitled to a place of considerable rank among the liberal arts." Thomas Whately, *Observations on Modern Gardening* (London: T. Payne, 1770), 1.

2   The title of Abbé Pluche's influential early eighteenth-century multivolume work on natural history, which was given added weight by Buffon, becomes a trope of subject recognition throughout *Théorie des jardins*.

3   Throughout *Théorie des jardins*, Morel adds copious footnotes on architecture and contrasts it with garden design. These notes, along with the discussion in the text, demonstrate Morel's mastery of the subject, which he acquired from his mentor, Jacques-François Blondel, the eighteenth century's most important architectural pedagogue; they also, by virtue of the differences he sets up, establish the professional territory of the new landscape designer.

4   Morel is signaling the importance of professional identity, picking up on an issue first raised by François-de-Paule Latapie in his translation of *Observations on Modern Gardening*. Latapie noted that "jardinier"—the French equivalent of the English "gardener"—was inadequate to describe the individual who designed in the new gardening idiom. The French term is restrictive, implying a tiller of ground, not a designer: "The word gardener is far from depicting the rare man whom M. Whately has described for us in his introduction, by the word, Gardener." Thomas Whately, *L'art de former les jardin modernes*, trans. François-de-Paule Latapie (Paris: C. A. Jombert, 1771), 197. Throughout his book, Morel would refer to the garden designer interchangeably as *l'artiste jardiner*, *compositeur*, and *jardinier*. As a measure of his lifelong preoccupation with professional nomenclature, Morel returns to the subject with an augmented footnote in the second edition: "Our language has still not adopted a word to designate the artist who professes this new art from, nor has the type of garden he creates been named." Morel, *Théorie des jardins*, 1:34n5. A few years later, he would self-define as an *architecte-paysagiste* (landscape architect), a neologism entirely of his own invention.

5   Morel's own footnote on the subject reinforces his belief that "regular" gardens have their place in the public domain and for palaces. He supports his argument on the basis of the architectural concept of *convenance*, which he will return to.

6   Morel returns to the charged phrase; the language of the chapter, and indeed of much of his book, is very much inspired by a read of Buffon, especially his essay "De la Nature: Première vue" and "De la Nature: Seconde vue," from *Histoire naturelle*, vol. 12 (1764) and vol. 13 (1765).

7   Morel's word is fermentation, here translated as "sweet infusion." His use of fermentation, and a host of other words suggesting infinitesimal changes or transformations from one state to another are redolent of what can be called the vocabulary of Lumières. Diderot and D'Alembert, editors of the *Encyclopédie*, were partial to the word. Morel's usage here recalls Abbé Dubos, who referred to the fermentation of air on the human spirit and how it affected artistic and literary expression, thought, and production. See Abbé Jean-Baptiste Dubos, *Réflexions critiques sur la poésie et sur la peinture* (Geneva: Slatkine Reprints, 1967).

8 Morel is alluding to the notion of art as a moral and edifying force in civilization, and the corollary argument that the arts are corrupted by the society that nurtures and sustains them. Claude-Henri Watelet, in his *Essai sur les jardins* (Paris: Prault, 1774), was first to address the theme, and was more emphatic in his language than Morel. Though this type of aesthetic-moral equivalency has a long pedigree, the immediate influence on Watelet and Morel was Jean-Jacques Rousseau, who warned of the corrupting influence of society on humans and their activities in such works as *Discours qui a remporté le prix à l'Académie de Dijon, en l'année 1750: Sur cette question proposée par la même académie; Si le rétablissement des sciences et des arts a contribué à épurer les moeurs* (Geneva: Barillot, 1750); *Discours sur l'origine et les fondemens de l'inégalité parmi les hommes* (Amsterdam: M. M. Rey, 1755); *Julie, ou la nouvelle Héloïse: Lettres de deux amants habitants d'une petite ville au pied des Alpes* (Amsterdam: Chez Pierre Erialed, 1761); and *Émile, ou De l'éducation* (1762). With these seminal works of Enlightenment political and social philosophy, Rousseau established nature as a norm, sanctioning a claim for the moral authority of rural living. Morel would argue more or less along these lines when discussing the farm, one of his classes of gardens.

9 These two charged words suggest Morel's reliance on Condillac's philosophy for much of the metaphysical language he uses throughout *Théorie des jardins*. Étienne Bonnot de Condillac, *Traité des sensations* (London and Paris, 1754).

10 In addressing the "principles and rules" for the new gardening style, Morel draws from Blondel, who recognized that new art forms must be structured to prevent them from becoming meaningless exercises in poor taste. Blondel writes: "The magic of art needs restraint. Too much audaciousness astonishes more than it satisfies." Jacques-François Blondel, *Cours d'architecture* (Paris: Desaint, 1777), 4:315.

11 Described by Ulysses in Homer's *The Odyssey*, book 7: a domesticated and tended garden, as much an orchard as vegetable garden. Alcinous was king of the Phoenicians; his garden was often evoked in literature as the exemplar of a luxuriant garden. Milton cites the garden in *Paradise Lost*.

12 In the following pages, Morel introduces his generic garden categories: *pays, parc, Jardin proprement dit,* and *ferme* (translated here as *countryside, park, Garden proper,* and *farm*). As he would explain, each broad category is subject to variations. In his first edition, he labeled the broader category, *espèce,* and its variation, *genre.* Perhaps as a sign of the newness of the theoretical nature of his subject, Morel got the hierarchy wrong: *espèce* is subordinate to *genre,* not the reverse. This was pointed out in an otherwise laudatory review of *Théorie des jardins* in the *Mercure* of September 1776, where La Harpe wrote: "Le lecteur a pu observer que des espèces ne pouvaient pas renfermer des genres. C'est un contresens dans les termes, l'espèce étant subordonnée au genre." (The reader can see that *espèces* cannot encompass *genres.* It is a contradiction of terms, for *l'espèce* is subordinate to *genre.*) Morel corrected the error in his second edition. In this English translation, Morel's broad, generic category is translated as "class" and the variation as "type."

13 "Constant variation," more of Morel's vocabulary of Lumières.

14 Morel's description of the duties of the landscape designer is a direct usurpation of those traditionally given to the architect. Throughout *Théorie des jardins,* he would expand on the duties in very clear terms, thus establishing the professional territory of the new landscape design professional.

15 Direct introduction of scientific terminology that will set the tone of following chapters. The phrase "reciprocal relationship" is indicative of language describing how the forms and shapes of the natural landscape are the result of natural processes.

16 Newton introduced the concept of refrangibility, or the refraction of white light into the color spectrum, in his work on optics. Buffon discusses the concept frequently in *Histoire naturelle.* La Harpe found the word jarring in an otherwise poetically inclined work

on garden theory. Morel replaces the word in his second edition with "rays divided into a million beams."

17 More of the vocabulary of Lumières, on concepts of infinitesimal change.

18 Morel is referencing Condillac's philosophy, in particular that aspect of human understanding made possible through comparisons with what precedes and follows a specific event. Rousseau broached the theme when writing of spring in *Émile*—"the imagination joins the spectacle of spring with the seasons that follow it"—which Morel cited in his note on page 67.

19 Morel is referring to a discovery reputedly made by Louis Bourguet in the first third of the eighteenth century about the equal and reciprocal angles of projecting and receding mountain valleys carved by rivers. The observation was included in almost all natural history discussions and texts of the era, including Demarest's entry on *géographie physique* in the *Encyclopédie*. Buffon, from whom Morel draws the history lesson without attribution, called this discovery "the key to the theory of the earth." Buffon, "Preuves de la théorie de la terre; Article V," in *Histoire naturelle* (1749), 1:189. Morel removes this lesson in historical geography from his second edition.

20 Morel is recalling Rousseau's description of the Alps given in *Julie, ou la nouvelle Héloïse*: "to the east, spring flowers; to the south, autumn's fruits; to the north the glaciers of winter. She [nature] unites all seasons at the same instant, all climates in one place" (79). Morel has taken Rousseau's horizontal distribution (north, east, south, and west) and made it vertical, which is a more astute ecological observation.

21 Here and throughout his discussion of mountains, Morel invokes the Burkean sublime. See Marjorie Hope Nicolson, *Mountain Gloom and Mountain Glory: The Development of the Aesthetics of the Infinite* (Ithaca, N.Y.: Cornell University Press, 1959). For a more comprehensive study of the sublime in France, see Baldine Saint Girons, *Fiat lux: Une philosophie du sublime* (Paris: Quai Voltaire, 1993).

22 The observation (taken from Buffon) that the irregularities of the earth, in addition to adding variety to the landscape, allow for life's diversity was ridiculed by Louis Carrogis de Carmontelle in a review of *Théorie des jardins*: "One important learned observation he recalls is that water follows the slope of the terrain. . . . He concludes that if the earth were smooth, without mountains, its surface would be covered by water. One can, also, conclude that its inhabitants would be fish." *Correspondance littéraire*, November 1776, 374. Carmontelle was not an unbiased reviewer. His Jardin de Monceau, under construction at the time Morel was writing *Théorie des jardins*, espoused a very different style of picturesque garden than that of Morel. Further along in his book, Morel would mock Carmontelle's Monceau. Thus, Carmontelle's review was a settling of scores. On Carmontelle and Monceau, see David Hays, "Carmontelle's Design for the Jardin de Monceau," *Eighteenth-Century Studies* 32, no. 4 (1999); and David Hays, "'This is not a Jardin Anglais': Carmontelle, the Jardin de Monceau, and Irregular Garden Design in Late-Eighteenth Century France," in *Villas and Gardens in Early Modern Italy and France*, ed. Mirka Beneš and Dianne Harris (Cambridge: Cambridge University Press, 2001). Dora Wiebenson, *The Picturesque Garden in France* (Princeton: Princeton University Press, 1978), is still worth reading.

23 In the following pages, until the end of the section, Morel, following Buffon, enters an unprecedented discussion of the water cycle and the importance of water in modeling the land. He concludes with the observation that, short of catastrophic events, water is the principal natural agent in giving shape to land. Compare Whately's chapter "Of Ground," whose opening lines are: "The shape of ground must be either a convex, a concave, or a plane. By combinations of these are formed all the irregularities of which ground is capable" (Whateley, *Observations on Modern Gardening*, 2). His is a purely descriptive discussion, devoid of any of the natural processes that Morel has put into play. The only other contemporary picturesque theorist

who broached the subject, but to much less degree, was Antoine Nicolas Duchesne in his *Sur la formation des jardins* (Paris: Dorez, 1775). Perhaps acknowledging that he had provided too much information on natural process, Morel removes much of this remarkable passage from the second edition. The thrust of the theory, however, is intact.

24 Morel is making an analogy with William Harvey's seventeenth-century discovery of the blood circulation system of the human body. He removes the analogy, including the offending technical language ("se bifurquent") that La Harpe objected to, from the second edition.

25 In this oddly placed conclusion to his subsection on principles of landscape formation, Morel describes the practical challenges a landscape designer faces with the new garden style—namely, working with clients and executing the designs in the field. Just as the method of designing in the new genre was not codified, the means of construction were not clear. Morel is, once again, entering into a discussion of the professional territory of the new garden designer. While he dismisses plans—the client can't read them, they can't possibly express all the intentions of the design, the worker can't follow them, etc.—he ultimately produced them. Six surviving Morel garden plans, all for private properties, date from the early nineteenth century: one each for Arcelot (Côte-d'Or), Champgrenon (Saône-et-Loire), Couternon (Côte-d'Or), and Heudicourt (Eure); and two for Saint-Trys (Anse).

26 Morel alludes to Newton's Third Law, "for every action there is an equal and opposite reaction." The trope is removed from the second edition.

27 Morel's use of "machine" implies a "great work of genius" rather than something mechanical.

28 One arpent equals 0.845 acres.

29 Morel's discussion here gives perhaps his clearest expression of the contingency and variability associated with the garden types and of his concept of the continuity of landscape style.

30 Morel's metaphor is derivative of Roger de Piles: "A landscape owes a large part of its soul to the water placed there by the painter." (Le paysage doit une grande partie de son âme à l'eau que le Peintre y introduit.") *Cours de peinture par principes* (Paris: Jacques Estienne, 1708), 175.

31 Morel's reference to air as a fluid, while scientifically correct, is a curious usage.

32 Morel is the only garden theorist among his contemporaries to address island formation. The subject will appear in nineteenth-century garden theory texts, but these discussions are not given the same hydrodynamic rigor.

33 In this paragraph, Morel gives perhaps his clearest expression of his version of artistic mimesis as applied to the art of gardening. To a large degree, he is following Watelet, who wrote: "Art that shows itself too clearly destroys the effect of Art." (L'art qui se montre détruit l'effet de l'art.") *Essai sur les jardins*, 61.

34 Perhaps the most succinct understanding of Morel's theory: gardening is the judicious application of the laws of nature with taste.

35 This long, evocative passage depicting a Burkean sublime, is quickly followed with an explanation derivative of empirical philosophy.

36 In this paragraph, Morel comes tantalizingly close to expressing the ecological concept of natural vegetative succession and plant associations, using the phrase "distribution indiquée par la Nature." No claim can be made for Morel's thinking "ecologically"; however, this passage does demonstrate his attention to plant associations and successions in nature, and can be said to foreshadow such thought once the science was put in place.

37 Morel may be making a veiled attack on Girardin, who wrote of the possibility of bringing rocks (even large ones) to a site: "To place a new, large rock, find a suitable one for your purposes in the vicinity and break it up into manageable sizes to move." René Louis de Girardin,

De la composition des paysages: Suivi de promenade ou itinéraire des jardins d'Ermenonville (Paris, 1777), 57n1.

38 Morel's interest in architecture within a landscape setting was a professional interest and lifelong preoccupation. He prepared a paper on the subject of rural architecture, which he read before the Société d'agriculture de Lyon in 1798. The paper was concerned with the siting, composition, character, and style of rural dwellings. (Minutes of the Société d'agriculture de Lyon, August 22, 1798, Bibliothèque municipal, Lyon, MS 5530 B.) Morel was working on a book of rural architecture at the time of his death, and reputedly left a manuscript and several engravings. Neither have been located.

39 In his reference to the "primitive hut," Morel is alluding to, and disagreeing with, the architecture theory of Marc-Antoine Laugier, who was first to present a coherent theory of architecture based on a return to first principles. The frontispiece to the second edition of Marc-Antoine Laugier, *Essai sur l'architecture* (Paris: Chez Duchesne, 1755), depicts the now famous *première cabane*.

40 Morel is referring to a very real architectural problem. As bathroom suites became important in home design, determining how to incorporate them was complicated because of the rigid architectural theory of the day, which prescribed strict rules for the function, composition, and arrangement of internal spaces. Incorporating a bathroom in a rigidly constructed building was not easy or evident. Morel suggests that rather than putting a bathroom in the damp basement or placing it in a newly constructed level (which would change the mass, volume, and character of the building), a new, entirely self-contained structure should be built. He took his cues from Jacques-François Blondel, who had addressed such a problem in his *De la distribution des maisons de plaisance, et de la décoration des édifices en général* (Paris: C. A. Jombert, 1737), 1:71–72.

41 Morel's critique on a superabundance of structures in a picturesque garden is a not too subtle attack on Carmontelle's Jardin de Monceau, which was chock a block filled with *fabriques*, including Chinese and Gothic structures. In *Jardin de Monceau: Près de Paris* (Paris: Delafosse, 1779), Carmontelle speaks whimsically of creating a garden for "all times and all places"—something Morel seems to have had knowledge of when he derisively questioned the idea of putting into one garden "les quatres parties du monde dans un petit espace, & tous les siècles dans le même instant." It is interesting to note that each designer was attached to an important French noble household: Carmontelle's patron was Louis-Philippe-Joseph d'Orléans, Duke of Chartres, subsequently Duke of Orléans, and in the immediate post-Revolutionary era, Philippe Égalité. He was a Prince of the Blood (Prince du sang), and ultimately head of the cadet branch of the House of Orléans. Morel's patron, Louis-François de Bourbon, Prince of Conti, was a matrilineal descendent of Louis XIV. His grandmother, Louise Françoise de Bourbon, was the monarch's legitimized daughter with Madame de Montespan; his mother was Louise Élisabeth de Bourbon-Condé. The fact that these two households employed garden designers with so diametrically opposed views of the picturesque garden, is suggestive that no single "read" can be made regarding the picturesque garden and a political agenda.

42 "Heaps" (*monceau*): more of Morel's witty attack on Carmontelle's Monceau.

43 There is little dispute that Morel worked with René Louis de Girardin, the owner of Ermenonville, on the design of the garden, but other than Morel's description, given in this chapter of *Théorie des jardins*, it is uncertain what he actually did. Morel and Girardin had a falling-out over *fabriques* in the garden, and Morel—as seen—differed with Girardin over the use of rocks. Girardin went on to write his own, better known, treatise on the picturesque garden (*De la composition des paysages*), and it is to be assumed that he and Morel had a mutual influence on each other. However, Morel's theory contains more scientific language and discussions of natural process than that of Girardin. For more on Girardin and his work, see Michel Conan, postface to *De la composition des paysages* (Seyssel: Champ Vallon, 1992).

44 Guiscard was designed for Louis-Marie-Augustin Aumont, Duke of Aumont. Morel's contemporary, the acclaimed Scottish garden designer Thomas Blaikie praised Guiscard as among the finest gardens of the new genre. See Thomas Blaikie, *Diary of a Scotch Gardener at the French Court at the End of the Eighteenth Century* (London: Routledge and Sons, 1931).

45 Morel is referring to Latapie's translation of Whately's *Observations on Modern Gardening.* Whately named four garden archetypes—garden, farm, park, and riding—the latter term was translated by Latapie as *carrière*, which Morel retained in his book. In the preface to the second edition of *Théorie des jardins*, Morel remarked on how similar Whately's garden divisions were to his own, except for the *riding*, which—as evident in his discussion in the chapter on Guiscard—is not equivalent to the generic garden category of the *countryside*, but is a circuit for pleasure riding. Despite the difference, in the second edition's preface, Morel congratulated himself on the correspondence between Whately's garden divisions and his own, noting that they had never communicated on the subject. Morel is being a bit disingenuous: he may have never corresponded with Whately, but he did read his book.

46 In this paean to the *Cultivateur*, Morel is not only expressing his admiration and esteem for the farmer, but describing a stable, stratified society: the administrator, the middleman, and the producer. Such a division resonates with his garden classification system.

47 Over the next two pages, Morel entertains his most sustained discussion of sensationist metaphysics and the mechanisms on how feelings are produced. The theme, first introduced in his chapter on the seasons, is expanded and elaborated. It is very much derivative of Condillac. Morel apologizes for the digression, "un peu métaphysiques," and removes the discussion entirely from the second edition.

48 "Fluttering of the eyelids": the word Morel uses, *papilloter* (fluttering) was introduced into French usage only in the mid-eighteenth century. It was a favorite word of Diderot in his Salon critiques, and had an entry in the *Encyclopédie.* That Morel incorporates it directly into his book is further evidence of the quickness with which he introduced such new and technical language into his theory.

49 The word "seigneuriale"—and others that speak of a pre-Revolutionary France—are omitted in the second edition. Such changes are evidence of Morel "republicanizing" the vocabulary of the second edition.

50 With this barb, Morel may again be attacking Carmontelle's Monceau. He retains the anecdote in the second edition, however he replaces *Jardins modernes* with *Jardins anglais*, which is indicative of the pejorative connotation the term had taken on among the French.

51 In this concluding chapter, Morel returns to ongoing themes of sensationist metaphysics and aesthetic theories of imitation.

52 This is the first time that Morel has specifically identified by name the overall generic type of gardens he is addressing in his theory. His qualification on this type of garden as being "de la Nature" enters the subtitle of the second edition.

53 Claude Lorrain (1604–1682), Philips Wouwerman (1619–1668), and Claude-Joseph Vernet (1714–1789) were well-known painters of landscapes of the seventeenth and eighteenth centuries.

54 Servandony: Giovanni Niccolò Servandoni (1695–1766), an architect best known for his exuberant theater and interior decorations.

55 Morel is the only picturesque theory author to characterize the changing style of garden design as a "revolution." He uses the analogy to suggest the many "obstacles" confronting the "advancement" of the gardening art: "on n'arrive au vrai qu'après avoir parcouru un long cercle d'erreurs."

ex horto
DUMBARTON OAKS TEXTS
IN GARDEN AND LANDSCAPE STUDIES

Published by
Dumbarton Oaks Research Library and Collection, Washington, D.C.

Ex horto is devoted to classic works on the philosophy, art, and techniques of landscape design. Augmented with contemporary scholarly commentary, the series offers historical texts from numerous languages and reintroduces valuable works long out of print. The volumes cover a broad geographical and temporal range, from ancient Chinese poetry to twentieth-century German treatises, and constitute a library of historical sources that have defined the core of the field. By making these works newly available, the series provides unprecedented access to the foundational literature of garden and landscape studies.

Further information on Garden and Landscape Studies publications can be found at www.doaks.org/publications.

Garden Culture of the Twentieth Century
    Leberecht Migge, author; and David H. Haney, editor and translator

Travel Report: An Apprenticeship in the Earl of Derby's Kitchen Gardens and Greenhouses at Knowsley, England
    Hans Jancke, author; Joachim Wolschke-Bulmahn, editor;
    and Mic Hale, translator

Thirty-Six Views: The Kangxi Emperor's Mountain Estate in Poetry and Prints 避暑山莊三十六景詩圖
    Kangxi Emperor, author; Richard E. Strassberg, translator;
    and Stephen H. Whiteman

Letters of a Dead Man
    Prince Hermann von Pückler-Muskau, author; and Linda B. Parshall,
    editor and translator

Theory of Gardens
    Jean-Marie Morel, author; Joseph Disponzio; and Emily T. Cooperman,
    translator